LAWS

OF THE

TERRITORY OF MICHIGAN.

VOL. IV.

SUPPLEMENTAL.

Embracing all Laws enacted by the Legislative Authority of the Territory, not printed in Vols. I., II., and III., Territorial Laws, being Acts from 1806 to 1811, and also those Passed at the Special Session of the 6th Legislative Council, August 17th--25th, 1835.

BY AUTHORITY.

LANSING:
W. S. GEORGE & CO., STATE PRINTERS AND BINDERS.
1884.

TITLE AND DATE OF APPROVAL OF ACTS CONTAINED IN THIS VOLUME.

TITLE AND DATE OF APPROVAL OF ACTS.—CONTINUED.

TITLE AND DATE OF APPROVAL OF ACTS.—CONTINUED.

PREFACE.

In the preface to the compilation of the Territorial laws of Michigan, made in 1874, the compiler states that in 1870 the Board of Auditors ordered a reprint of those laws prior to the compilation of 1827. It was taken for granted that the printed laws extant contained all laws that were of value. This reprint was made, but there were many omissions and needless repetitions. In 1873 the Legislature provided for the collection and printing of *all* the Territorial laws. This the compiler in his preface states has been accomplished with the exception of twenty-six acts, of which the titles and dates of adoption were known. Since then manuscript, not heretofore known to be in existence, has been discovered, embracing Legislation of the Governor and Judges, or, as they were sometimes called, the Legislative Board, from 1805 to 1811, included in which are all of the acts mentioned by Mr. Cook as missing, thirteen acts not known to have been adopted; fourteen acts of which only the title or a digest of has heretofore been printed, are here given in full, twenty-nine acts printed in full in other of the preceding volumes are here inserted, as they occur in the manuscript, by title only, with foot notes to show where they may be found.

The second part of this volume contains the acts passed at the special session of the Sixth Legislative Council of the Territory held in Detroit August 17-August 24, 1835. Although the same were printed at the time, the copies seem to have disappeared and their existence been overlooked. The original acts of this session, with the exception of one, are on file in this office and were in the possession of the compiler of 1874, who, for some unexplained reason, did not see fit to incorporate them in his work.

It is confidently asserted that this volume contains all heretofore missing from the compilations of the laws of the Territory of Michigan, and that the same are now complete in all respects.

OFFICE OF THE SECRETARY OF STATE,
Lansing, March 9, 1884.

H. C. T.

LAWS

OF THE

TERRITORY OF MICHIGAN. 1806.

AN ACT concerning the town of Detroit.* No. 1. Sept. 13.

AN ACT concerning the city of Detroit. † No. 2. Sept. 13.

Be it enacted by the Governor and the Judges of Michigan, That the town of Detroit, that is to say the section laid off, surveyed, and numbered from time to time, under the act entitled, "An act concerning the town of Detroit," shall be a city, and the government thereof as such shall be vested in a Mayor, to hold his office for one year, and to be appointed and commissioned by the Governor; and in a city council, which shall consist of two chambers, the first chamber of which shall be composed of three members, to be elected annually by ballot, on the last Monday in September, by the inhabitants of the said city above the age of twenty-one years, and having resided within the same one year, and paid their public taxes; and the second chamber of which shall be composed of three members, to be elected annually by ballot on the last Monday in March, by the inhabitants similarly qualified: *Provided,* That the first election of the second chamber shall be held on the first Monday in October next, and the members shall continue in office until the next annual election in March: *And provided,* That the number of members in the respective chambers, and the manner of electing them shall afterwards be as prescribed by the city council by law. A majority of each chamber shall be a quorum for the transaction of business, but a smaller number may adjourn from time to time and compel the attendance of absent members and issue warrants to supply any vacancy in their respective chambers. Each chamber shall elect its own president and other officers, and judge of the elections, returns, and qualifications of their own members, and may, with the concurrence of two-thirds of the whole, expel any member for disorderly behavior or mal-con-

Boundaries. Mayor. City council: First chamber. Annual election. Qualification of voters. Second chamber. Proviso. Proviso. Quorum, how constituted. Vacancy, how supplied. President, etc. Election; qualification and expulsion of members.

*Printed in full on page 283, vol. 1, Ter. Laws. See also Cass' Code, p. 141, vol. 1, T. L.
† See Cass code, page 142, vol. 1, Ter. Laws, and page 221, vol. 2, Ter. Laws for earliest acts relative to city of Detroit heretofore published.

1806.

Journal.

duct in office, but not a second time for the same offense. Each chamber shall keep a journal of their proceedings, and the names of those voting in the affirmative and of those voting in the negative on any question, at the request of any member, shall be entered on the journal. Elections shall be held by the mayor between the rising and setting of the sun, and the ballots shall be opened and counted on the day succeeding the election in the presence of the two chambers, and the members elected shall be notified by the mayor of their election, and shall commence their functions on the first Monday in October, and the first Monday in April respectively after their election: *Provided,* That at the first election the presence of the two chambers shall not be required at the opening and counting of the votes, and the members of the second chamber shall commence their functions immediately after their notification of their election by the mayor, the same being adopted from the laws of one of the original States, to wit, the State of Maryland, as far as necessary and suitable to the circumstances of the Territory of Michigan.

Elections, time and mode of, etc.

Term of office commences.

Proviso.

Mayor vested with veto power.

And be it enacted, That every bill or act having passed by a majority of both chambers, before it become a law, shall be presented to the mayor, and if not approved by him, shall not take effect or become a law, but shall be returned with his objections to the chamber which it last passed, within ten days after its presentation to him, and if not so returned it shall become a law, unless the city council, by adjournment, prevent its return. The mayor may at any time convene the city council if the public good require their deliberations. The mayor shall appoint and commission all officers created by the laws of the city, the same being adopted from the laws of one of the original States, to wit, the State of Maryland, as far as necessary and suitable to the circumstances of Michigan.

Mayor, power and duties.

Seal.

And be it enacted, That the city council shall have power to make and use a common seal, alterable at their pleasure, to be deposited with the mayor, and affixed by him where necessary; and shall be capable, in the name of the mayor of Detroit, to sue and be sued in courts of law and equity, and in the same name shall have succession, and shall be capable to acquire, hold, and alien property, real and personal; the same being adopted from the laws of one of the original States, to wit: the State of Maryland, as far as necessary and suitable to the circumstances of Michigan.

May sue and be sued, hold property, etc.

Name.

Powers of council.

Absent members.
Nuisances, health of city, patrols, lighting.
Vessel regulations.
Licenses.
Markets, bridges.
Streets, parks.

And be it enacted, That the city council of Detroit shall have power by law to provide the manner of compelling the attendance of absent members, to prevent and remove nuisances, to provide for the health of the city, to establish watch and patrols, and erect lamps, to regulate the stationing, anchorage, and mooring of vessels, and the discharge and laying of ballast from ships and vessels, to provide for licensing and regulating hackney carriages, wagons, carts, and drays, and theatrical and other public amusements, to establish and regulate markets, to erect and repair bridges, to make, name, and keep in repair all streets, lanes, avenues, and public spaces of ground in conformity to the plan of the city, to make regulations for landing and laying materials for building said city, for disposing and laying earth which may be dug out of the wells, cellars, and foundations, and for ascertaining the thickness of the walls of houses, to erect and keep in repair drains and sewers, and to make regulations necessary for the preservation of the same, to regulate weights and measures in conformity to the constitution and laws of the United States, and of Michigan, to regulate the cleaning of chimneys, to provide for the prevention and extinction of fires, and to establish and regulate fire companies and wards, to establish and regulate the size of bricks made or used in the said city, to provide for regulating the measuring of boards, planks, scantling, timber, and lumber of every kind, to regulate the measuring of coals and firewood, and the weighing of hay, to sink wells, and erect and repair pumps, to impose and appropriate fines and forfeitures for breach of their laws recoverable before justices, where not exceeding twenty dollars, and before courts when exceeding that sum; to establish and regulate the inspection of flour, tobacco, potash, and salted provisions; to regulate the gauging of casks and liquors, the storage of gunpowder, not the property of the United States, or of Michigan; to regulate the weight and quality of bread, not affecting the price; to preserve the navigation of the river Detroit, adjacent to the city, to erect, repair, and regulate public wharves, and to deepen docks and basins; to provide for the education of youths, to lay and collect taxes, and to pass all laws necessary to give effect and operation to their powers; the same being adopted from the laws of one of the original States, to wit: the State of Maryland, as far as necessary and suitable to the circumstances of Michigan.

Building materials and regulations. Sewers. Weights and measures. Chimneys. Fire companies. Bricks. Lumber. Fuel. Hay. Wells. Fines. Flour, tobacco, etc. Liquor. Powder. Bread. Navigation of river. Wharves. Education of youths. Taxes. Laws.

And be it enacted, That all lands belonging to minors, persons absent, out of the territory, married women, or persons *non compotes mentis,* shall be subjected to the same terms and conditions as other proprietors. In every case where the proprietor is an infant or married woman, insane, absent out of the territory, or shall not attend on three months' notice, the governor, and the judges, or any three of them may allot and assign the portion or share of such proprietor, as near the old situation as may be, and to the full value of what the party might claim under the general terms and conditions of other proprietors: *Provided,* In the case of coverture and infancy, if the husband, guardian, or next friend will agree with the public, then an effectual division and allotment may be made, by consent, and in case of contrary claims, if the claimants will not jointly agree, the proceedings shall be the same as if the proprietor was absent, and all persons to whom allotments and assignments shall be made on consent and agreement, or pursuant to this act without consent, shall hold the same in their former state and interest in lieu of their former quantity. In all cases where the proprietor or possessor is tenant in right of dower, or by the courtesy, the annual value of the lands, and the gross value of such estate therein shall be ascertained as in other

Lands belonging to minors, etc. How allotted. Proviso. Tenant in right of dower, etc.

1806.

cases, and upon paying such gross value, or securing to the possessor the payment of the annual valuation, at the option of the proprietor or possessor, the public shall be vested with the whole estate of such tenant for squares, avenues, streets, lanes, or other public uses. Certificates granted of allotments, assignments, or purchases, with acknowledgments of the payment of all purchase money and interest being recorded, shall be sufficient to vest a legal estate without any more formal conveyance; the same being adopted from the laws of one of the original States, to wit: the State of Maryland, as far as necessary and suitable to the circumstances of Michigan.

Certificates sufficient title.

Register of deeds, appointment, duties, powers, etc.

And be it enacted, That the governor of Michigan shall appoint and commission a register for recording deeds and other writings within the said city, and all divisions and allotments of lands and lots made in pursuance of this act, and the register shall receive the same compensation as are or may be allowed to the clerk of the Supreme court in similar cases, and the governor may make a seal of office of the said register, which shall be kept by him; the same being adopted from the laws of one of the original States, to wit: the State of Maryland, as far as necessary and suitable to the circumstances of Michigan.

Providing for second sale of lots when not promptly paid for, etc.

And be it enacted, That on sales of lots in the said city under terms, or conditions of payment being made therefor at any day or days after such contract entered into, if any sum of the purchase money or interest, shall not be paid for the space of thirty days after the same ought to be paid, the same lots may be re-sold at vendue, at any time after sixty days' notice of such sale; the principal and interest due on the first contract, together with the expenses of advertisements and sale shall be retained, and the balance paid to the original purchaser, or his heirs or assigns, and all lots so sold shall be freed and acquitted of all claims legal and equitable of the first purchaser, his heirs and assigns; the same being adopted from the laws of one of the original States, to wit, the State of Maryland as far as necessary and suitable to the circumstances of Michigan.

Adopted and published at Detroit the thirteenth day of September, one thousand eight hundred six.

Attest:
PETER AUDRAIN,
Secretary of the Governor and Judges in their legislative department.

WILLIAM HULL,
Governor of Michigan.
AUGUSTUS B. WOODWARD,
Chief Judge of Michigan.
FREDERICK BATES,
Senior Associate Judge of Michigan.

No. 3.
Sept. 14.

AN ACT concerning the surveyor of Michigan.*

Be it enacted by the Governor and the Judges of Michigan, In pursuance of the act of congress of the United States, entitled,

*See Cass code page 221, volume 1, Territorial Laws.

"An act to provide for the adjustment of titles of land in the town of Detroit, and territory of Michigan and for other purposes" that there shall be a surveyor of Michigan to be appointed and commissioned by the governor, whose duty it shall be to lay out, survey, mark, and bound the town of Detroit agreeably to the provisions of an act entitled "An act concerning the town of Detroit," and all lands, lots, sections, avenues, streets, lanes, squares, and public spaces of ground within the same. It shall be the duty of the said surveyor to lay out and survey all adjudicated claims to lands, both within the city of Detroit and within the territory of Michigan; to lay out, survey, mark, and bound all public lands which are or may become the property of the territory; to lay out, survey, mark, and bound all public roads, to execute all orders of court relating to surveying, and all directions of the legislative authority of the territory from time to time, all directions of the governor and the judges of the territory, and of the mayor of Detroit, and the city council of the same; and generally all public business of every kind relative to surveying. He shall have power to appoint such deputies as he may deem expedient. The surveyor and his deputies, in addition to the oath to support the constitution of the United States, shall take an oath well and faithfully to execute their offices. Fair plots and certificates of all surveys shall be made and recorded.

1806.

Appointment.

To lay out town of Detroit, etc.

Other duties.

Appointment of deputies.

Oath.

Made and published at Detroit the fourteenth day of September one thousand eight hundred six.

Attest:
PETER AUDRAIN,
Secretary of the Governor and Judges in their legislative department.

WILLIAM HULL,
Governor of Michigan.
AUGUSTUS B. WOODWARD,
Chief Judge of Michigan.
FREDERICK BATES,
Senior Associate Judge of Michigan.

AN ACT concerning the bank of Detroit.*

No. 4.
Sept. 19.

Be it enacted by the Governor and the Judges of Michigan, That a bank shall be established at the city of Detroit, the capital stock whereof shall not exceed one million of dollars, divided into ten thousand shares, and subscriptions towards constituting the said stock shall, on Saturday, the twentieth day of September, in the present year, be opened in the city of Detroit, under the superintendance of such person or persons, not more than two, as shall be appointed for that purpose by the Governor. It shall be lawful for any person, copartnership, or body politic to subscribe for so many shares as he, she or they shall think fit. The subscription shall be closed in four days from the evening of the same, that is to say, at sunset, on Wednesday, the twenty-fourth day of September, in the present year. The same being adopted from the laws of two of the original States, to wit: the States of Maryland

Capital stock.

Subscriptions for, how made, etc.

*This act was disapproved by Congress March 3, 1807, although as will be seen by subsequent acts the Territory had subscribed for shares and partly paid for same.

1806. and Virginia, as far as necessary and suitable to the circumstances of Michigan.

And be it further enacted, That all those who shall become subscribers to the said bank, their successors and assigns shall be, and are hereby created and made a body corporate by the name of the President, Directors, and Company of the Detroit Bank, and shall so continue until the expiration of one hundred and one years from and after the passing of this act, and by their name aforesaid shall be capable to sue and be sued in courts of law and equity; to acquire, hold, and alien lands, tenements, and hereditaments, and personal goods and effects of every kind, provided their real property at no time exceed the value of fifty thousand dollars; to make and use a common seal alterable at their pleasure, and to enact and give effect to such laws as may be necessary and convenient for the government and regulation of the said corporation not being contrary to the constitution and laws of the United States, or of Michigan. The same being adopted from the laws of six of the original States, to wit: the States of Kentucky, Maryland, Massachusetts, New York, Pennsylvania, and Virginia, as far as necessary and suitable to the circumstances of Michigan.

Body corporate. Name. To exist. Sue and be sued, etc. Proviso. Shall enact by-laws, etc.

And be it enacted, That for the well ordering the affairs of the said corporation, there shall be a president and four directors who shall be elected in the present year on the last Saturday of September, and thereafter on the first Monday in July, annually, by the proprietors of the capital stock of the said corporation, by the plurality of the votes actually given. Absent stock-holders may vote by proxy authorized in writing. The number of votes to which each proprietor shall be entitled shall be according to the number of shares he shall hold, each share giving one vote. After the first election no share shall confer a right of suffrage which shall not have been holden three months previous to the day of election. In case an election of president and directors shall not be made upon any day when it ought to have been made, an election shall be held on any other day in such manner as may be regulated by the laws of the said corporation, and in the same manner vacancies shall be supplied. The same being adopted from the laws of two of the original States, to wit: The States of Maryland and Virginia, as far as necessary and suitable to the circumstances of Michigan.

Officers. How elected, etc.

And be it enacted, That the President and Directors shall have powers to appoint and compensate such officers and clerks as shall be necessary, and of exercising all other powers and authorities for the well governing and ordering the affairs of the said corporation. A majority shall constitute a quorum for the transaction of business. A number of stockholders who together shall be proprietors to the amount of twenty thousand dollars, shall have power at any time to call a general meeting of the stockholders, giving at least four months' previous notice, in at least one public gazette, and specifying in such notice the object or objects of such meeting. The cashier or treasurer shall give bond with two or more sureties to the satisfaction of the president and directors, in a sum not less than ten thousand dollars, with condition for his good

Powers of president and directors. Quorum. Meeting may be called by stockholders. Cashier and treasurer's bond.

behavior. The lands, tenements, and hereditaments, which it shall be lawful for the said corporation to hold, shall be only such as shall be requisite for its immediate accommodation, for the convenient transaction of business, and such as shall have been mortgaged to it by way of security or conveyed to it in satisfaction of debt previously contracted in the course of its dealings, or purchased upon judgments which shall have been obtained for such debts. The stock of the said corporation shall be assignable and transferable according to such regulations as shall be provided by the laws of the same. Bills under the seal of the said corporation shall be assigned by a written assignment under the hand of the obligee or payee for value received, and the assignee or assignees may bring and maintain an action thereupon in his, her, or their own name or names. Bills signed by the president, and countersigned by the principal cashier or treasurer thereof, promising the payment of money to any person or persons, his, her, or their order, or to bearer shall be binding on the corporation, as if by a private person and shall be assigned and negotiable in like manner as if issued by a private person, that is to say, by indorsement where payable to order, and by delivery where payable to bearer. If there shall be a failure in the payment of any part of any sum subscribed, the party failing shall lose the benefit of any dividend during the delay of the same. Every subscriber failing to make any of the payments required on his subscription shall forfeit such sum, not exceeding one hundred dollars, as by law of the corporation may be provided. It shall be lawful for the president and directors to establish offices wheresoever they shall think fit for the purpose of discount and deposit. The same being adopted from the laws of three of the original States, to wit: The States of Maryland, Pennsylvania, and Virginia, as far as necessary and suitable to the circumstances of Michigan.

Conditions of holding lands, etc.

Stock transferable, etc.

Bills, how assignable, etc.

Penalty for failure to pay subscription for stock.

Offices, how established.

And be it enacted, That the bills of the said corporation originally made payable or which shall become payable, on demand, in gold and silver, shall be receivable in all payments to the territory; the same being adopted from the laws of one of the original States, to wit: The State of Virginia, as far as necessary and suitable to the circumstances of Michigan.

Bills to be received by Territory.

And be it enacted, That the governor of Michigan may make or cause to be made a subscription to the stock of said corporation, on behalf of the Territory, as proprietor of the same; the same being adopted from the laws of three of the original States, to wit: The States of Maryland, New York, and Virginia, as far as necessary and suitable to the circumstances of Michigan.

Subscription for stock by the Territory.

Adopted and published at Detroit the nineteenth day of September, one thousand eight hundred six.

Attest:
PETER AUDRAIN,
Secretary of the Governor and Judges in their legislative department.

WILLIAM HULL,
Governor of Michigan.
AUGUSTUS B. WOODWARD,
Chief Judge of Michigan.
FREDERICK BATES,
Senior Associate Judge of Michigan.

1806.

No. 5.
October 7.

AN ACT in addition to an act entitled "An act concerning the militia of Michigan."

Fines, how appropriated.

Be it enacted by the Governor and the Judges of Michigan, That all fines and forfeitures which hereafter shall be incurred by virtue of the act to which this is an addition, shall be appropriated for the use of the companies to which the delinquents respectively belong, for purchasing and maintaining trumpets, drums, and fifes, and said fines and forfeitures are to be paid over to the commanding officers of the companies, to which the delinquents belong, for said purposes. And should there be any over-plus of fines remaining in the hands of the commanding officers of companies, they shall pay it over to the commanding officer of the regiment or corps to which they belong, which shall be applied to procuring and keeping in order colors and a band music for said regiment or corps; the same being adopted from the laws of one of the original States, to wit: The State of Connecticut, as far as necessary and suitable to the circumstances of Michigan.

Adopted and published the seventh day of October, one thousand eight hundred six.

Attest:
PETER AUDRAIN,
Secretary to the Governor and Judges in their legislative department.

WILLIAM HULL,
Governor of Michigan.
AUGUSTUS B. WOODWARD,
Chief Judge of Michigan.
FREDERICK BATES,
Senior Associate Judge of Michigan.

No. 6.
October 24.

AN ADDITIONAL ACT concerning highways and roads. *

No. 7.
November 3.

AN ACT concerning certain appropriations.

Salary of clerk of Supreme Court.

Be it enacted by the Governor and the Judges of Michigan, That for the payment of the annual salary of the Clerk of the Supreme Court, for the year one thousand eight hundred six, there is appropriated a sum not exceeding twenty-five dollars; for the payment of the annual salaries of the clerks of the courts of the districts of Detroit, Erie, and Michillimackinac, for the same year, there is appropriated a sum not exceeding forty-four dollars; for the payment of the annual salary of the treasurer, for the same year, there is appropriated a sum not exceeding fifty dollars; for the payment of the annual salary of the secretary of the legislature for the same year, there is appropriated a sum not exceeding fifty dollars; for the payment of special services rendered by Peter Audrain there is appropriated a sum not exceeding sixty dollars; for the payment of Joseph Côté, for chain carrying, there is appropriated a sum not exceeding ten dollars; for rendering the road from the river to the site of the court-house, and on the other side of the same, suit-

Salary of clerks of district courts. Salary of treasurer. Salary of secretary of the Legislature. Services of Peter Audrain. Services of Jos. Cote. For repairing road.

* Printed in full p. 1, Vol. 2, Ter. Laws; also see Cass code page 180, Vol. 1, Ter. Laws, date of year given as 1805, which is error, should be as above.

1806.

able for the transportation of material for building the same, by the removal of obstructions, and construction of small bridges, chargeable to the fund thereof, there is appropriated a sum not exceeding one hundred and twenty dollars; for the payment of the services rendered by Ezskiel Solomon, as a chain carrier, there is appropriated a sum not exceeding forty-five dollars; for the payment of services rendered by Esa Jones, in chain carrying and attending the legislature, there is appropriated a sum not exceeding seventy-five dollars; for the erection of pumps in the vicinity of the site of the court house, to supply water for (struition) of the same, chargeable to the fund therefor, there is appropriated a sum not exceeding one hundred and twenty dollars; for the payment of the first installment on the shares of the Territory in the bank of Detroit, there is appropriated a sum not exceeding twenty dollars; for the payment of David McClain for the support and burial of a pauper, there is appropriated a sum not exceeding twenty dollars; for the payment of the services of Abijah Hull for the year one thousand eight hundred and six, there is appropriated a sum not exceeding one hundred and fifty dollars; for the relief of the poor during the year one thousand eight hundred five, there is appropriated a sum not exceeding sixty dollars; for the relief of the poor during the year one thousand eight hundred seven, there is appropriated a sum not exceeding one hundred forty dollars; for the payment of the salaries of the clerks of courts during the year one thousand eight hundred seven, there is appropriated a sum not exceeding seventy dollars; for the payment of other salaries established by law, for the same, a sum not exceeding two hundred dollars; for the payment of installments on the shares of the Territory in the bank of Detroit during the same year, there is appropriated a sum not excceeding fifty dollars; for the relief of the poor during the same year, there is appropriated a sum not exceeding one hundred fifty dollars: for the services of the militia during the year one thousand eight hundred six, there is appropriated a sum not exceeding twenty dollars; for the services of the militia during the year one thousand eight hundrod seven, there is appropriated a sum not exceeding thirty-five dollars; for the payment of John Dodemead for the use of his house two days for the Supreme Court, at two dollars fifty cents for one day, there is appropriated a sum not exceeding five dollars; for the payment of Richard Smyth for the use of his house eleven days for the court of the district of Detroit, at three dollars for one day, there is appropriated a sum not exceeding thirty-three dollars; for the payment of James May for the use of his house fourteen days for the Supreme Court, at three dollars for one day, there is appropriated a sum not exceeding forty-two dollars; for the erection of a court-house and prison agreeable to the act of Congress and the acts of this Territory, chargeable to the fund directed by the same, there is appropriated a sum not exceeding twenty thousand dollars. The same being adopted from the laws of four of the original States, to wit: the States of Kentucky, Ohio, Pennsylvania, and Virginia, as far as necessary and suitable to the circumstances of Michigan.

Services of Ezskiel Solomon

Services of Esa Jones.

For pumps.

Stock of Bank of Detroit, 1st installment.

David McClain.

Abijah Hull.

Relief of the poor.

Salaries, clerks of courts.

Other Salaries.

Stock bank of Detroit, 2nd installment.

Relief of the poor.

Services of the militia.

John Dodemead and others, use of houses for courts.

For erection of court house and prison.

1806.

Adopted and published at Detroit the third day of November one thousand eight hundred six.

Attest:
PETER AUDRAIN,
Secretary of the Governor and Judges in their legislative department.

WILLIAM HULL,
Governor of Michigan.
AUGUSTUS B. WOODWARD,
Chief Judge of Michigan.
FREDERICK BATES,
Senior Associate Judge of Michigan.
JOHN GRIFFIN,
Junior Associate Judge of Michigan.

No. 8.
December 8.

AN ACT making certain appropriations for the services of the years one thousand eight hundred five, six, and seven.*

No. 9.
December 11.

AN ACT to repeal certain parts of the act relative to ferries, taverns, retailers, auctions, and taxes.

Licenses reduced to sixteen dollars.

SECTION 1. *Be it enacted by the Governor and Judges of Michigan,* That so much of the acts concerning ferries, tavern keepers, and retailers of merchandise, as requires the price of license to retail merchandise to be twenty dollars, be repealed, and the same shall be sixteen dollars.

Tax on winter vehicles reduced.

SEC. 2. *And be it enacted,* That so much of the act imposing certain taxes, as requires the tax on sleighs, carrioles, or other carriage for riding in winter to be two dollars, be repealed, and the same shall be one dollar.

Tax on stud horses.

SEC. 3. *And be it enacted,* That so much of said act as requires the tax on stud horses to be four dollars, be repealed, and the same shall be two dollars, except when the stud horse is kept for covering, in which case the tax shall remain four dollars.

Taxes become due, when collectible.

SEC. 4. *And be it enacted,* That so much of the said act, or any other act, as requires one-half of any taxes to become due on the first day of April and the first day of October in every year, be repealed, and the whole shall become due on any day of the year after the first day of January in every year, and may be collected on any day of the year after the same at the most early period of the year that shall be possible.

Acts repealed as to date of payment.

SEC. 5. *And be it enacted,* That so much of the acts relative to ferries, tavern keepers, retailers, auctions, and taxes, as would require the payment of money to the public between the first day of October and the thirty-first day of December, one thousand eight hundred six, be repealed.

Provisions as to tax collections by marshal.

SEC. 6. *And be it enacted,* That so much of the act relative to taxes as requires the marshal to pay the moneys collected quarterly be repealed, and he shall pay them every two months, and shall

Treasurer to audit.

render with them when paid an exact account to the treasurer of the sources from which they have been derived, and the treasurer

*This act printed in full pp. 1-4, vol. 2, Ter. Laws.

shall audit the said accounts and certify to the governor its correctness or incorrectness. **1806.**

SEC. 7. *And be it enacted,* That so much of the act relative to auctions as imposes a duty of three dollars be repealed, and the same shall be two dollars and fifty cents. Licenses for auctions reduced.

SEC. 8. *And be it enacted,* That the taxes on dogs be repealed. Dog tax repealed.

SEC. 9. *And be it enacted,* That so much of the act respecting auctions as requires the return to be made semi-annually be repealed and the same shall be made every two months. Auction returns.

Made and published at Detroit the eleventh day of December one thousand eight hundred six.

Attest:
PETER AUDRAIN,
Secretary to the Governor and Judges in their legislative department.

WILLIAM HULL,
Governor of Michigan.
AUGUSTUS B. WOODWARD,
Chief Judge of Michigan.
JOHN GRIFFIN,
Junior Associate Judge of Michigan.

No. 11.
December 12.

AN ACT concerning attachments and absent defendants.

Be it enacted by the Governor and Judges of Michigan, That it shall be lawful for the Clerk of the Supreme Court, or any district court, on the application of any creditor, whose debt exceeds two hundred dollars, and for the clerk of any district court, on the application of any creditor whose debt exceeds twenty dollars, and does not exceed two hundred dollars, and for a justice of the peace, on the application of any creditor, whose debt does not exceed twenty dollars; on affidavit of the amount due to him, and of the manner in which the same became due, and of the credits which are justly due and allowable, to the debtor, and that he has reason to believe, and does believe the debtor absconds or conceals himself, so that the ordinary process of law cannot be served upon him and is removing privately, or intends to remove his effects, to issue a writ of attachment accompanied by a capias, or warrant, as the case may be, and returnable in the same manner with other process, as the case may be, directed to the marshal, by virtue whereof it shall be lawful for the marshal to seize the estate and effects of such debtor, or so much thereof as shall be sufficient to satisfy the debt and costs and to serve and levy the same upon such estate and effects wherever the same shall be found, or in the hands of any person indebted to the debtor, or having any of his effects, and to summon such person to appear at the return of the writ, or process and answer upon oath what he is indebted to such debtor, or what effects of such debtor he has in his hands, or had at the service of the process and being returned summoned, the court or justice may, on failure, compel such person to appear and answer, and security shall be given to the satisfaction of the officer issuing in double the amount demanded, payable to the opposite party, for satisfying and paying all costs and damages recovered against the plaintiff for such attachment, and all estate and effects attached

Clerks of Supreme or district courts, or justices of the peace may issue. On affidavit stating. Writ of attachment and capias, etc. Marshal to make seizure, etc. Examination on oath. Compel answer. Security. May be replevied.

1806.

shall be repleviable by appearance and putting in good bail, if so ruled. On the return of the execution of the process, the court or justice shall proceed to judgment, as in all other cases, except where a trial is by a jury, and then the verdict shall be in the nature of an inquest, and the estate and effects attached shall be sold on the execution, as if originally taken on a writ of *fieri facias*, and judgment and execution shall in like manner go against the person indebted to the debtor, or having any of his effects. Where live stock is taken, the marshal shall provide sufficient sustenance, and the court or justice shall cause the reasonable cost thereof to be taxed against the plaintiff, to be again taxed against the debtor, if the plaintiff recover, but to remain taxed against the plaintiff, if he should be cast. It shall be lawful to issue and serve the attachment, capias, or warrant the same on Sunday as on any other day; the same being adopted from the laws of three of the original States, to wit, Maryland, New York, and Virginia, as far as necessary and suitable to the circumstances of Michigan.

Judgment by judge or jury, how given.

Sustenance for live stock, costs, etc., how provided for.

Writ may be served on Sunday.

SEC. 2. *And be it further enacted*, That in any suit in law or equity against any defendant or defendants who are out of Michigan and another or others within the same, having in their hands effects of, or being indebted to such absent defendant or defendants, upon proper affidavit, the court or justice, as the case may be, may make any order and require security, if it shall appear necessary, to restrain the defendant or defendants in Michigan from paying, conveying away, or secreting the debts, or effects in his, her, or their hands, of such absent defendant, or defendants, and for that purpose may order such debts to be paid and effects delivered to the plaintiff or plaintiffs, upon their giving sufficient security for the return thereof to such person and in such manner as the court shall direct. In any suit in equity against any absent defendant or defendants, on satisfactory proof made that the defendant or defendants are out of Michigan, or cannot be found, the court may appoint a day for the defendant or defendants to appear, which shall be advertised two months, as the court shall direct, and if he or they do not appear and the court shall be satisfied of the justice of the demand, the bill may be taken for confessed, and such order and decree may be made as shall appear just, and the court shall enforce due performance and execution thereof, and may require security from the plaintiff or plaintiffs for the future restoration of the estate or effects, or the same may remain under the direction of the court, in the hands of a receiver, or otherwise, and eventually disposed of, as the court shall deem just. If the opposite party, his, her, or their representatives, shall, within seven years appear and contest the merits against the plaintiff, his, her, or their representatives, and comply with the reasonable order of the court relating to costs and security, the cause shall be heard as if no former decree had been made, and the court may make such further order for quieting possession and title to the estate and effects as to them shall appear just and reasonable; the same being adopted from the laws of one of the

When security may be required.

Defendants, out of Territory and not appearing.

As confession of judgment.

Plaintiffs to give security for restoration.

Receiver.

Case may be reopened within seven years.

original States, to wit: Virginia, as far as necessary and suitable to the circumstances of Michigan.

Adopted and published at Detroit the twelfth day of December, one thousand eight hundred six.

Attest
PETER AUDRIAN,
Secretary of the Governor and Judges in their legislative department.

WILLIAM HULL,
Governor of Michigan.
AUGUSTUS B. WOODWARD,
Chief Judge of Michigan.
JOHN GRIFFIN,
Junior Associate Judge of Michigan.

1807.

AN ACT to prevent certain acts hostile to the peace and tranquility of the United States within the jurisdiction of this Territory. * No. 11. January 23.

AN ACT concerning the appointment and duties of an Attorney General.† No. 12.

Be it enacted by the Governor and the Judges of Michigan, That it shall be the duty of the attorney general, who shall be appointed by the Governor, to prosecute and defend all suits, both civil and criminal, for and against the United States or this territory, and to perform all proper official duties required of him by the legislative, executive, or judicial power of Michigan, or of the United States of America; the same being adopted from the laws of two of the original States, to wit: The States of Massachusetts and New York, as far as necessary and suitable to the circumstances of Michigan. Appointment by Governor. Duties.

Adopted and published at Detroit the twenty-ninth day of January, one thousand eight hundred seven.

Attest:
PETER AUDRIAN,
Secretary to the Governor and Judges in their legislative Dapartment.

WILLIAM HULL,
Governor of Michigan.
AUGUSTUS B. WOODWARD,
Chief Judge of Michigan,
JOHN GRIFFIN,
Junior Associate Judge of Michigan.

AN ACT making certain appropriations.‡ No. 13. March 20.

AN ADDITIONAL ACT concerning District Courts. ‖ No. 14. April 2.

---

* Printed in full, vol. 2, Ter. Laws, pp. 4-6. Digest of in Cass code, p. 224, vol. 1, Territorial Laws, date given as January 23, 1816, should be as above.
† See Cass code p. 138, vol. 1, Ter. Laws. Title only given.
‡ Printed in full, page 6, Vol. 2, Ter. Laws.
‖ Printed in full, page 7, Vol. 2, Ter. Laws.

1807.

AN ACT concerning religious societies.*

No. 15.
April 3.

Any religious society.
Trustees. Election of.
May hold property.

SECTION 1. *Be it enacted by the Governor and the Judges of Michigan,* That it shall be lawful for any religious societies in Michigan to elect a trustee or trustees of the society, at such times, in such manner, and of such number as the society shall think proper. The person or persons so appointed, and his or their successor or successors, shall have power to acquire, hold and alien property, real and personal, slaves excepted, in trust for the use and benefit of the society, and shall be capable of suing and being sued. The society may at any time cause the trustee or trustees to account for matters committed to his or their trust, and in case of refusal, to appoint any agent or agents to bring suits respecting the same. No one society shall hold more land at one time than two thousand acres, and all the property of the society shall be subject to taxation in the same manner as other property; the same being adopted from the laws of one of the original States, to wit: North Carolina, as far as necessary and suitable to the circumstances of Michigan.

Sue and be sued.
Require accounting.
Limitation as to real estate.
Taxation of property.

Roman Catholic organization.

SEC. 2. *And be it enacted,* That the members of the church usually denominated Catholic, Apostolic, and Roman, within the Territory of Michigan, may convene and adopt such regulations for the management of their estates and temporalities, as shall seem advisable to a majority; and shall choose such person or persons as they shall think proper, who shall assume the style, name, and title by which they are to be designated, and shall certify the same under their hands to the clerk of the Supreme Court who shall record the same, and thereupon the same person or persons, his and their successors, shall be a body politic and corporate by the name and description so assumed, for carrying into execution such regulations as may have been or may at any time be adopted as aforesaid, and for giving effect to the provisions of this act, which said body corporate shall be immediately seized and possessed of all the present property, estate, and temporalities of the said church, and which shall from thenceforth be under the sole control and management of the said corporation and their successors subject to taxation as aforesaid; and all vacancies occasioned by death, resignation, or other disqualification shall be supplied by other person or persons elected or appointed according to the regulations of the said church, and separate congregations may be established according to the first section of this act, which shall also be bodies corporate in the same manner; the same being adopted from the laws of one of the original States, to wit: The State of Maryland, as far as necessary and suitable to the circumstances of Michigan.

Title to be filed with Clerk of Supreme Court.
Body politic and corporate.
Title to property to vest in.
Sole control.
Taxation.
Vacancies, how filled.
Establishment of new congregations.

Power to repeal, etc., retained by Legislature, etc.

SEC. 3. *And be it enacted,* That this act and all acts additional or supplementary thereto, and all other acts whatsoever relating to the said societies as corporations, shall be repealed at the pleasure of the legislative power of the territory of Michigan for the time being, and at the pleasure of the legislative power of the

*Digest of this act printed Cass code, p. 209, vol. 1, Ter. Laws.

United States of America, anything whatsoever to the contrary thereof notwithstanding; the same being adopted from the laws of two of the original States, to wit: The States of Connecticut and Massachusetts as far as necessary and suitable to the circumstances of Michigan. 1807.

Adopted and published at Detroit the third day of April, one thousand eight hundred seven.

Attest:
PETER AUDRAIN,
Secretary of the Governor and Judges in their legislative department.

WILLIAM HULL,
Governor of Michigan.
A. B. WOODWARD,
JOHN GRIFFIN.

AN ACT repealing part of the additional act concerning district courts. * No. 16. April 13.

AN ADDITIONAL ACT concerning compensations. † No. 17. April 14.

SECTION 1. *Be it enacted by the Governor and the Judges of Michigan,* That the judges of the District Courts shall be entitled to receive one dollar on every action entered in the said courts, and fifty cents for every judgment rendered by them, which sums shall be taxed in the bills of cost against the person or persons against whom judgment shall be rendered, and shall be collected and paid by the clerk of the court, to be equally divided among said Judges; the same being adopted from the laws of one of the original States, to wit: The State of Massachusetts, as far as necessary and suitable to the circumstances of Michigan. Judges' fees. How taxed, collected, etc.

SEC. 2. *And be it enacted,* That the Attorney General in addition to the taxable fee recoverable from the defendants, in case of conviction, shall receive an annual salary of fifty dollars, to be paid semi-annually from the treasury; the same being adopted from the laws of one of the original States, to wit: The State of Massachusetts, as far as necessary and suitable to the circumstances of Michigan. Attorney General, salary.

SEC. 3. *And be it enacted,* That the surveyor shall be entitled to receive an annual salary of two hundred fifty dollars, to be paid from the treasury semi-annually; and the expenses of chain carriers and necessary attendants shall be audited by the treasurer and paid at the treasury, not exceeding one dollar for the services of one person for one day; the said salary and the said expense to be charged to the Detroit fund when the services relate to the city of Detroit, and the salary in an equitable proportion, to be settled by the treasurer, where part of the services relate to the city of Detroit and part to the Territory of Michigan; and for services rendered at the request of private persons, the surveyor shall receive from Surveyor, salary. Other salaries. To be charged to, and when.

* Printed in full p. 9, vol. 2, Territorial Laws.
† Digest of, Cass code, p. 140, vol. 1, Territorial Laws.

1807.

Schedule of fees allowed for surveying.

the party, payable when service is rendered, for surveying a lot in the city of Detroit, sixty-two and one-half cents; for the plat and certificate of the courses of the same, sixty-two and one-half cents; for surveying in the country, two dollars and fifty cents for one day; for the plat and certificate of a tract in the country, one dollar and fifty cents; the same being adopted from the laws of two of the original States, to wit: The States of New York and Virginia, as far as necessary and suitable to the circumstances of Michigan.

Part of act regulating fees of justices of the peace repealed and new schedule made.

SEC. 4. *And be it enacted,* That so much of the act concerning compensations, as allows to a justice of the peace for making any entry relative to a case, six and one-fourth cents, and so much of the said act as allows to a justice of the peace, for filing any paper, six and one-fourth cents, be repealed; and so much of the said act as would operate to give to a justice of the peace twenty-five cents for a judgment, where the same is by confession, is also repealed; and there shall be allowed to a justice of the peace for a judgment in cases, where the same is by confession, twelve and one-half cents, and such judgment by confession may be entered by consent without any previous process.

Fee of attorney appearing before a justice of the peace.

SEC. 5. *And be it enacted,* That so much of the said act as would operate to give the usual compensation to a counsel or attorney appearing in cases before a justice of the peace be repealed, and where counsel or attorney appear in cases before a justice of the peace, there may be taxed on every final judgment for the use of the counsel or attorney of the party in whose favor the judgment is, one dollar.

Fee of witnesses before justice of the peace.

SEC. 6. *And be it enacted,* That so much of the said act as would operate to allow the usual compensation to witnesses in cases before a justice of the peace, be repealed, and there shall be allowed to a witness in cases before a justice of the peace the usual compensation where such witness resides five miles or more from the place where he attends.

Adopted, made, and published at Detroit the fourteenth day or April, one thousand eight hundred seven.

Attest:
PETER AUDRIAN,
Secretary of the Governor and Judges in their legislative department.

WILLIAM HULL,
Governor of Michigan.
AUGUSTUS B. WOODWARD,
JOHN GRIFFIN.

No. 18.
April 16.

AN ADDITIONAL ACT concerning the recovery of small sums to the amount of twenty dollars.*

No. 19.
May 7.

AN ADDITIONAL ACT concerning compensations.†

Act relative to paupers, clause repealed.

Be it enacted by the Governor and Judges of Michigan, That so much of the act relative to paupers as would operate to require

* Printed in full p. 9, vol. 2, Territorial Laws.
† Digest of, Cass code, p. 140, vol. 1, Territorial Laws.

1807.

the justices of the peace to give a certificate without allowing them any compensation therefor be repealed, and there shall be allowed to each justice for such certificate twelve and one half cents, to be paid at the public treasury.

Fees, justice of the peace.

SEC. 2. *And be it enacted,* That there shall be allowed to a justice of the peace for a certificate of an oath or affidavit, twenty-five cents, to be paid by the party applying for the same, on the service being rendered; and for a notification under the act for the relief of poor prisoners committed by execution for debt, there shall be allowed to a justice of the peace, twenty-five cents, to be paid in the same manner; and for a certificate under the said act, there shall be allowed to the justices giving the same, twelve and one half cents each, to be paid in the same manner; the same being adopted from the laws of three of the original States, to wit: The States of Maryland, Massachusetts, and Pennsylvania, as far as necessary and suitable to the circumstances of Michigan.

Repealing provisions.

SEC. 3. *And be it enacted,* That so much of the last act on the subject of compensations, as provides that where counsel or attorney appear in cases before a justice of the peace, there may be taxed on every final judgment, for the use of the counsel or attorney, of the party in whose favor the judgment is, one dollar, be and the same is hereby repealed.

Made, adopted, and published at the city of Detroit, in the Territory of Michigan, the seventh day of May, one thousand eight hundred seven.

Attest: (Signed) WILLIAM HULL,
Governor of Michigan.
JOS. WATSON,
Secretary of the Governor and Judges in their legislative department.
A. B. WOODWARD,
JOHN GRIFFIN.

No. 20.
No date given.

AN ACT making certain appropriations.*

No. 21.
May 18.

AN ADDITIONAL ACT concerning the town of Detroit. †

No. 22.
May 22.

AN ACT repealing part of the act relative to the marshal. ‡

Be it enacted by the Governor and Judges of the Territory of Michigan, That so much of the acts relating to the marshal as requires that officer to be appointed and commissioned for the whole Territory, without separate marshals for the several districts, and to give security to the amount of ten thousand dollars, be repealed, and a marshal of the Territory shall be appointed and commissioned by the Governor, who shall give security in the same manner as heretofore to the amount of four thousand dollars; and one

* Printed in full page 11, vol. 2, Territorial Laws.
† Printed in full p. 286, vol. 1. Territorial Laws.
‡ Digest of, Cass code, p. 219, vol. 1, Territorial Laws.

1807.

marshal shall be appointed and commissioned by the Governor for each judicial district in the Territory of Michigan, who shall give security, in the same manner as the marshal of the Territory, to the amount of one thousand dollars, and who shall be charged within his district with all powers and duties vested by law in the present marshal, excepting such as relate to the Supreme Court or business which relates to the United States.

Made and published at the city of Detroit, in the Territory of Michigan, the twenty-second day of May, one thousand eight hundred seven.

Attest:
JOSEPH WATSON,
Secretary to the Governor and Judges in their legislative department.

WILLIAM HULL,
Governor of Michigan.
A. B. WOODWARD,
JOHN GRIFFIN.

No. 23.
June 2.

AN ACT making appropriations for the service of the year one thousand eight hundred and eight. *

No. 24.
June 2.

AN ACT to repeal a certain appropriation. †

No. 25.
June 2.

AN ADDITIONAL act concerning compensation. ‡

Secretary Legislature, salary reduced.

Be it enacted by the Governor and the Judges of the Territory of Michigan, That from and after the thirtieth day of June, one thousand eight hundred seven, so much of the act relative to compensations as allows an annual salary of fifty dollars to the legislative secretary be repealed, and the same shall be twenty-five dollars.

Treasurer, salary reduced.

SECTION 2. *And be it enacted*, That after the said day so much of the acts relative to compensations as allows to the Treasurer an annual salary of fifty dollars be repealed, and the same shall be twenty-five dollars.

Clerk Supreme Court, salary abolished.

SEC. 3. *And be it enacted*, That after the said day so much of the said act as allows to the clerk of the Supreme Court an annual salary of twenty-five dollars be repealed.

Attorney General, salary reduced.

SEC. 4. *And be it enacted*, That after the said day so much of the said acts as allows an annual salary to the attorney general of fifty dollars be repealed, and the same shall be twenty-five dollars.

Surveyor, salary reduced.

SEC. 5. *And be it enacted*, That after the thirtieth day of September, one thousand eight hundred seven, so much of the said acts as allows an annual salary to the surveyor of two hundred fifty dollars be repealed, and the same shall be twenty-five dollars.

---

* Printed in full p. 11, vol. 2, Territorial Laws.
† Printed in full p. 12, vol. 2, Territorial Laws.
‡ Digest of, Cass code, p. 140, vol. 1, Territorial Laws.

1807.

Made and published at the city of Detroit, in the Territory of Michigan, the second day of June, one thousand eight hundred seven.

Attest:
JOS. WATSON,
Secretary of the Governor and Judges in their legislative department.

WILLIAM HULL,
Governor of Michigan.
AUGUSTUS B. WOODWARD,
Chief Judge of the Territory of Michigan.
JOHN GRIFFIN.

AN ACT concerning the taxes of the year one thousand eight hundred and eight.* No. 26. June 2.

1808.

AN ACT to fix the times of meeting of the Legislature of the Territory of Michigan, and for other purposes. No. 27. November 9.

Be it enacted by the Legislature of the Territory of Michigan, That the legislature shall hold two stated sessions in every year, which shall commence respectively, on the second Thursdays of May and October, at eleven of the clock in the forenoon, and shall continue until all business requiring legislation shall be finished; the same being adopted from the laws of two of the original States, to wit: The States of Connecticut and Vermont, as far as necessary and suitable to the circumstances of the Territory of Michigan. Sessions—number of, when to commence and duration of.

SEC. 2. *Be it enacted,* That the Governor and three Judges appointed and commissioned by the President of the United States shall compose the legislative board of said Territory, three of whom shall be necessary for a majority; but any three of them in the absence of the other, shall constitute a quorum for transacting business, in which case two shall be deemed a legal majority on any question, and when any law shall have received the assent of a majority as provided in either of the cases aforesaid, it shall be taken and deemed to have been regularly passed by the legislative board, and shall be signed by the presiding officer thereof at the time of its passage, and attested by the person acting as secretary to the Governor and Judges in their legislative capacity; the same being adopted from the laws of one of the original States, to wit; The State of Vermont, so far as necessary and suitable to the circumstances of the Territory of Michigan. Legislative Board, who to compose. Majority. Quorum. Laws, when passed. To be signed by.

Adopted and published in and at the city of Detroit, within the Territory of Michigan, this ninth day of November, one thousand eight hundred and eight.

Attest:
JOS. WATSON,
Secretary.

WILLIAM HULL,
President of the Legislative Board.

---

*Printed in full p. 12, vol. 2, Territorial Laws.

1808.

AN ACT for the punishment of crimes and misdemeanors.

No. 28. December 9.

Treason.

SECTION 1. *It is hereby enacted by the Governor and Judges of the Territory of Michigan,* That if any person or persons owing allegiance to this Territory shall levy war or conspire to levy war against the same, or shall in any way, within this Territory or elsewhere, give aid and comfort to the enemies of this Territory, and shall be thereof convicted before the Supreme Court thereof, either on confession in open court or on the testimony of two witnesses to the same overt act of treason, of which such person or persons is or are indicted, such person or persons shall be adjudged guilty of treason against this Territory, and shall suffer death.

Misprision of treason.

SEC. 2. *And it is hereby enacted,* That if any person or persons knowing any such treason to have been committed, or having knowledge of the intent of any person or persons to commit any such treason, shall not within fourteen days from the time of his having such knowledge, give information thereof to the governor of this Territory or some one of the judges of the Supreme Court, or some justice of the peace, such person or persons, on conviction before the Supreme Court, shall be adjudged guilty of misprison of treason, and shall be imprisoned or confined to hard labor not exceeding seven years and fined not exceeding two thousand dollars.

Murder.

SEC. 3. *And be it enacted,* That if any person shall commit murder or the wilful killing of any person with malice prepense, or such other detestable practices, such person, on conviction thereof before the Supreme Court, shall suffer death.

False witness.

SEC. 4. *And be it enacted,* That if any person shall bear false witness wilfully and of purpose to take away any person's life and the life of any person be taken away in consequence of such false witness, the person so offending, on conviction thereof before the Supreme Court, shall suffer death; but if no person's life shall be taken in consequence of such false witness, the offender, on conviction as aforesaid, shall be punished as in this act is hereafter provided for the punishment of manslaughter.

Arson with murder.

SEC 5. *And be it enacted,* That if any person shall wilfully or maliciously burn the dwelling house of another, any out building adjoining thereto, or any other building, by means of which any person shall suffer death or be injured in his or her body or members, such offender, on conviction thereof before the Supreme Court, shall suffer death.

Arson.

SEC. 6. *And be it enacted,* That if any person shall wilfully and maliciously burn the dwelling house of another or any out building adjoining thereto or any other building, or if any person shall wilfully and maliciously burn any barn, warehouse, shop, mill, malt house, distillery, out-house, any meeting-house, court-house, goal, school-house, or any other building erected for public or private uses, or any vessel, cutter, or boat used on the rivers or lakes within this Territory, or if any person shall wilfully and maliciously burn any stacks of corn, hay, or grain, the person so offending in either of the cases aforesaid, on conviction thereof before the Supreme Court, shall be sentenced to sit in the pillory, whipped, imprisoned, or confined to hard labor not exceeding seven years, bound to good behavior, or fined a sum not exceeding three thousand dollars, or any or all the foregoing punishments, according to the nature and aggravation of the offense.

SEC. 7. *And be it enacted,* That if any person shall commit manslaughter and be thereof convicted before the Supreme Court, he or she so offending shall be sentenced to stand in the pillory or be whipped not exceeding one hundred stripes, imprisoned, or confined to hard labor not exceeding ten years, bound to good behavior, and fined not exceeding three thousand dollars or any or all the above punishments, according to the nature and aggravation of the offense; and, provided, that if any person shall kill another in the just defense of his or her own life or the life of a wife, husband, parent, brother, sister, master, mistress, or servant, or if any person shall kill another attempting to murder or to commit rape, burglary, or robbery with force and violence; or if any officer shall kill any person in supporting an opposition against him in the just and necessary discharge of his duty, such persons respectively, shall be holden guiltless. Manslaughter.

SEC. 8. *And be it enacted,* That if any person shall wilfully and maliciously cut out or disable the tongue, put out the eye or eyes, or cut off all or any part of the privy members of any person, or shall aid or assist therein, such person on conviction thereof before the Supreme Court, shall pay a fine not exceeding three thousand dollars, and be imprisoned or confined to hard labor for a period not exceeding ten years. Mayhem

SEC. 9. *And be it enacted,* That if any man shall ravish or carnally know any woman, maid, or damsel, committing carnal copulation with her by force against her will, and being thereof convicted before the Supreme Court, he shall be fined not exceeding one thousand dollars, and be imprisoned or confined to hard labor during life. Rape.

SEC. 10. *And be it enacted,* That if any person over the age of fifteen years shall unlawfully and carnally know and abuse any woman child under the age of eleven years, with her will or against her will, and being thereof convicted before the Supreme Court, he shall suffer the same punishment as directed in the ninth section of this act. Unlawfully knowing a woman child under eleven years.

SEC. 11. *And be it enacted,* That if any person shall in the night time burglariously break and enter any dwelling house, store, or shop for merchandise, or workshop, with intent to kill, rob, steal, commit rape, or to do or perpetrate any other high crime or misdemeanor, the person so offending, on conviction thereof before the Supreme Court, shall be punished by whipping not exceeding one hundred stripes, and be imprisoned or confined to hard labor not exceeding twelve years, and pay a fine not exceeding three thousand dollars, or any or all the foregoing punishments, according to the nature and aggravation of the offense. Burglary.

SEC. 12. *And be it enacted,* That if any person shall feloniously assault, rob and take from another person, any money, goods or chattels, or other property, that may be the subject of theft, the Robbery.

1808.

person so offending, on conviction thereof before the Supreme Court, shall be punished as is directed in case of burglary; and if any person shall make an assault upon another person with intent to commit murder or robbery, the person so offending, and being thereof convicted, before the Supreme Court, shall pay a fine not exceeding eight hundred dollars, and may be imprisoned or kept to hard labor for a term not exceeding ten years, and shall give bond, with sufficient sureties, for his or her good behavior in such sum as the court shall direct.

Perjury.

SEC. 13. *And be it enacted,* That if any person shall knowingly, wilfully and corruptly commit perjury in any cause or matter pending before any court of law or equity, auditors, referees, or arbitrator, or in any other case in which an oath or affirmation is, or may be administered, by direction of law, such person, on conviction thereof, before the Supreme Court, shall be punished by standing in the pillory for the space of two hours, pay a fine not exceeding one thousand dollars, and suffer imprisonment, without bail or main prize, for a term not exceeding six months, or a part or all of the aforesaid punishments, at the discretion of the said court, and shall thereafter be discredited and disabled from being sworn or giving evidence, or verdict in any case whatever until judgment on such conviction be reversed, and the person so convicted shall forfeit and pay treble damages to the parties aggrieved by such offense, to be recovered by an action brought on this statute.

Subornation of perjury.

SEC. 14. *And be it enacted,* If any person shall unlawfully and corruptly procure any witness or witnesses by letters, by rewards, promises, or by any other similar or unlawful labor, or means whatever, to commit wilful and corrupt perjury in any cause or matter pending before any court of law, or equity, auditors, referees, or arbitrators, or in any other case, such person, on conviction thereof, before the Supreme Court, shall suffer the same punishment, penalties, and forfeitures, and be subject to the same disabilities in all respects as is provided in the last preceding section.

How indictments for perjury are to be set out.

SEC. 15. *And be it enacted,* That in any presentment or indictment to be procured against any person for wilful and corrupt perjury, or subornation of perjury, it shall be sufficient to set forth the substance of the offense charged upon the defendant, and by what court and before whom the oath or affirmation was taken, averring such court, or person, or persons to have a competent authority to administer the same, together with the proper averment or averments to falsify the matter or matters in which the perjury or perjuries is or are assigned, without setting forth the bill, answer, information, indictment, declaration, or any part of any record or proceeding, either in law or equity, other than as aforesaid, and without setting forth the commission or authority of the court or person or persons before whom the perjury was committed.

Forgery.

SEC. 16. *And be it enacted,* That if any person shall wittingly, falsely, and deceitfully forge or alter, or wittingly, falsely, and deceitfully cause to be forged, or altered, or procure, aid, or counsel the forging or altering any matter of record, any writ, process, or

1808.

other proceedings in the courts or other course of justice in this Territory, any deed of conveyance, last will and testament, obligation or writing sealed, any promissory note, bill of exchange, order, acceptance, assignment, or endorsement on them, any acquittance, or receipt for money, goods, or other things, or any order, warrant, or request for the payment of money or the delivery of goods, or chattels of any kind, any certificate, or accountable receipt for money or other things, any lottery ticket, or any evidence or assurance of money, or other thing whatever, with intent to defraud any person, or if any person shall utter or publish as true, any of the above false, forged, altered and counterfeited deeds and other matters or instruments, as above specified, or shall in anywise be aiding or assisting therein with intent to deceive or defraud any person, the person so offending, on conviction thereof before the Supreme Court, shall be punished by sitting in the pillory, imprisonment not exceeding three years, and pay a fine not exceeding two thousand dollars, or a part or all the aforesaid punishments according to the nature and aggravation of the offense, and shall thereafter be disabled from giving evidence or verdict in any cause or case whatever, and the person so convicted shall forfeit and pay treble damages to the party aggrieved by such offense, to be recovered by action brought on this statute.

Horse stealing.

SEC. 17. *And be it enacted,* That if any person shall hereafter steal any horse or horses, or any horse kind, on conviction thereof before the Supreme Court, shall be whipped not exceeding one hundred stripes and be imprisoned or confined to hard labor not exceeding seven years and be further punished by fine not exceeding three hundred dollars, and the court before whom the conviction is had may award to the party from whom such horse or horses was or were stolen, treble damage, and such party is hereby empowered to assign such convict in service to satisfy the same, and any person to whom such convict is assigned may, in any manner without cruelty, chain or otherwise shackle or confine him in the common goal or elsewhere in such manner as may be necessary for his performing from day to day the task or labor enjoined on him; *Provided,* That if the cost and treble damages be paid the court may remit the fine which may have been adjudged in the premises, and every person who shall be convicted as aforesaid shall, on a second conviction, be punished by whipping not exceeding one hundred stripes and confined to hard labor a term not exceeding ten years, or any or any part or all of the aforesaid punishment, at the discretion of the court before whom conviction was had.

Proviso.

Adultery.

SEC. 18. *And be it enacted,* That if any person shall commit adultery and be thereof convicted before the Supreme Court, he or she shall be punished by fine not exceeding five hundred dollars.

Defaming civil authority.

SEC. 19. *And be it enacted,* That if any person shall defame any court of justice or any sentence or proceedings thereof, or shall defame any of the magistrates, judges, or justices of any such court touching any act or sentence therein passed, on conviction

1808.

thereof before the Supreme Court, shall be punished by fine not exceeding two hundred dollars.

Forgery of coins, or counterfeiting.

SEC. 20. *And be it enacted,* That if any person shall forge, counterfeit, or utter any of the coins which shall be made current by the laws of this Territory or of the United States, or shall pass or put off, or shall offer, or shall procure to be offered, passed, or put off, any such forged, false, or counterfeited coins, knowing them to be such, or shall make or mend, or have in possession, any die, stamp, or any other instrument or tool, or shall buy or sell any such die, stamp, or other instrument or tool, for the purpose of forging or counterfeiting any of the coins aforesaid, every person so offending, and being thereof convicted before the Supreme Court, shall be punished by whipping not exceeding one hundred stripes, and may be sentenced to stand in the pillory not less than one hour each day for three days successively, and be committed to any goal or house of corrrection within the Territory, and be there kept to hard labor, for so long a time as the Supreme Court shall adjudge, not exceeding seven years, and shall pay a fine not exceeding seven hundred dollars to the treasury of this Territory, and if any person shall counsel, advise, procure, or in any way assist in forging, counterfeiting, falsifying, or in altering, or in passing or putting off any of the coins aforesaid, knowing the same to be such, and be thereof convicted before the Supreme Court, such person or persons so offending shall be punished by whipping not exceeding one hundred stripes, and stand in the pillory one hour in each day for three days successively, and shall pay to the treasury of this Territory in the discretion of the Supreme Court a sum not exceeding four hundred dollars.

Counterfeiting bank bills.

SEC. 21. *And be it enacted,* That if any person shall counterfeit, or cause, or procure to be counterfeited, or aid or assist in counterfeiting any bill or note issued or to be issued by the President, directors and company of the bank of the United States, or by the directors of any other bank, by whatever name it may be called or denominated by or under the authority of the Legislature of this Territory, or any of the United States of America, or Territories thereof, shall alter any such bill or note issued or to be issued as aforesaid, or shall utter, pass, or give in payment, orprocure to be offered, passed or given in payment, any such counterfeited or altered note or bill, knowing the same to be counterfeited or altered, or shall make and engrave any plate or other instrument, or shall cause or procure the same to be made or engraved, or shall have any such plate or instrument in his or her possession for the purpose of counterfeiting, every person so offending, on conviction thereof before the Supreme Court, shall suffer the same punishment as is directed in the twentieth section of this act.

Theft of good chattels, etc.

SEC. 22. *And be it enacted,* That if any person shall steal any money, goods, or chattels, or any bond, bill, note, accountable receipt or other written security, assurance or promise for the payment of money, or performance of any covenant, contract, or agreement, or any acquittance, release, or discharge of any debt, due, demand, covenant, contract, or agreement, any person so

1808.

offending, his or her councilors, aiders, or abettors knowing of or privy to the offenses aforesaid, on conviction thereof before any district court or the Supreme Court, shall be fined not exceeding three hundred dollars or be whipped not exceeding thirty-nine stripes, and the said court shall further award to the party from whom the money, goods, or other articles were stolen treble the value thereof, and any of the articles stolen being returned undamaged, to be accounted part according to the value thereof, and if such offender shall be unable to make restitution or pay such treble damage, he may be assigned in service to make satisfaction, and the party to whom satisfaction is to be made is hereby empowered to dispose of such convict in service for such term of time as shall be ordered by the court before whom the conviction shall be had.

Receiving or concealing stolen goods.

SEC. 23. *And be it enacted,* That if any person shall buy or receive any goods, chattels, or other thing taken or stolen from any other person, knowing the same to be stolen, or shall receive or harbor any thief or thieves, knowing him, her, or them to be such, the person so offending, on conviction thereof, shall be liable to the same punishment as is prescribed in the preceding section.

Fruit stealing.

SEC. 24. *And be it enacted,* That if any person shall steal any fruit from any orchard, garden, or other enclosure, whether such fruit had been previously severed from the tree, plant, or vine on which it had grown or not, he or she shall be punished by fine not exceeding fifty dollars, and the court before which the conviction shall be had shall award to the party injured treble damages and costs, and in case of inability to pay such damages and costs, may assign such person in service to make satisfaction.

Impeding officers in the execution of their office.

SEC. 25. *And be it enacted,* That if any person or persons shall impede or hinder any officer, judicial or executive, civic or military, under the authority of this Territory, in the execution of his office, such person or persons, on conviction thereof, shall pay a fine not exceeding two hundred dollars each to the treasury of the district in which the offense was committed, and if any such person or persons shall not be of sufficient ability to pay such fine and cost of prosecution, the court may assign such person or persons in service to any citizen of this Territory for so long a time as shall be necessary to make satisfaction of such fine and costs, and if any person shall be convicted a second time of the aforesaid offense, he shall pay a fine not exceeding two hundred dollars, and shall be imprisoned in any goal in the Territory one whole year, and if, at the expiration of said term, he be not of sufficient ability to pay such fine and costs he shall be liable to be assigned to service as aforesaid.

Breaking of goal.

SEC. 26. *And be it enacted,* That if any person or persons shall directly or indirectly break open or counsel, aid, or assist in breaking open any goal or place of confinement in which any prisoner shall be confined by the authority of this Territory or of the United States within this Territory, such person or persons, on conviction thereof, shall pay a fine not exceeding two hundred dollars to the treasury of the district where the offense is committed and be imprisoned six months, and if any such person or

1808.

persons, at the expiration of said term, shall not be of sufficient ability to pay such fine and the costs of prosecution, he, she or they may be assigned in service as directed in the last preceding section, and if any person shall be convicted a second time of the aforesaid offense, he, she, or they shall pay a fine not exceeding three hundred dollars and be imprisoned one year.

Fraudulent conveyance.

SEC. 27. *And be it enacted,* That all fraudulent and deceitful conveyances of goods or chattels and all bonds, bills, notes, contracts and agreements, and all suits and judgments and executions made or had to avoid any right, debt, or duty of others shall, as against the party or parties only whose right, debt, or duty is endeavored to be avoided, their heirs, executors, administrators, or assigns, be utterly null and void, any false pretense or feigned consideration to the contrary notwithstanding, and every of the parties to such fraudulent and deceitful conveyance of goods or chattels, bond, bill, note, contract, agreement, suit, judgment, or execution, or any conveyance of houses, lands, tenements, hereditaments made with like fraudulent intent, who, being privy thereto, shall justify the same to be made, had, or executed bona fide and upon good consideration, or shall alien or assign any houses, lands, tenements, hereditaments, so to him, her, or them conveyed as aforesaid, shall forfeit the full value of such houses, lands, tenements, hereditaments, and the full value of such goods or chattels; and also so much money as shall be contained in such covenant, bond, bill, note, contract, or agreement, which forfeiture shall be equally divided between the parties aggrieved and the district treasurer when the conviction is had, for the use of such district to be recovered by an action brought on this statute.

Private banks restrained.

SEC. 28. *And be it enacted,* That if any person or number of persons, society or company of men, within this Territory, without authority and license first had and obtained from the legislative authority thereof, shall strike, emit, or put in circulation any bills of credit or notes on any fund or credit of any person or persons, society, or company, to be passed and used as a general currency or medium of trade, traffic, or commerce in lieu of money (other than promissory notes of hand and bills of exchange), every person herein offending, on conviction thereof, shall forfeit treble the nominal value of the bills or notes so emitted or put in circulation, one-third part to him, her, or them who shall sue for and prosecute the same to effect, and the other two-thirds to the treasury of the district in which the conviction shall be had.

Bills of private banks prohibited.

SEC. 29. *And be it enacted,* That if any person or persons within this Territory shall utter, vend, or pass any bills or notes or other currency whatever, which either have been or which shall hereafter be struck, emitted, or put in circulation to be passed and used as a general currency or medium of trade, traffic, or commerce in lieu of money, as mentioned in the last preceding section, on the fund or credit of any person or persons or private society or company of men, either in this Territory or any of the United States or Territories thereof, shall forfeit double the value expressed in such bill, note, or other currency, the one moiety thereof to him,

1808.

her, or them, who shall sue for and prosecute the same to effect, and the other moiety to the treasury of the district in which the conviction shall be had; *Provided, nevertheless*, That nothing in this or the preceding section shall be construed to prevent any person or persons from demanding and receiving payment from any person or persons, society, or company of persons, on any bill or note which may have been emitted or issued by him or them before the passage of this act.

Proviso.

SEC. 30. *And be it enacted*, That if any person or persons, after the first day of June next, shall pass or offer to pass within this Territory any cut, mutilated, or altered coins, which coins, before they were cut, mutilated, or altered passed as current money in this Territory or in any of the United States, such person or persons shall forfeit double the value of such cut, mutilated, or altered coins which they shall have passed or offered to pass as aforesaid, one moiety to him or them, who shall prosecute for the same, and the other moiety to this Territory, to be recovered by action brought on this statute for that purpose, with cost of prosecution.

Passing of cut or mutilated money prohibited.

SEC. 31. *And be it enacted*, That if any person or persons within this Territory without authority and license first had and obtained from the legislative authority thereof, shall publicly or privately set up or make any lottery, game, or device of chance of any nature or by any name whatever, or shall, by any such means, expose for sale any houses, lands, tenements, or real estate, or any goods, wares, merchandise, or other thing or things whatever, every person so offending, on conviction thereof, shall forfeit the amount of the whole sum or value for which such lottery was made, to be recovered by action brought on this statute, one moiety thereof to him or them, who shall sue for and prosecute the same to effect, and the other moiety to the treasury of the district in which such conviction shall be had; and every person who shall vend, sell, or barter, or who shall offer to vend, sell or barter any ticket or tickets of such private lottery, game, or device of chance, or if any person shall purchase or become an adventurer or adventuress therein, or in any wise whatever be aiding or assisting in the same, any person so offending, on conviction thereof, shall pay a sum not exceeding thirty dollars, to be sued for and applied as above directed, and every ticket or other assurance purporting to entitle any person, bearer or possessor, to any prize or prizes in money or to any houses, lands, tenements, or other real estate, or to any other article or thing, for the disposition of which such lottery was erected, shall be utterly null and void, and no action shall be maintained thereon in any court in this Territory.

Private lotteries restrained.

SEC. 32. *And be it enacted*, That all contracts, promises, bills, notes, bonds, judgments, and other assurances, and all mortgages, conveyances, or sureties made and executed by any person or persons whatever, in which the whole, or any part of the consideration of the same was for any money, goods, or chattels won on any game, horse racing, or any other sport, or for any money, goods, or chattels lent or borrowed for such purpose at the time

Gambling contracts void.

1808.

and place of gaming, be and they are hereby declared to be utterly null and void to all intents and purpose.

Riotous assemblages.

SEC. 33. *And be it enacted,* That when three or more persons shall meet or assemble themselves together with intent to do any unlawful act, with force and violence, against the person of another, or against his or her goods or possessions, or to do any unlawful act against the peace or to the manifest terror of the people, and being required or commanded by proclamation to be made in the form and by the authority hereinafter directed, shall not disperse themselves and peaceably depart to their homes or lawful business, or being so assembled as aforesaid, shall do any unlawful act against the person, goods, or possessions of any person, or against the peace, and be thereof convicted before any court proper to try the same, they shall be severally punished by fine not exceeding one hundred dollars or imprisonment not exceeding six months; any and every justice of the peace, marshal, or his deputies, within their respective jurisdictions, are hereby authorized, empowered, and required, on notice or knowledge of any such unlawful and riotous assembly, to resort to the place where such assembly shall be, and after commanding silence, shall, with a loud voice make proclamation nearly as followeth, namely: "In the name of the Territory I command all persons being assembled immediately to disperse themselves and depart to their habitations, or to their lawful business, under the pains and penalties of the law."

Not dispersing when ordered.

SEC. 34. *And be it enacted,* That if such persons so unlawfully assembled, or any three or more of them, after proclamation made as aforesaid, shall continue together and not disperse themselves, it shall and may be lawful for every justice of the peace, marshal, and his deputies who shall be present, and for every other person or persons who shall be commanded to assist such justice, marshal, or deputy marshal who are hereby authorized and empowered to command all or any of the inhabitants of this territory to assist them respectively to seize and apprehend, and they are hereby required to seize and apprehend such persons unlawfully and riotously assembled and continuing together after proclamation made as aforesaid, that they may be proceeded with according to law.

Killing of rioters not criminal.

SEC. 35. *And be it enacted,* That if any of the persons so unlawfully and riotously assembled and continuing together as aforesaid to the number of twelve, for the space of one hour after proclamation made as aforesaid, shall happen to be killed, maimed, or hurt in dispersing or apprehending, or in endeavoring to disperse or apprehend them, by reason of their resisting the person or persons dispersing or endeavoring to disperse or apprehend them, every justice of the peace, marshal, or deputy marshal, and all and singular the persons aiding or assisting them, or any of them shall severally be freed, discharged, and indemnified from any bill, complaint, indictment, or action that may be commenced against him or them on that account.

Obstructing proclamation.

SEC. 36. *And be it enacted,* That if any person or persons shall forcibly, wilfully, or knowingly oppose or obstruct any person

1808.

who shall begin or attempt to make proclamation as herein directed, whereby such proclamation shall not be made, or after such attempt and obstruction shall continue together and not disperse, having knowledge thereof, each and every person so offending shall be punished by fine not exceeding one hundred dollars, and imprisoned not exceeding six months: *Provided always,* that no person shall be punished by the two preceding sections of this act, unless prosecution be commenced within six months after the offense is committed.

Breaking of the peace.

SEC. 37. *And be it enacted,* That if any person shall in any manner disturb and break the peace by tumultuous and offensive carriage, by threatening, quarreling, challenging, assaulting, beating, or striking any other person, the person or persons so offending shall be liable to pay such fine as the court, taking into consideration the situation of the party smiting or being smitten, the instrument and danger of the assault, the time, place, and provocation, according to the nature of the offense, shall adjudge, and if such offense be aggravated by any high handed violence, it shall be the duty of a justice of the peace to bind over the offender to the next district court in the district where the offense shall be committed.

Persons standing mute, how proceed against.

SEC. 38. *And be it enacted,* That in all indictments founded on this act when the persons arraigned shall obstinately stand mute, or refuse to plead and be tried by due course of law, such standing mute, or refusal to plead and be tried, as aforesaid, shall be judged to amount to and be a proper traverse or denial of the facts charged in the indictment, and the trial shall thereupon proceed in like manner, and the record shall be in the same form, and the same judgment shall be given against the said party if found guilty as if he or she had, on being arraigned, plead not guilty, and for trial had put himself or herself on the country.

Grand jury.

SEC. 39. *And be it enacted,* That when the grand jury, attending the Supreme or District Court, are empaneled and sworn, the court shall appoint a foreman, who shall have power to swear all witnesses to testify before them, and who shall, where the grand jury or any twelve of them find a bill of indictment to be supported by good and sufficient evidence, write thereon "a true bill," and if they do not find any bill to be supported by sufficient evidence, the foreman shall endorse thereon "this bill not found," and the accused person shall thereupon be discharged; and no person shall be held to trial for a capital offense unless a bill of indictment be found against such person for such crime by a grand jury legally empaneled and sworn, and no bill of indictment shall be presented by a grand jury unless twelve of the jurors shall be agreed in the same, and no person shall be compelled to plead to any indictment or information until he or she shall have been furnished with a copy of such indictment or information at least twenty-four hours, and it is hereby made the duty of the attorney prosecuting to furnish the same.

Right of challenging jurors.

SEC. 40. *And be it enacted,* That any person indicted for any crime, mentioned in this act, who shall have duly pleaded to the

1808.

indictment or information against him, and put himself on the country for trial shall be permitted to challenge peremptorily six of the jurors, and as great a number farther as he or she can shew good cause for challenging; and if any person indicted as aforesaid shall refuse to put himself or herself on the country for trial, or shall peremptorily challenge a greater number than six of the jurors as aforesaid, the court shall disallow such peremptory challenges, above the number of six, and the jury shall be charged and the trial proceed in like manner in all respects, and the like judgment shall be given as if the person so refusing to put himself on the country for trial or so challenging a greater number than six jurors without assigning any cause, had duly put himself or herself on the country for trial, and had not peremptorily challenged a greater number of jurors than by law he or she might or could have done, and no peremptory challenges to jurors shall be made in behalf of the Territory.

Defendant may have witnesses, etc.

SEC. 41. *And be it enacted,* That every person who shall be arraigned or tried for any criminal offense shall be admitted to make any proof that he or she can produce by lawful witness or witnesses who shall then be under oath for his or her just defense in that behalf, and shall have the like process of the court in which he or she shall be tried to compel his or her witnesses to appear for him or her at such trial as is usually granted to compel witnesses to appear against him or her.

May find verdict of manslaughter

SEC. 42. *And be it enacted,* That every person arraigned and tried on an indictment for murder, burglary, or robbery, and the evidence in the opinion of the jury shall not be sufficient to prove the crime alleged, it shall be lawful for the jury, on an indictment for murder, to acquit the person indicted for the murder, and to find him or her guilty of manslaughter if the evidence shall be sufficient thereto, and on all indictments for burglary and robbery the jury may acquit of the crimes alleged and convict of stealing if the evidence shall be sufficient thereto.

Death penalty, how inflicted.

SEC. 43. *And be it enacted,* That the manner of inflicting the punishment of death shall be hanging the person convicted by the neck until dead.

Justices of the peace, jurisdiction of in criminal cases.

SEC. 44. *And be it enacted,* That every justice of the peace, within his respective district, be, and he is hereby fully authorized and empowered to hear, try, and determine all cases and actions of a criminal nature, where the fines and forfeitures are within the sum of seven dollars.

Idem.

SEC. 45. *And be it enacted,* That every justice of the peace within his district be and he is hereby empowered to cause to be apprehended and committed to prison, or bound over to be tried at the district or Supreme Court, all criminal offenders, the enormity of whose misdemeanors surpass his power to try, and it shall be the duty of each justice of the peace who shall bind over any respondent to appear before any district or Supreme Court to bind over the necessary witnesses, who shall attend before such justice to appear before the same court to which such respondent shall be bound in the same sum in which the respondent shall be bound,

1808.

and in case any witness shall refuse to become recognized as aforesaid, such justice shall have power to commit the person so refusing to the common goal in such district, and the goaler is hereby directed to detain such person until he or she shall enter such recognizance and pay the cost of commitment: *Provided*, that if the respondent shall be committed such justice shall bind each witness severally in such sum as he shall judge proper, considering the nature and aggravation of the offense.

Right of appeal.

SEC. 46. *And be it enacted*, That in all criminal causes cognizable before a justice of the peace, any person who shall think him or herself aggrieved by the sentence or judgment given by such justice shall have liberty to appeal to the next district court to be holden within and for the same district, and the party claiming such appeal shall enter the same within two hours from the time of rendering such sentence or judgment, and shall give sufficient security by way of recognizance to the treasurer of the district where the offense is committed when the prosecution is on behalf of the Territory, and if otherwise to the prosecutor, conditioned that he shall personally appear before said district court and there prosecute his appeal so taken to effect and abide the order or sentence of said court, and the party so appealing shall remain in the custody of an officer until he, she, or they have given such security, and the party appealing shall procure and enter the court in which trial on such appeal is to be had, attested copies of the complaint, warrant, writ, sentence, or judgment, and all the evidence filed in the court from which said appeal was allowed, and in all criminal causes tried before a justice of the peace, in which sentence shall be given when no appeal is entered as aforesaid, the justice shall immediately issue his warrant to carry the same into effect, and the several marshals and the deputy marshals are empowered and required to serve any warrant or precept issuing from a justice of the peace within their respective districts.

Bonds, court may lessen, etc.

SEC. 47. *And be it enacted*, That in all actions brought for the recovery of the penalty or forfeiture annexed to any bond of recognizance given or taken in any criminal cause, the several district courts and the Supreme Court respectively are hereby authorized and empowered to lessen the sum of any such bond or recognizance and render such judgment thereon as the nature and circumstances of the case shall require, any law, usage, or custom to the contrary, notwithstanding.

Repealing.

SEC. 48. *And be it enacted*, That the sixth and eighth sections of an act entitled "An act concerning the marshal of the Territory of Michigan," adopted and published on the tenth day of July, one thousand eight hundred five, be, and the same hereby is repealed; the same being adopted from the laws of one of the original States, to wit: The State of Vermont, as far as necessary and suitable to the circumstances of the Territory of Michigan.

Adopted and published at the city of Detroit, in the Territory of Michigan, this ninth day of December, one thousand eight hundred and eight.

WILLIAM HULL,
Governor of Michigan, and President of the Legislature.

Attest:
JOSEPH WATSON, *Secretary.*

1808.

No. 29.
December 10.

AN ACT to repeal an act for the encouragement of literature and the improvement of the town of Detroit.

Be it enacted by the Governor and Judges of Michigan, That an act for the encouragement of literature and the improvement of the city of Detroit, adopted and published at Detroit the ninth day of September, one thousand eight hundred and five be, and the same is hereby repealed.

Made and published at the city of Detroit, in the Territory of Michigan, this tenth day of December, one thousand eight hundred and eight.

Attest: WILLIAM HULL,
JOS. WATSON, *Governor of Michigan and President*
Secretary. *of the Legislature.*

No. 30.
December 10.

AN ACT in addition to an act making appropriations for service of the year one thousand eight hundred and eight.

For officers, etc., of Legislature.

Be it enacted by the Governor and the Judges of the Territory of Michigan, That for the payment of the daily compensation of the secretary of the legislature, the daily compensation of the sergeant at arms, and the expenses of firewood and other necessary expenses of the legislature for the present year, and likewise for the daily compensation of the legislative secretary previous to the present year, there is appropriated a sum in addition to the sum or sums heretofore appropriated not exceeding one hundred and seventy dollars, the same being adopted from the laws of one of the original States, to wit: The State of Pennsylvania, as far as necessary and suitable to the circumstances of the Territory of Michigan.

Adopted and published at the city of Detroit, in the Territory of Michigan, this tenth day of December, one thousand eight hundred and eight.

Attest: WILLIAM HULL,
JOS. WATSON, *Governor of Michigan and President*
Secretary. *of the Legislature.*

No. 31.
December 15.

AN ACT concerning limitations to claims for donation lots in the city of Detroit.

Sec. previous act repealed.

Be it enacted by the Governor and Judges of the Territory of Michigan, That the last section of the act entitled "An act concerning the town of Detroit," passed the thirteenth day of September, one thousand eight hundred and six, be, and the same is hereby repealed, and that all persons who are entitled to donation lots in the town of Detroit, by the act of Congress of the twenty-first of April, one thousand eight hundred and six, be allowed until the fifteenth day of January, one thousand eight hundred and nine, to exhibit the same to the Governor and Judges as commissioners under said act.

Time for claiming extended.

1808.

Made and published at the city of Detroit, in the Territory of Michigan, this fifteenth day of December, one thousand eight hundred and eight.

Attest: WILLIAM HULL,
JOSEPH WATSON, *Governor of Michigan and President*
Secretary. *of the Legislature.*

AN ACT for laying out and opening a road from the city of Detroit to the foot of the rapids of the Miami, which enters into Lake Erie.

No. 32. December 19.

Lottery—managers appointed.

SECTION 1. *Be it enacted by the Governor and Judges of the Territory of Michigan,* That the Governor be, and hereby is authorized to appoint three persons as managers of a lottery, and the same three persons when appointed as aforesaid shall cause to be raised, by lottery, six thousand dollars.

To raise $6,000.

Bond.

SEC. 2. *And be it further enacted,* That each of the managers who shall be appointed as aforesaid shall, before they enter upon the execution of the duties of their office, enter into a bond to this Territory, with such sureties as the Governor and the Judges of the Supreme court, or any two of them, shall approve, in the sum of two thousand dollars, conditioned for the faithful and honest discharge of the duties required of them by this act, and for rendering a just account of all their proceedings from time to time when called on by the legislative authority of this Territory.

Disposition of funds.

SEC. 3. *And be it further enacted,* That the managers who shall be appointed as aforesaid shall from time to time, and as often as they shall receive the sum of two hundred dollars for the sale of tickets, deposit the same in the treasury of this Territory.

Power to adopt scheme of lottery, etc.

SEC. 4. *And be it further enacted,* That the managers to be appointed as aforesaid, or a majority of them, shall have full power to adopt such scheme or schemes, or to manage the lottery in such manner as they shall think proper; to divide the same into classes not exceeding four, and to provide by their scheme or schemes that a portion of the prizes in the first, not exceeding fifty per cent., shall be paid by tickets in the second class, and in the same manner until the lottery is completed, and the classes shall be drawn without delay after the sale of tickets in the city of Detroit.

Commissioners to lay out road, appointment, duties of, etc.

SEC. 5. *And be it further enacted,* That the Governor of this Territory be, and he hereby is authorized to appoint three commissioners, a majority of whom shall have authority to lay out a road from the city of Detroit to the foot of the rapids of the river Miami, which enters into Lake Erie, of the width of one hundred and twenty feet, in the best and most convenient route, and to have the same surveyed under their direction by such surveyor as shall be appointed by the Governor, and each of said commissioners shall be entitled to a sum not exceeding four dollars a day, to be paid from the proceeds of the lottery, and immediately after the survey is made they shall return a plan of the same to the Legislature of this Territory.

1808.

Damages, how assessed and determined.

SEC. 6. *And be it further enacted,* That if any part of the road shall be laid through inclosed or improved lands the owners thereof shall be paid such damages as may be sustained by reason thereof, which damages shall be determined and assessed in the manner prescribed in like cases in and by the third section of an act entitled "An act concerning highways and roads," adopted the eighteenth day of September, one thousand eight hundred and five, and the payment shall be made from the proceeds of the lottery.

Net proceeds of the lottery to be used to pay for road.

SEC. 7. *And be it further enacted,* That the net proceeds of the lottery, after paying all the expenses of surveying and laying out the road and the expenses of managing the lottery, shall be, and hereby are appropriated to the opening and making the road aforesaid, and such bridges as may be necessary on the same, and for no other purpose, and it shall be done in such manner and under the direction of such agent or agents as the legislative authority of this Territory shall hereafter direct; the same being adopted from the laws of one of the original States, to wit: The State of New York, as far as necessary and suitable to the circumstances of the Territory of Michigan.

Adopted and published at the city of Detroit, within the Territory of Michigan, this nineteenth day of December, one thousand eight hundred and eight.

Attest:
JOSEPH WATSON,
Secretary.

WILLIAM HULL,
Governor of Michigan and President of the Legislature.

No. 33.
December 21.

AN ACT in addition to an act entitled "An act concerning the militia of the Territory of Michigan."

Governor may make detail of the militia.

SECTION 1. *Be it enacted by the Governor and Judges of the Territory of Michigan,* That the Governor of this Territory is hereby authorized and empowered to make detachments of the militia for actual service, or to be held in readiness for the same, in conformity to any requisitions which have been or hereafter shall be made by the President of the United States, pursuant to law, and likewise in case of threatened invasion, insurrection, or other public dangers, when he shall think it necessary, and it shall be the duty of the adjutant general to detail the number of non-commissioned officers, music, and privates, which each regiment and other corps are to furnish, and after the commanding officers of regiments or corps have proportioned the number to the respective companies, the persons to be detached shall be determined by lot in such manner as the commanding officer of the company shall direct; and any person absent or refusing to draw, the commanding officer of the company shall draw for him, and it shall be equally binding as if he was present and drew for himself; *Provided,* however, that no person or persons enrolled in the militia under the age of eighteen years and over the age of forty-five years, shall be liable to be detached by virtue of any requisition

Adjutant Gen. to detail requisite number.

Determination by lot of those to be detached, how performed, etc.

Proviso as to age.

from the President of the United States or marched out of the Territory, by virtue of any orders from the Governor thereof.

1808.

SEC. 2. *And be it further enacted,* That every person who shall be ordered or detached in conformity to the provisions of the foregoing section, who shall neglect or refuse to appear at the place of rendezvous, armed and equipped as the law directs, after having been duly notified, or shall not, in twenty-four hours after he shall have been notified as aforesaid, pay a fine of thirty-four dollars to the commanding officer of the company which he is ordered to join, or procure an able bodied man in his place, such as shall be accepted by the said commanding officer, shall be liable to be apprehended by a warrant from any justice of the peace in the district where he resides, and committed to the common goal in the district, there to remain without bail or mainprize until he pays the fine of thirty-four dollars aforesaid, or procures an able bodied man in his place, such as shall be accepted by the said commanding officer, or offers himself to join the detachment at the place of rendezvous, and pays all the costs of his arrest and confinement.

Penalty for not appearing when notified.

SEC. 3. *And be it further enacted,* That every person who shall be detached as aforesaid, after he shall have marched to the place of rendezvous, and after having been committed to the charge of the officer or officers appointed to command him, shall be considered as a soldier in such detachment and shall be liable to trial by court martial for disobedience of orders.

When considered a soldier and liable to court martial.

SEC. 4. *And be it further enacted,* That if any person shall abscond or desert from such detachment, and shall attempt to evade the punishment by law provided for desertion, he shall pay a fine of forty dollars, to be sued for and recovered by the captain or commanding officer of the company to which such person belongs at any time within twelve months after the discharge of such detachment, which said fines shall be disposed of and equally divided among the men of said company who actually performed their duty in such detachment.

Desertion.

SEC. 5. *And be it further enacted,* That all officers, non-commissioned officers, and soldiers detached and called into actual service in manner aforesaid, shall be entitled to the same pay and emoluments of every kind, bounty excepted, as the troops of the United States, and be subject to the same rules and regulations.

Pay and emoluments.

Rules and regulations.

SEC. 6. *And be it further enacted,* That if any officer, non-commissioned officer, or private of the militia shall be killed, or die of his wounds received in the service of this Territory, his widow, child, or children shall be entitled to similar relief and under the same regulations and restrictions as is provided by law in such cases for the relief of widows and orphans of persons killed or dying of wounds received in the service of the United States.

Pension.

SEC. 7. *And be it further enacted,* That if any officer, non-commissioned officer, or private of the militia, shall be wounded or otherwise disabled in the service of this Territory, he shall be entitled to similar relief, and under the same regulations and restrictions as is provided by law in such cases for the relief of

Idem.

1808. persons wounded or disabled in the service of the United States; the same being adopted from the laws of two of the original States, to wit: The States of Vermont and Connecticut, so far as necessary and suitable to the circumstances of the Territory of Michigan.

Adopted and published at the city of Detroit, within the Territory of Michigan, this twenty-first day of December, one thousand eight hundred and eight.

Attest: WILLIAM HULL,
JOS. WATSON, *Governor of Michigan and President*
Secretary. *of the Legislature.*

No. 34.
December 27.

AN ADDITIONAL ACT concerning compensation.*

No. 35.
December 27.

AN ACT to provide for the assessment and collection of a territorial tax.

Licenses, for what required.

Be it enacted by the Governor and Judges of the Territory of Michigan, That no person shall be permitted to retail any goods, wares, or merchandise within this Territory other than the growth or manufacture of the United States, or keep a tavern or public house, or occupy or employ any ferry boat or other water craft for transporting persons or property across any rivers or other waters within or bounding this Territory, for hire, after the tenth day of January next unless he shall have received a license therefor from three justices of the peace, within the district where such person resides, and any three justices as aforesaid are hereby authorized, on application, to grant such license, and shall assess such persons respectively in a sum they shall deem equitable, according to the profits arising from their respective operations; *Provided*: That no retailers of merchandise shall be assessed more than twenty dollars nor less than five dollars, nor any tavern keeper more than twenty dollars nor less than one dollar, nor any keeper of a ferry at more than fifteen dollars nor less than one dollar, and the justices assessing as aforesaid shall furnish the treasurer of the Territory with a certificate of the names of the several persons licensed by them and the sums in which they have assessed each person, on or before the first day of February next, and shall likewise fix and certify the rates of ferriage each ferry keeper is authorized to demand; and if any person shall retail any goods, keep a tavern or ferry after the said tenth day of January without having obtained a license as aforesaid, he shall be liable to pay a sum not exceeding fifty dollars to the treasury of the Territory, to be recovered in the name of the treasurer thereof with costs of prosecution in an action brought on this statute before any court of competent jurisdiction.

Any three justices may grant and fix amount of.

Proviso, maximum and minimum rate.

Certificate of license to be sent to the Treasurer, etc.

Rate of ferriage.

Penalty for neglect to obtain license.

Auctioneers.

SEC. 2. *Be it enacted,* That there shall be collected from each

* Printed in full, p. 13, vol. 2, Territorial laws.

1808.

auctioneer a tax of twenty dollars, and from every person keeping one or more stud horses the sum of two dollars for each horse.

Stud horses.

SEC. 3. *Be it enacted,* That the treasurer shall make a list of the persons liable to pay taxes either by the first or second section of this act, and affix the sums severally to their names and sign the same in his official capacity and deliver it to the marshal of the Territory, taking his receipt for the same, and the said marshal shall collect and pay the amount thereof into the treasury on or before the first day of June next.

Treasurer to make up list, etc.

Marshal to collect tax, etc.

SEC. 4. *Be it enacted,* That if any person shall neglect or refuse to pay the sum whereof he stands assessed in such roll or rate bill, the marshal is empowered and required to destrain the goods or chattels of such person, and after having given six days' notice thereof to the owner, may sell the same at public auction to the highest bidder, and after deducting a sufficient sum to pay the tax and reasonable costs, shall return the surplus, if any, to the owner of such property.

Penalty for refusal to pay tax.

SEC. 5. *Be it enacted,* That the several acts and parts of acts hereinafter mentioned be, and the same are hereby repealed, viz.: "An act in addition to an act entitled, 'An act concerning ferries, tavern keepers, and retailers of merchandise,'" adopted the twenty-sixth day of September, one thousand eight hundred and six; "An act imposing certain taxes," adopted the tenth day of September, one thousand eight hundred and five; the first, fourth, fifth, sixth, seventh, and eleventh sections of "An act concerning ferries, tavern keepers, and retailers of merchandise," adopted the twenty-ninth day of August, one thousand eight hundred and five; "An act concerning the taxes of the year one thousand eight hundred and eight," adopted the second day of June, one thousand eight hundred and seven; "An act to repeal certain parts of the act relative to ferries, taverns, retailers, auctioneers, and taxes," adopted the eleventh day of December, one thousand eight hundred and six; "An act in addition to an act entitled, 'An act imposing certain taxes and to repeal certain parts of the said act,'" adopted the twenty-sixth day of September, one thousand eight hundred and five; "An act repealing in part an act concerning ferries, taverns, and retailers of merchandise, and so much of an act concerning auctions, as imposed a duty of fifteen dollars on auctioneers, adopted the thirtieth day of August, one thousand eight hundred and five, the same being adopted from the laws of two of the original States, to wit: The State of New York and the State of Ohio, as far as necessary and suitable to the circumstances of the territory of Michigan.

Repealing.

Adopted and published at the city of Detroit, within the Territory of Michigan, this twenty-seventh day of December, one thousand eight hundred and eight.

Attest: WILLIAM HULL,

JOS. WATSON, *Governor of Michigan and President*

Secretary. *of the Legislature.*

1809.
No. 36.
January 17.

AN ACT prescribing the mode of assessing and collecting taxes within this Territory.

Judges of district court to appoint.

Be it enacted by the Governor and Judges of the Territory of Michigan, That the judges of the respective district courts within this Territory, or a majority of them, shall, some time in the month of March, annually, appoint in each respective district three discreet persons, who shall be denominated district assessors, who shall, between the first day of June and the fifteenth day of July in each year, make out a roll of all the free male inhabitants of the district over the age of twenty-one years and under sixty, and also a roll of all those over eighteen years and under twenty-one, on which roll, agreeable to a form to be furnished by the treasurer of the Territory, they shall make assessment in the manner following, to wit: on each head or poll over twenty-one years and under sixty, twenty dollars; on each head or poll over eighteen and under twenty-one, ten dollars; on each acre of improved land other than orchardings, one dollar and seventy-five cents; on each acre of orchard, ten dollars; on each house of the value of two hundred dollars and upward, at the rate of two per cent on its just value; on each pleasure wheel carriage, eight per cent on its just value; on each horse kind of three years old and upwards, thirteen dollars and fifty cents; on each ox, bull, cow, steer, or heifer of three years old and upward, six dollars and fifty cents; on each house clock, other than wooden clocks, and gold watches, ten dollars, and on other watches, three dollars; and shall assess each practicing attorney, physician, merchant, auctioneer, or peddler, and each keeper of tavern or ferry such sum as shall seem proportionable and just according to the profits arising to them respectively from their professions or employments, not exceeding two hundred dollars, nor less than twenty dollars each; which roll of assessments made up as aforesaid shall be signed by said assessors, or any two of them, and delivered to their respective district treasurers, and an exact duplicate returned to the treasurer of the Territory on or before the thirty-first day of July following, except the assessors for the district of Michilimackinac shall be allowed until the tenth day of September to make their returns to the treasurer of the Territory; and the assessors previous to entering upon the duties prescribed by this act, shall severally take an oath before some magistrate within this Territory, faithfully and impartially to discharge the same; and when any person liable to be assessed by the provisions of this section, shall, on request made by any assessors, neglect or refuse to exhibit or disclose any matter or thing within his knowledge or possession which is made subject to assessment by this section, it shall be lawful for the assessors to assess double the assessment on such matter or thing which they shall have good reason to believe such person is possessed of and refuses to exhibit or disclose as aforesaid, and shall note it in their roll of assessment as being two-fold: *Provided,* That the judges of the district of Michilimackinac shall be allowed until the first day of July of the present year to make

District assessors, duties of, etc. — Poll tax. — Land, improved. — Orchards. — Houses. — Carriages. — Horse. — Cattle. — Clocks. — Watches. — Professions and business pursuits. — Tax roll to be delivered to treasurers,—when. — Time extended for Michilimackinac. — Oath, assessor's. — Refusal to disclose, penalty for. — Proviso—Michilimackinac district.

1809.

the appointment of assessors, and the assessors until the fifteenth day of August to make the return of the assessment of that district to the treasurer of the territory.

Territorial Tax, how assessed and collected.

SEC. 2. *And be it enacted*, That when it is necessary to collect a territorial tax the same shall be first assessed by the legislature thereof, declaring what sum shall be raised upon the dollar of the aggregate of the whole of the last preceding district assessments, made and returned to the treasurer of the territory, agreeable to the provisions of the first section of this act, and thereupon it shall be the duty of the treasurer of the territory to make out a roll or rate bill on which shall be written the names of the several persons found on the returns made by the district assessors as aforesaid, annexing to the names severally the sum of which they stand assessed, and on another column, in which shall be entered the sum of the tax to be collected, and shall sign the same, affixing the office of treasurer of the territory, and shall deliver the same to the marshal of the territory, taking his receipt for the amount of the said tax, specifying the time within which the marshal is to collect and account for the same at the said treasury, which shall not exceed the first day of the following October.

Penalty for non-payment, how enforced, etc.

SEC. 3. *And be it enacted*, That it shall be the duty of the marshal of the territory to receive and receipt the said rate bill as aforesaid, and when any person whose name shall be on said rate bill shall refuse or neglect to pay to the said marshal the sum annexed to his name as aforesaid within a reasonable time after notified thereof by the marshal, in case of such refusal or neglect the marshal is hereby empowered and directed to distrain the goods and chattels of such person, and sell the same at public auction to the highest bidder, after first having given six days' notice of such sale by posting up an advertisement thereof in some conspicuous place where such sale is to be made, and after having retained so much of the money arising from the sale as will pay the tax for which such property was sold and the just costs attending the same, he shall return the overplus money (if any) to the owner of such property, and in cases where the marshal cannot find property whereon to levy, he is hereby empowered and directed to take the body of such delinquent and commit him to the goal within the same district, and the keeper of the prison is hereby required to detain such person until he shall have paid his said tax and the cost which has accrued on the same, or be otherwise liberated by order of law; *Provided*, That in cases where the tax is wholly on the poll, if the person against whom such poll tax is about to be collected procures a certificate from two disinterested justices of the peace within the same district setting forth and declaring that they consider such person wholly unable to pay such tax, and that they do believe such person has not fraudulently concealed or disposed of any property for the purpose of evading the payment thereof, the body of such person shall not be imprisoned for such tax.

Proviso, as to poll tax.

District taxes, levying and collecting of.

SEC. 4. *And be it enacted*, That in levying and collecting district taxes the same mode shall be pursued as is pointed out by

1809.

the second and third sections of this act, except the tax shall be assessed by the district courts, and the rate bill shall be made by the district treasurer, and delivered to the marshal of the district, and the treasurer and marshal of each respective district shall have the same powers and be subject to the same accountability in the making up and collecting of district taxes as are by this act given to or imposed on the treasurer and marshal of the Territory in making up and collecting territorial taxes.

Appeal from excessive assessment.

SEC. 5. *And be it enacted,* That when any person shall think himself oppressed by any assessment made pursuant to this act, he shall have a right to make application to the judges of the court of the district where the assessment was made, who, or any two of them, on a consideration of the complaint, are hereby authorized and empowered to make such abatement in such assessment as they shall deem equitable and just, and transmit immediately a certificate thereof to the district and territorial treasurers:

Proviso—reduction limited.

Provided, That in no case shall the judges have power to lessen any assessment more than one-fourth part.

District treasurer, appointment of.

SEC. 6. *And be it enacted,* That there shall be appointed a treasurer in each district by the judges thereof, who, before he enters upon the duties of his office, shall enter into bonds to the district in such sum and with such sureties as shall be prescribed and approved by said judges, which bond shall be lodged in the office of the clerk of the district court for the security of the district; and the said treasurer shall take an oath before one of the judges of the district court for the faithful discharge of his duty as treasurer to the district, and shall, annually, and oftener if required by the district court, or the legislature of the territory, render a full, fair, and accurate account of the state of the treasury, and no money shall be paid out of the treasury but in consequence of an appropriation thereof made by the judges of the district, or a majority of them. And it shall be the duty of the treasurer to examine, state, settle, and audit the claims against the district, and to give the claimant a certificate of the sum due; and the person holding such certificate, before he shall be entitled to draw the money from the treasury thereon, shall procure an order founded on such certificate from one of the judges of the district court, which certificate and order as aforesaid, together with the receipt of the person in whose favor the money shall be drawn, shall be good accounting for the treasurer in his settlement with the district.

Bonds. Oath. Report. Money to be paid. Settle and audit claims, etc.

Compensation of treasurer; of assessors.

SEC. 7. *And be it enacted,* That the judges of the several district courts may respectively allow such compensations to the treasurer for his services as shall be equitable, not exceeding twenty dollars per annum; and likewise compensations to the assessors, not exceeding one dollar per day each for each day actually spent in the business required of them by this act.

Allowance to marshal for collecting tax.

SEC. 8. *And be it enacted,* That there shall be allowed to the marshal of the Territory six per cent on all territorial taxes by him collected and paid into the treasury, and six per cent to the marshals of the several districts on all district taxes by them collected and paid into the district treasury.

1809.

SEC. 9. *And be it enacted*, That the fifth section of the act entitled "An additional act concerning district courts," passed the second day of April, one thousand eight hundred and seven, be and the same is hereby repealed: *Provided*, That nothing in this section shall be construed to affect the assessments already made in any district or the disposition of money already collected, or to be collected agreeable to said assessments; the same being adopted from the laws of one of the original States, to wit: The State of Vermont, as far as necessary and suitable to the circumstances of the Territory of Michigan.

Repealing.

Proviso—act not to be retroactive.

Adopted and published at the city of Detroit within the Territory of Michigan, this seventeenth day of January, one thousand eight hundred and nine.

Attest;
JOS. WATSON,
Secretary.

WILLIAM HULL,
Governor of Michigan, and President of the Legislature.

AN ACT concerning highways.

No. 37.
January 18.

Be it enacted by the Governor and Judges of the Territory of Michigan, That the judges of the respective district courts shall, before the month of April next, divide each district by suitable designating descriptions into such parts as they shall deem necessary, to be denominated highway districts, and shall cause such divisions to be recorded in the district treasurer's office, subject to be altered by said judges.

Highway districts—how constituted.

SEC. 2. *And be it enacted*, That the judges aforesaid shall, in the month of March, annually appoint a suitable person in each highway district who shall be denominated surveyor of highways, and shall furnish the district treasurer with a list of their names, who shall, before they enter on the duties assigned them by this act, take an oath before some magistrate in this territory faithfully and impartially to perform the same, and any person appointed as aforesaid, who shall neglect or refuse to be qualified and serve in such capacity, unless he show satisfactory cause to the said judges for neglecting or refusing, shall pay a fine to the treasurer of the district of thirty dollars, with costs of prosecution, and the judges shall appoint another person in his room.

Surveyor of highways, appointment of, etc.

Oath.

Penalty for refusal to qualify or serve.

SEC. 3. *And be it enacted*, That the said surveyors shall have a right to lay out and survey any new road within their respective districts, and alter any old roads when necessary; accurate surveys of which, if approved by the judges of the district courts, shall be recorded in the office of the district clerk: *Provided*, That no road or street which has already been or shall hereafter be laid out or surveyed by special act of this legislative board, shall be shut up or altered without its express authority therefor.

May survey, lay out, and alter roads.

If approved by Judges to be recorded with clerk.

Proviso.

SEC. 4. *And be it enacted*, That there shall be done in each district in each year to the amount of ten days' work to every taxable poll, apportioned to each person according to his last preceding assessment, at the rate of one dollar per day.

Ten days' road work.

1809.

Rate bill—how made up, etc.

Proviso, one day at least.

Proviso, new residents.

SEC. 5. *And be it enacted,* That the district treasurers shall, in the month of March, annually furnish each district surveyor with a rate bill made up agreeable to the provision of the fourth section of this act, taking his receipt for the amount of the days' work contained in it; *Provided, always,* That no one shall be made up at less than one whole day: *Provided, also,* That each surveyor be authorized to place on his rate bill, warn, and call upon every person subject to pay taxes who may come to reside in his district after he has received his rate bill, to do one day's work on the highway, who are hereby made liable to perform the same, unless they can make it to appear that they have done their highway work for the same year in some other district within this territory.

Time for performing road work.

SEC. 6. *And be it enacted,* That each surveyor shall cause two-thirds of the work contained in his rate bill to be done in the month of June, and the other third in the month of September.

Three days' warning.

How given.

May pay tax in money instead of labor.

SEC. 7. *And be it enacted,* That it shall be the duty of each surveyor to give each person whose name is in his rate bill at least three days' warning before the day he shall set for doing the work, by personal notice, or leaving word at his usual place of abode with some person of discretion, and if any person shall prefer to pay his tax in money instead of labor, the surveyor is hereby authorized to accept it and cancel the same at the rate of one dollar per day, and procure therewith some other person to perform said work.

Teams, allowance for.

Can not be commuted for.

Penalty for refusal.

SEC. 8. *And be it enacted,* That when it shall be necessary to employ a team in doing highway work, there shall be allowed therefor at the rate of one dollar per day for each horse and cart, or a horse and plow, and one dollar for a yoke of oxen and cart or plow, to every person who shall furnish the same by request of a surveyor; and any person who shall be warned as provided in the preceding section of this act to furnish such team and implements as he is the owner of, shall not be allowed to commute therefor by paying the money, but shall furnish the same, and on neglect shall be proceeded against as is provided in the ninth section of this act, in case of refusal to work, or commute by paying the money therefor.

Penalty for refusal to perform work or pay tax.

SEC. 9. *And be it enacted,* That every person made liable to do highway work by the provisions of this act, who shall neglect or refuse to perform the same, or commute therefor by paying the money, agreeable to the provisions of the seventh section of this act, shall pay a fine to the treasurer of the district wherein he resided at the time of such neglect or refusal, of treble the value of the tax, with costs of prosecution, to be recovered in the name of the treasurer thereof, and it shall be the duty of the surveyor to return the name of any person so neglecting or refusing to the district treasurer immediately on such neglect or refusal.

Repair of bridges and roads, special call may be made, etc.

SEC. 10. *And be it enacted,* That whenever any bridge or road shall get impaired or obstructed so as to make it dangerous or difficult passing the same, it shall be the duty of the surveyor of the same district to call out so many of the persons on his rate

1809.

bill, with such teams or implements as shall be necessary for the immediate repairing or clearing the same, in which case he shall not be obliged to give three days' notice, and any such person being so called upon, who shall neglect or refuse to give immediate assistance, shall pay a fine not exceeding five dollars, with costs of prosecution, to be received and applied as provided in the ninth section of this act; and the fines and forfeitures which shall be received by this or the ninth section of this act, shall be expended in making or repairing bridges and highways within the district, except so much as may be necessary to compensate persons for labor done on the highways in extraordinary cases, over and above their rate.

Without notice.

Penalty for refusal.

SEC. 11. *And be it enacted*, That it shall be the duty of each surveyor, at the end of the year for which he was appointed, to return to the district treasurer his rate bill, together with a full and just statement of all his proceedings thereon, and if necessary, may be examined on oath relative thereto, which oath the said treasurer is hereby authorized and empowered to administer.

Report of year's doings to be made to treasurer, etc.

SEC. 12. *And be it enacted*, That if any person shall dam or obstruct any waters made highways, by erecting any mill, wier, or other works, or by throwing timber in the same, or shall obstruct any public road or highway, every person so offending shall, for each offense, pay a fine not exceeding thirty dollars, to be recovered in the name of the treasurer of the district where the offense is committed, and is to be applied as is provided by the ninth section of this act.

Water or road obstructions, penalty for.

SEC. 13. *And be it enacted*, That when any person through whose land a public highway or road shall be opened, conceives himself aggrieved thereby, may set forth his grievances in writing to the judges of the district court where the road or highway is opened as aforesaid, and thereupon the said judges shall appoint five disinterested persons who shall be summoned by the marshal of the district to meet on the land, and being first sworn by a justice of the peace truly and impartially to assess the damages such complainant will sustain, the party having six days' notice previous of the day they shall proceed to view the highway or road, and take into consideration how much less valuable the property of such complainant will be rendered by the highway or road, and they, or a majority of them, shall assess the damage, if any, and report the same to the judge of the district court, who shall order the same to be paid out of the district treasury; and if a majority of the said appraisers assess no damages, or less than the costs would amount to, the complainant shall pay the cost.

Damages—how fixed, etc.

SEC. 14. *And be it enacted*, That an act entitled "An act concerning highways and roads," adopted and published at Detroit on the eighteenth day of September, one thousand eight hundred and five, be and the same is hereby repealed; *Provided, nevertheless, and it is hereby enacted and expressly declared*, That the aforesaid repealed act shall be in full force as to all matters or things done or transacted during its existence to which it relates, to all intents and purposes, as though this act had not been

Repealing.

Proviso.

1809. made; the same being adopted from the laws of two of the original States, to wit: The State of New York and the State of Vermont, as far as necessary and suitable to the circumstances of the Territory of Michigan.

Adopted and published at the city of Detroit, within the Territory of Michigan, this eighteenth day of January, one thousand eight hundred and nine.

Attest: WILLIAM HULL,
JOSEPH WATSON, *Governor of Michigan and President*
Secretary. *of the Legislature.*

No. 38. January 31

AN ACT for the probate of wills and the settlement of testate and intestate estates.*

No. 39. February 1.

AN ACT for the support of the poor.†

No. 40. February 4.

AN ACT for the maintenance and support of illegitimate children.

Persons accused of begetting bastard children may be brought before justices.

SECTION 1. *Be it enacted by the Governor and Judges of the Territory of Michigan,* That on complaint made to any justice of the peace within this Territory, by any unmarried woman resident therein, who shall hereafter be delivered of a bastard child, or being pregnant with a child, which if born alive may be a bastard, accusing any person of being the father, of said child, the justice shall take such accusation in writing, and thereupon issue his warrant, directed to the marshal, or one of his deputies within said district, commanding him forthwith to bring such accused person before said justice to answer to such complaint, and on return of such warrant, the justice, in the presence of the accused person, if he may be taken, and if not, then in his absence, shall proceed to examine the complainant, under oath, respecting her cause of complaint, and such accused person shall be allowed to ask the said complainant, when under oath, any questions he may think necessary for his justification, and such questions and answers, with every other part of the examination, shall be reduced to writing by the justice, and if, on examination of such accused person, he shall pay, or secure to be paid to the woman complainant, such sum or sums of money, or other property as she may agree to receive in full satisfaction, and shall further enter into bonds with one or more sufficient sureties, to be approved by the justice, to the treasurer of the district, in the penal sum of two hundred dollars, in which such woman shall reside, conditioned to save such district free from all charge towards the maintenance of

Complainant to be examined on oath.

When such persons may be discharged.

* Printed in full p. 13, vol. 2, Territorial laws.
† Printed in full p. 40, vol. 2, Territorial laws.

1809.

said child; in such case the justice shall discharge such person, on his paying the costs of prosecution.

Women having bastard children failing to complain or prosecute, overseers of the poor may.

SEC. 2. *And be it enacted*, That when a woman has a bastard child and neglects to bring forward a suit for its maintenance, or commences a suit and fails to prosecute to final judgment, the overseers of the poor, in any district interested in the support of any such bastard child, when sufficient security is not offered to save the district from expense, may bring forward suit in behalf of the district, against him who is accused of begetting such child, or may take up and prosecute a suit begun by the mother of the child.

Persons accused to be recognized to appear at the next district court.

SEC. 3. *And be it enacted*, That in case such accused person does not comply with the provisions in the first section in this act contained, the justice to whom such complaint was made, shall bind such person in a recognizance to the treasurer of the district, to appear at the next district court, with sufficient security, in a sum not less than one hundred dollars, nor more than five hundred dollars, to answer such accusation, and to abide the order of said court thereon, and, on neglect or refusal to find such security, the justice shall cause him to be committed to the jail of the district, there to be held to answer to such complaint.

Not giving security to be committed to jail.

Recognizance may be renewed by district court when woman cannot attend.

SEC. 4. *And be it enacted*, That if, at the time of such court, the woman be not delivered, or be unable to attend, the court shall order the renewal of the bonds of recognizance that the person complained of shall be forthcoming at the next court after the birth of the child, at which the mother of said child shall be able to attend, and the continuance of such bonds shall be entered by order of said court, and shall have the same force and effect as a recognizance taken in court for that purpose.

On plea of not guilty issue to be tried by jury.

SEC. 5. *And be it enacted*, That when such accused person shall plead not guilty to such charge, before the court to which he is recognized, the court shall order the issue to be tried by a jury, and on the trial of such issue, the examination before the justice shall be given in evidence, and the mother of the bastard child shall be admitted as a competent evidence, and her credibility be left to the jury: *Provided, always*, That no woman shall be admitted as a witness as aforesaid, who has been convicted of any crime which would by law disqualify her from being a witness in any other case, and on the trial of the issue, the jury shall, in behalf of the man accused, take into consideration any want of credibility in the mother of the bastard child; also any variation in testimony before the justice and that before the jury, and also any other confession of her, at any time, which does not agree with the testimony, or any other pleas or process made and produced on behalf of such accused person.

Mother of child a competent witness.

Proviso.

Judgment and proceedings on verdict of guilty.

SEC. 6. *And be it enacted*, That in case the jury find the defendant guilty, or such accused person before the trial shall confess in court that the accusation is true, he shall be judged the reputed father of such child, and shall stand charged with the maintenance thereof in such a sum or sums as the court shall order and direct, with payment of costs of prosecution, and moreover be

1809.

liable to the suit of the complainant for damages, and the court shall require the reputed father to give security to perform the aforesaid order; and in case the reputed father shall neglect or refuse to give security as aforesaid, and pay the costs of prosecution, he shall be committed to the jail of the district, there to remain till he shall comply with the order of the court, or until the court shall, on sufficient cause shown, direct him to be discharged, and the judgment of the district court herein shall be final, any law, usage, or custom to the contrary notwithstanding.

Repealing clause.

SEC. 7. *And be it enacted,* That all other laws, or parts of laws on this subject be and the same are hereby repealed. This act shall take effect and be in force from and after the first day of March, one thousand eight hundred and nine; the same being adopted from the laws of one of the original States, to wit: The State of Ohio, as far as necessary and suitable to the circumstances of Michigan.

Adopted and published at the city of Detroit, within the Territory of Michigan, this fourth day of February, one thousand eight hundred and nine.

Attest: WILLIAM HULL,
JOS. WATSON, *Governor of Michigan and President*
Secretary. *of the Legislature.*

No. 41.
February 4.

AN ACT subjecting real estate to the payment of debts.*

No. 42.
February 9.

AN ACT directing the mode of taking inquisitions on the body of a person found dead by casualty or violence.

Inquisition of death.

Duties of the marshal thereto

Jury summoned.

Be it enacted by the Governor and the Judges of the Territory of Michigan, That the marshal as soon as he shall be certified of the dead body of any person supposed to have come to his or her death by violence or casualty, found or lying within any district of the territory, shall forthwith summon a jury of good and lawful men of the district, at such time and place as he shall appoint. The marshal shall repair to the place where the dead body is at the time mentioned.

Penalty for non-appearance.

Every person summoned as a juror as aforesaid that shall fail of appearance without having a reasonable excuse therefor shall forfeit thirteen dollars thirty-three and

---

* Printed as first adopted, p. 40, vol. 2, Territorial laws. Printed as after amendment p. 154, vol. 1, Territorial laws.

The following from page 235 of the manuscript volume, will explain itself:

September 5, 1810.

The act entitled "An act subjecting real estate to the payment of debts," which is to be found on the 135, 136, 137, 138, 139, and 140 pages of this book, was this day signed by William Hull, Governor of the Territory of Michigan, Augustus B. Woodward, one of the Judges of the Territory of Michigan, John Griffin, one of the Judges of the Territory of Michigan, and attested by Jos. Watson, Secretary, after having undergone the following alterations and amendments, to wit: By striking out in the seventh line from the top of the 136th page after the word "manner," the words "and method," and by placing the words "the State of Pennsylvania" before the words "the State of Vermont," in the adopting clause on the 140th page.

WITNESS MY HAND: JOS. WATSON.
Secretary to the G. and J.

1809.

one-third cents, which forfeiture shall be recovered before any authority having cognizance of the same and shall be applied to the use of the territory. The marshal shall swear the jurors upon a view of the body in the form following: "You solemnly swear or affirm that you will diligently inquire, and true presentment make, on behalf of the Territory of Michigan, how and in what manner this man or woman, as the case may be, who here lies dead, came to his or her death, and you shall render to me a true inquest thereof, according to such evidence as shall be laid before you, and according to your knowledge, so help you God." The jurors being sworn, the marshal shall give them a charge upon their oaths, to declare of the death of the person, whether he of felony, or mischance, or accident; and if of felony who were the principals, and who were accessories, with what instrument he was struck or wounded, and so of all circumstances and matters which may come by presumptions and if by mischance or accident, whether by the act of man or whether by hurts, fall, stroke, drowning, or otherwise; to inquire of the persons who were present, the finders of the body, his or her relations and neighbors, whether he or she was killed in the same place where he or she was found, and if elsewhere by whom and how he or she was brought from thence, and of all circumstances relating to said death; and if he or she died of his or her own act, then to inquire of the manner, means, instrument, and of all circumstances concerning it. The jury being charged shall stand together and proclamation shall be made for any person that can give evidence to draw near, and that they shall be heard. The marshal is hereby empowered to send out his warrant for witnesses, commanding them to come before him to be examined and to declare their knowledge concerning the matter in question, and he shall administer to them an oath in form following: "You solemnly swear that the evidence which you shall give to this inquest concerning the death of this man or woman, or calling the name of the person, if known, here lying dead, shall be the truth the whole truth, and nothing but the truth, so help you God." The evidence of such witnesses shall be in writing, subscribed by them. If they relate to the trial of any person concerned in the death, then shall the marshal bind such witnesses by recognizance, to the treasurer of the territory, in a reasonable sum for their personal appearance at the next court having jurisdiction there to give evidence accordingly and take into his custody such witness or witnesses as shall refuse to recognize as aforesaid, and shall return to the same court the inquisition, written evidence, and recognizance by him taken.

Oath.

Charge.

Witnesses.

Oath.

Evidence to be in writing.

When to be recognized to appear at next term of court.

Refusal to give recognizance.

SEC. 2. *And be it enacted,* That the jury having viewed the body, heard the evidence, and made all the inquiry within their power, they shall draw up and deliver to the marshal their verdict upon the death under consideration, in writing, under their hands, in the following or equivalent form: Territory of Michigan, district of (inserting here the name of the district), to-wit: An inquisition taken at (here mention the name of the place), within the said district (inserting here the date), before (inserting here

Form of the inquisition.

1809. the name of the marshal aforesaid), upon the view of the body of (inserting here the name of the deceased), there lying dead, by the oaths of (inserting here the names of the jurors), good and lawful men, who, being charged and sworn to inquire for the territory of Michigan, when, how, and by what means the said (here inserting the name of deceased), came to his death, upon their oaths do say (inserting how, when, and by what means, and with what instrument he was killed).—If it appears that he has been murdered by a person known, then the inquisition shall be concluded in this form: And so the jurors aforesaid, upon their oath aforesaid, do say that the aforesaid, (inserting here the name of the supposed felon) in manner and form aforesaid, then and there of his malice aforethought, the said (inserting here the name of the deceased), did kill and murder, against the peace and dignity of the Territory of Michigan, and the laws of the same. If it appears to be self-killing then shall the inquisition be concluded thus; and so the jurors aforesaid, upon their oaths aforesaid, do say that the said (inserting here the name of the deceased), in manner and form aforesaid, then and there voluntarily did kill himself. If it appears that the death was by misfortune; and so the jurors aforesaid, upon their oaths say that the said (inserting here the name of the deceased) in manner aforesaid, came to his death by misfortune. If innocently by the hands of any person: The jurors upon their oaths aforesaid, do say that the said (inserting here the name of the person supposed to be the innocent cause of the death of the deceased), the aforesaid (inserting here the name of the deceased), by misfortune and against and contrary to the will of him, the said (inserting here the name of the person supposed to be the innocent cause of the death of the deceased), in manner aforesaid did kill. In witness whereof, the marshal and jurors to this inquisition have set their hands, the day and year above said. Upon an inquisition found of the death of any person by the felony or misfortune of another, the marshal shall speedily inform one or more of the justices of the district thereof, to the intent that the person killing, or being any way instrumental to the death, may be apprehended, examined, and secured in order for trial.

Marshal to inform justices, when.

Punishment of the marshal for neglect.

SEC. 3. *And be it enacted,* That if the marshal be remiss, and make not inquisition upon the view of the body slain or murdered, or shall not endeavor to do his office upon any person dead by misadventure, or shall not certify the inquisition by him taken, in the manner directed by this act, he shall for every such offense forfeit the sum of one hundred dollars, one-half thereof to the use of the informer, the other half to the use of the territory; the same being adopted from the laws of two of the original States, to-wit: the States of Massachusetts and Virginia, as far as necessary and suitable to the circumstances of the Territory of Michigan.

Adopted and published at the city of Detroit, within the Terri-

1809.

tory of Michigan, this ninth day of February, one thousand eight hundred and nine.

Attest: WILLIAM HULL,
JOS. WATSON, *Governor of Michigan and President*
Secretary. *of the Legislature.*

No. 43.
February 9.

AN ACT concerning ferries.

Ferry keepers to always have boat ready for service.

Be it enacted by the Governor and Judges of the Territory of Michigan, That every person obtaining a license to keep a ferry shall provide and keep in complete repair, a good and sufficient boat for the safe conveyance of persons and property and shall, with a sufficient number of hands to work and manage the boat, give due attendance from daylight in the morning until nine of the clock in the evening, at all times when the creek or river over which the ferry is kept is passable; and shall, moreover, at all such times, at any hour of the night or day when called upon, convey the mail, or other public express across said ferry, and if any person obtaining a license as aforesaid shall refuse or neglect to perform the duties herein enjoined, or any of them, the person so offending shall forfeit and pay for every such offense, a sum not exceeding one hundred dollars.

Hours of service.

Penalty for non compliance.

Penalty for overcharging.

SEC. 2. *And be it enacted*, That if any keeper of a ferry as aforesaid, shall demand a higher rate or sum for ferriages than shall be allowed by law, the person so offending shall forfeit and pay a fine not exceeding one hundred dollars, the same being adopted from the laws of two of the original States, to wit: The States of Ohio and New York, as far as necessary and suitable to the circumstances of the Territory of Michigan.

Adopted and published at the city of Detroit, in the Territory of Michigan, this ninth day of February, one thousand eight hundred and nine.

Attest: WILLIAM HULL,
JOS. WATSON, *Governor of Michigan and President*
Secretary. *of the Legislature.*

AN ACT concerning the treasurer of the Territory of Michigan.*

No. 44.
February 9.

No. 45.
February 9.

AN ACT concerning tavern keepers.

Penalty for refusal to provide for man and horse.

Be it enacted by the Governor and Judges of the Territory of Michigan, That every person obtaining license for a tavern, shall provide and furnish suitable entertainment and accommodation for man and horse, and for failure therein shall be liable to prosecution and fine to any amount not exceeding one hundred dollars; *Provided*, that nothing in this section contained shall be construed so as to compel any tavern keeper to entertain any person

Proviso.

* Printed in full p. 46, vol. 2, Territorial Laws.

1809. living in the neighborhood whose situation is not such as reasonably requires entertainment.

Penalty for allowing rioting, drunkenness, etc.

SEC. 2. *And be it enacted,* That if any person licensed to keep a tavern, or any retailer of wine, spirituous liquors, or strong drink, shall knowingly permit or allow of any rioting within their houses, out-houses, shed, arbor, or other place in their occupancy, or shall suffer any disorder, reveling, or drunkenness therein, every such tavern keeper or retailer on being thereof legally convicted, shall for every such offense be fined not exceeding one hundred dollars, besides costs; the same being adopted from the laws of one of the original States, to wit: The State of Ohio, as far as necessary and suitable to the circumstances of the Territory of Michigan.

Adopted and published at the city of Detroit, in the Territory of Michigan, this ninth day of February, one thousand eight hundred and nine.

Attest:
JOS. WATSON,
Secretary.

WILLIAM HULL,
Governor of Michigan and President of the Legislature.

No. 46.
February 9.

AN ACT concerning auctions.

Governor to appoint.

Be it enacted by the Governor and Judges of the Territory of Michigan, That the Governor of the Territory of Michigan shall annually appoint so many persons, within the Territory, to be auctioneers as he shall judge proper. No person whatsoever, other than persons appointed and authorized as aforesaid, shall sell, or expose to sale at public auction or vendue, within the Territory, any goods, wares, merchandise, or effects whatsoever; and every person offending shall forfeit the sum of one hundred dollars for each article so exposed to sale. Every auctioneer, before he enter upon the execution of his office, shall give bond to the treasurer of the Territory in one thousand dollars, with two sufficient sureties, conditioned for the faithful execution of his office according to law, to be taken by any justice of the peace and returned to the clerk of the district. All goods, wares, merchandise, and effects whatsoever, exposed to sale at public auction or vendue within the Territory, shall be struck off to the highest bidder, and shall be subject, if the auction be in the city or district of Detroit, to a duty of three dollars, and if in any other place in the Territory, to a duty of two dollars for every one hundred dollars of the value or price at which the same shall be sold, and at and after the same rate for every greater or less sum, to be paid by the person who shall so sell the same, to the marshal of the Territory, at or within ten days from the day of the sale. In all cases when the auctioneer or the owner of such goods so exposed to sale, or any person employed by them, or either of them, shall be the highest bidder, the goods shall be subject to the payment of the said duties, as if they had been sold to any

None other to act. Penalty for non-compliance. Bond. Must sell to highest bidder. Tax on sales. Goods bid in by owner, etc.

1809.

other person. Every auctioneer who shall sell any goods, shall, within twenty days after the expiration of every six months, to be computed from the first day of April and the first day of October in every year, render a just and true account in writing, subscribed by him, to a justice of the peace of the district, of all goods by him sold, of the days when the same were respectively sold, and the amount of the sales of each day, and shall thereupon take before the said justice the following oath or affirmation: "I do solemnly swear, or affirm that the account now exhibited by me, and to which I have subscribed my name, contains a just and true account of all the goods, wares, and merchandise or effects sold by me, subject to a duty by law, within the time mentioned in the said account, and of the days upon which the same were respectively sold, and the amount of the sales of each day." The account, with the oaths endorsed, shall be immediately transmitted to the clerk of the district. Every auctioneer neglecting or refusing to pay the moneys due for the duties, according to law, or to render his account thereof, or otherwise violating the law, shall forfeit his appointment, and shall thereafter be disqualified from being an auctioneer, and shall forfeit for every offense one hundred dollars. All auctions shall be in open day, between sunrise and sunset. No auctioneer shall sell at private sale any goods, wares, merchandise, or effects, excepting when such auctioneer being a merchant shall sell his own goods and merchandise as such. No auctioneer shall receive or accept any higher or further reward for his services in the sale of any goods, wares, merchandise, or effects than at and after the rate of two and one-half per cent in value to which the said goods or effects by him actually sold shall amount, unless a previous agreement be made in writing between the owner of such goods or effects and such auctioneer for such further and higher reward. Every auctioneer guilty of any fraud or deceit in the execution of this act, or in eluding or defeating the operation thereof, shall forfeit one hundred dollars for each offense; the same being adopted from the laws of one of the original States, to wit: The State of New York, as far as necessary and suitable to the circumstances of the Territory of Michigan.

Auctioneers to make semi-annual reports.

Penalty for non-payment of tax, etc.

Auctions to be in day light.

Private sales forbidden.

Commission allowed.

Penalty for fraud, deceit, etc.

Adopted and published at the city of Detroit, in the Territory of Michigan, this ninth day of February, one thousand eight hundred and nine.

Attest: WILLIAM HULL,
JOS. WATSON, *Governor of Michigan and President*
Secretary. *of the Legislature.*

1809. AN ACT concerning the militia of the Territory of Michigan.*

No. 47.
February 10.

No. 48. AN ACT defining the powers of justices of the peace in causes of a civil nature.†

No. 49.
February 18.

AN ACT concerning depositions and witnesses.

Deposition of witnesses, when same may be taken out of court and how.

Be it enacted by the Governor and Judges of the Territory of Michigan, That when any witness shall be more than fifty miles from the place of trial in any civil cause, or is going out of the territory not to return before the time of trial, or by reason of age, sickness, or other bodily infirmity, he or she are rendered incapable of traveling and appearing at court, every justice of the peace be and he is hereby empowered to take the deposition of such witness, out of court, and every justice to whom application is made to take a deposition out of court, shall issue a subpœna for the appearance of the witness before him, in the usual form, and shall also issue citation to the adverse party if he, she, or they live within this territory and within fifty miles of the place of caption; of the following tenor:

Territory of Michigan, }
................district. } ss.

Form of citation.

To the marshal..........district, or to.........., an indifferent person, greeting:

In the name of the Territory of Michigan, you are hereby required to notify............, of the district of............, to appear before me at............, in the district of............, on the............day of ...., at .... o'clock, ...noon, to be present at the taking of the deposition of ...., to be used in a cause to be heard and tried before

---

* Printed in full, page 48, Vol. 2, Ter. Laws.
The following, found page 235 of manuscript volume containing these laws, will explain itself:

September 5, 1810.

The act entitled "An act concerning the militia of the Territory of Michigan," which is to be found on the 148, 149, 150, 151, 152, 153, 154, and 155 pages of this book was this day signed by William Hull, Governor of the Territory of Michigan, Augustus B. Woodward, one of the judges of the Territory of Michigan, John Griffin, one of the judges of the Territory of Michigan, and attested by Joseph Watson, secretary, after having undergone the following alterations and amendments, to wit: By inserting after the word "summons" in the 12th line from the top of the 152 page, the words "and warrant," and after the form of the summons, on the 152 page, a form of a warrant in these words: "Brigade..........Regiment...... To............orderly sergeant (or other sergeant as the case may be) of........company, in the regiment aforesaid, Greeting: By the military authority of this Territory you are hereby commanded to levy and collect from the goods, chattels, or estate of..................of.............the sum.............fine, and..........costs, amounting in the whole to............and for want of such goods, chattels, or estate, commit him, the said.............to the keeper of the jail in............. within the said prison, who is hereby directed to receive the said..............and him safely keep until he shall pay the same, together with all legal fees. Make return of this precept to me within sixty days from this date. Dated at.........." And by inserting after the words "light infantry" in the 10th line from the top of the 153 page the word "artillery."

WITNESS MY HAND,

JOS. WATSON,
Secretary to the G. and J.

† Printed in full, page 53, vol. 2, Territorial Laws.

1809.

.... court, to be holden within and for the .... on the .... day of .... next, in which cause ...., of ...., is plaintiff, and ...., of ...., defendant. Hereof fail not, but of this precept and your doings herein due return make.

Given under my hand at ...., this ....day of ...., A. D. ....

....

Justice of the Peace.

A copy of which citation shall be delivered to such adverse party, or left at his, her, or their usual place of abode, by a proper officer or an indifferent person, whose return shall be made under oath, so that he, she, or they may have a reasonable time to appear and be present at taking such deposition, and if any person on whom a subpœna as aforesaid shall be served, having been tendered with his or her legal fees, shall refuse or neglect to appear at the time and place therein mentioned before the authority issuing the same to make his or her deposition, the said authority shall have power to issue an attachment to compel the appearance of such person, and if upon appearance by virtue of such attachment such person shall refuse to make his or her deposition, the said authority, by his warrant directed to the marshal of the district, or some other meet person who shall have power, respectively, to command necessary assistance against the person so opposing and forthwith cause him or her to be committed to the common goal in said district, there to remain till such person shall make his or her deposition as required and discharge the costs of commitment; a copy of such warrant attested by the officer or person serving the same, shall be sufficient authority to the goaler to detainsuch person. And every such witness shall be carefully examined and duly cautioned to testify the whole truth and nothing but the truth, and being sworn the justice shall certify the same in manner following:

Action taken in case of refusal to respond to subpœna or make deposition.

Testimony to be certified to by justice, form of.

"Territory of Michigan, district of ...., ...day of ...., A. D. ...., then ...., of ...., personally appearing and after being carefully examined and duly cautioned, made solemn oath that the foregoing deposition by him subscribed contains the whole truth and nothing but the truth. .... before ...., justice of the peace, the above deposition taken at the request of ...., to be used in a cause to be heard and tried before the .... next, to be holden at .... within the district of .... in which cause ...., is plaintiff, and ...., is defendant, the deponent (living more than thirty miles from the place of trial, or was going out of the territory not to return before the time of trial, or rendered incapable of traveling and appearing at said court by reason of age, sickness, or bodily infirmity as the case may be), and the adverse party (living more than fifty miles from the place of caption), was or was not notified and did or did not attend, certified by ...., justice of the peace," which deposition the said justice shall seal up and

1809.

superscribe in the following manner, namely, "the within deposition of ...., was taken and sealed up by ...., justice of the peace;" and shall deliver the same to the party or person if desired at whose request it shall be taken.

Deposition to be delivered to party at whose request made.

Attorneys or interested persons forbidden to draw up deposition.

SEC. 2. *And be it enacted,* That no agent, attorney, or person interested in any cause shall write or draw up the deposition of any witness to be used in such cause, and if it shall appear that any agent or attorney, or any other person interested or engaged in the cause, shall write or draw up such deposition, or if such deposition shall be returned into court unsealed, or with the seal broken, all such depositions shall be rejected by the court, and every deposition taken and returned agreeable to the foregoing provisions, shall be admitted to be read in evidence in the causes for which they are taken, and depositions of witnesses living without this Territory shall be allowed to be read in evidence in any court in this Territory, if taken agreeable to the directions of this, or the laws of the State or country in which they are taken, and any judge of the supreme court may grant a *dedimus potestatem* to have depositions taken, either within or without this Territory, in any action, suit, or controversy pending in said court, or in any district court, on such terms and conditions as he shall, from time to time, prescribe.

Deposition, when to be rejected.

As evidence.

Dedimus potestatem.

Non-appeaance to testify, etc., penalty for.

SEC. 3. *And be it enacted,* That if any person upon whom any subpœna shall be legally served, commanding him or her to appear and testify concerning any cause or matter pending in any court in this Territory, or before auditors, referees, or arbitrators, there having been tendered unto him or her so much money, for his or her travel, and one day's attendance, as by law is or shall be allowed, do not appear according to the tenor of such subpœna, having no lawful nor reasonable excuse or impediment to the contrary, the person so making default, shall, for every such default forfeit the sum of ten dollars to the party in whose behalf he or she has been subpœnæd to appear and testify, and all just damages; which forfeiture and damages shall be recovered by the party aggrieved before any court proper to try the same: *Provided, nevertheless,* and it is hereby enacted that when any party in any cause pending before either the supreme court, or any district court, shall make it appear to the satisfaction of such court that he has caused a subpœna to be duly served on any witness to appear and testify in his cause, and has tendered so much money for his or her travel and attendance as is by law directed, and such witness has neglected to appear, such court shall have power to issue an attachment to compel the attendance of such witness, and on appearing, if any witness shall refuse to give his or her evidence, he or she may be committed to prison, there to remain until he or she will give his or her evidence, or be liberated by law; the same being adopted from the laws of two of the original States, to wit: The States of Massachusetts and Vermont, as far as necessary and suitable to the circumstances of Territory of Michigan.

Proviso.

Adopted and published at the city of Detroit, in the Territory of Michigan, this eighteenth day of February, one thousand eight hundred and nine. **1809.**

Attest: WILLIAM HULL,
JOS. WATSON, *Governor of Michigan.*
Secretary.

AN ACT concerning jails and jailors.* No. 50. February 18.

AN ACT concerning attachments.† No. 51. February 18.

AN ACT concerning the supreme court of the Territory of Michgan.‡ No. 52. February 18.

AN ACT concerning executions. No. 53. February 18.

Be it enacted by the Governor and Judges of the Territory of Michigan, That the party obtaining judgment in any civil action in any court of judicature within this Territory, shall be entitled to have his execution thereon at any time after the expiration of twenty-four hours after judgment rendered, and within one year next after entering up such judgment, when there is no appeal or review by law allowed, or where no appeal or review hath been entered on motion in arrest of judgment, or for a new trial has been made within the time allowed therefor, and execution issuing from a district court shall be made returnable within ninety days, or to the next stated session of the said court, at the election of the creditor; and those issuing from the supreme court shall be made returnable within six months, or at the next stated session of the court, as the creditor may elect; and those issuing from a justice of the peace shall be made returnable within sixty days from the day of their date, and when such execution shall be returned without any satisfaction made, or satisfied only in part, the clerk of the court from whence, or justice of the peace from whom such execution issued, shall upon application of the creditor, make out an alias or pluries execution for the whole, or the remainder as the case may be till the judgment shall be fully satisfied; but if the creditor shall neglect, for the space of one year next after obtaining judgment, to take out his execution, or shall not within one year next after his execution shall be returned not satisfied, take out his alias or pluries, he shall issue out his writ of scire facias, and shall cause the adverse party to be served with the same personally, or by leaving an attested copy thereof at his last and usual place of abode, fourteen days before the sitting of the court, notifying him to show cause, if any he hath, why exe-

Execution for judgment, when same may be obtained.

When returnable.

When unsatisfied.

Creditors neglect to take out, etc.

Scire facias.

* Printed in full, page 62, Vol. 2, Ter Laws.
† Printed in full, p. 59, vol. 2, Territorial Laws.
‡ Printed in full, p. 60, vol. 2, Territorial laws.

1809.

cution ought not to be done, and upon his non-appearance, or not shewing sufficient cause, the court shall award execution for what remaineth, with additional costs: *Provided*, That every marshal who shall neglect, for the space of ten days, after collecting any moneys on execution, or rate bill, to pay the same to the creditor, or the treasurer, shall be accountable to the creditor, or the treasurer, as the case may be, to pay interest at the rate of twenty per cent per annum, on all money by him so retained.

Proviso.

SEC. 2. *And be it enacted*, That when a writ of execution shall be issued on any judgment, recovered before any court within this territory, the marshal or other officers to whom it is directed shall repair to the debtor's usual place of abode if within his jurisdiction, and demand of such debtor the sum in debt, damages, or costs contained in such execution, with all legal charges for serving the same, and upon such debtor's refusal or neglect to pay such sum with the costs as aforesaid, the officer shall levy the same upon the proper goods or chattels of such debtor or such as shall be shown him by the creditor, always excepting one cow and ten sheep, and such suitable apparel, bedding, tools, arms, and articles of household furniture as may be necessary for upholding life, but not on such goods as last enumerated unless turned out by the debtor to satisfy such execution, and any such goods or chattels levied upon as aforesaid, shall be safely kept by the officer at the expense of the debtor, until they shall be sold as hereinafter directed or the debtor shall otherwise satisfy the execution, and the officer shall forthwith advertise the same setting up notifications wherein he shall enumerate the goods or chattels so levied upon at such places as will best give notoriety, that they are to be sold at public auction at the time and place therein mentioned, which shall not be less than fourteen days from the time of setting up such notification and if within the time such goods or chattels shall have been posted the owner shall not redeem the same by otherwise satisfying the execution, and the officer's costs and charges thereon, such goods or chattels shall be sold at public auction to the highest bidder, at the place of sale, or such part thereof as shall [be] sufficient to satisfy the execution with legal costs thereon and the moneys arising upon such sale shall be applied to the payment of the charges and the satisfaction of the execution, and the officer shall return the overplus, if any there be, to the debtor upon demand thereof made, and the officer serving the execution shall make return thereof with his doings thereon, particularly describing the goods or chattels taken and sold and the sum for which each article is struck off, and if any officer shall be guilty of any fraud or collusion in the sale or in the return as before directed he shall be liable to the debtor to pay him treble damages for the sum so defrauded to be recovered by action on the case with costs.

Manner of serving execution, etc.

Exemptions.

Advertisement of sale.

Sale.

Excess, if any, to be paid back to debtor.

To make return.

Fraud or collusion.

SEC. 3. *And be it enacted*, That when moveable or personal estate of the debtor cannot be found sufficient to satisfy the debts, damages, or costs in the execution and the legal fees thereon, the officer may take the body of the debtor, and him or her commit

When body of the debtor may be taken.

1809.

to the keeper of the goal in the district in which the executions shall be served, and the debtor shall there remain until he or she shall pay the debt, damages, and costs for which he or she is committed, with the officer's and prisoner's keeper's fees thereon or be otherwise discharged by order of law, and every officer who shall commit any person to goal by virtue of any writ or warrant of distress or execution, shall deliver a copy of such writ, warrant, or execution and of this return thereon signed by such officer to the keeper of the goal, which copy so delivered and signed shall be sufficient warrant or order to the keeper of the goal to receive such person, and him or her hold in safe custody until discharged by order of law.

What a sufficient warrant for detention in goal.

SEC. 4. *And be it enacted,* That this law shall take effect from and after the first day of April next, the same being from the laws of two of the original States, to wit: Massachusetts and Vermont, as far as necessary and suitable to the circumstances of the Territory of Michigan.

When to take effect.

Adopted and published at the city of Detroit, in the Territory of Michigan, this eighteenth day of February, one thousand eight hundred and nine.

Attest: WILLIAM HULL,

JOS. WATSON, *Governor of Michigan and President*

Secretary. *of the Legislature.*

No. 54.
February 18.

AN ACT concerning minors.

Be it enacted by the Governor and Judges of the Territory of Michigan, That as often as it shall be represented to the judge of probate of an probate district within this Territory that [there] are minor children in such district, who are living in idleness and indigence, and not in a situation to acquire useful instruction, or the habits of industry, it shall be the duty of such judge of probate to issue a citation calling such minor, and his or her parents [if he or she have any in the vicinity] to appear before him at a time and place therein named, to show cause why a guardian should not be appointed over such minor, and if no good cause be shown, or if neither minor or parent do appear, the said judge may, in his discretion, proceed to appoint a guardian over such minor, taking sufficient bond of such guardian for the faithful performance of his trust; and such guardian appointed as aforesaid, is hereby empowered to bind such minor, if a male until he shall arrive at the age of twenty-one years, and if a female till she arrive at the age of eighteen years; and the age of the minor at the time of binding shall always be inserted in the indenture, and among other covenants the master or mistress shall engage to cause such minor to be taught to read and write, and any indenture which is without such covenant shall not be binding on the minor; the same being adopted from the laws of one of the original States, to wit: The State of Ohio, as far as necessary and suitable to the circumstances of the Territory of Michigan.

Minors idle, etc. may have guardian appointed.

Guardian to give bond.

Authority of.

Indenture, must provide.

1809. Adopted and published at the city of Detroit, in the Territory of Michigan, this eighteenth day of February, one thousand eight hundred and nine.

Attest: WILLIAM HULL,
JOS. WATSON, *Governor of Michigan and President*
Secretary. *of the Legislature.*

No. 55.
February 18.

AN ACT concerning marshals*

No. 56.
February 21.

AN ACT repealing an act concerning aliens.

Be it enacted by the Governor and Judges of the Territory of Michigan, That the act entitled "An act authorizing aliens to hold lands in the Territory of Michigan," adopted and published at Detroit, on the twelfth day of August, one thousand eight hundred and five, be and the same is hereby repealed: *Provided, nevertheless,* That this act shall in no wise affect any rights which have already accrued under said act.

Made and published at the city of Detroit, in the Territory of Michigan, this twenty-first day of February, one thousand eight hundred and nine.

Attest: WILLIAM HULL,
JOS. WATSON, *Governor of Michigan and President*
Secretary. *of the Legislature.*

No. 57.
February 21.

AN ACT concerning trustees of concealed or absconding debtors.†

No. 58.
February 21.

AN ACT concerning the recording of deeds and other writings.

Clerk of court to record, what.

Be it enacted by the Governor and Judges of the Territory of Michigan, That the clerk of every court shall record all deeds and writings, acknowledged or proved before such court or any judge thereof, or any justice of the peace, or any notary public, together with the acknowledgments of married women, and all endorsements and papers thereto annexed, by entering them word for word in proper books to be carefully preserved, and shall afterwards re-deliver them to the parties entitled to them.

How.

Wife to be privately examined as to her signature before record is made.

SEC. 2. *And be it enacted*, That when husband and wife have sealed and delivered a writing, if the wife appear before such court, judge or justice, or notary public, and being examined privily and apart from her husband, shall declare that she did freely and willingly seal and deliver the said writing to be then shown and

---

* Printed in full, p. 64, vol. 2, Territorial Laws.
† Printed in full, p. 74, vol. 2, Territorial Laws.

explained to her, and wishes not to retract it, and consenteth that it may be recorded, a certificate of such privy examination being returned and recorded, with the writing, and the writing being acknowledged also by the husband, or proved by witnesses to be his act, in such the said writing shall not only be sufficient to convey or release any right of dower, thereby intended to be released, or conveyed, but be as effectual for every other purpose as if she were an unmarried woman.

Right of dower released.

SEC. 3. *And be it enacted,* That if the party reside not in Michigan the acknowledgement by such party or the proof by the number of witnesses requisite, of the sealing and delivery of the writing before any court of law or the mayor or chief magistrate of any city, town, or corporation in which the party shall dwell, certified by such court, mayor, or magistrate, in the manner such acts are usually authenticated by them, together with any relinquishment of dower shall be effectual.

Non-residents.

SEC. 4. *And be it enacted,* That the register of deeds for the city of Detroit, appointed by the Governor of the Territory, pursuant to an act entitled "An act concerning the city of Detroit," adopted on the thirteenth day of September, one thousand eight hundred and six, be and he is hereby directed to deliver over to the clerk of the court of the district of Huron and Detroit all the records and files in his possession in consequence of his said appointment, within ten days from and after the passage of this act, taking the receipt of the said district clerk for the same, who is hereby directed to execute such receipt; and all the records of deeds by the said register so delivering over the same, legally and properly made, shall be deemed good and valid in law for the purposes for which they were made; the same being adopted from the laws of one of the original States, to wit: The State of Virginia, as far as necessary and suitable to the circumstances of the Territory of Michigan.

Register of deeds of Detroit to turn over records, etc., to clerk of court., etc.

Adopted and published at the city of Detroit, in the Territory of Michigan, this twenty-first day of February, one thousand eight hundred and nine.

Attest: WILLIAM HULL,
JOS. WATSON, *Governor of Michigan and President*
Secretary. *of the Legislature.*

AN ACT concerning interest on contracts.

SECTION 1. *Be it enacted by the Governor and Judges of the Territory of Michigan,* That no person or persons upon any contract hereafter to be made shall receive or take directly or indirectly more than the value of six dollars for the forbearance of one hundred dollars for a year, and so after that rate for a greater or less sum, or for a longer or shorter time, and any person who shall, upon any contract, take, accept, or receive by ways or means of any corrupt bargain, or by covin, or by deceitful conveyance, or by

Rate of, allowed.

1809.

Penalty for usury.

any other ways or means whatever for the forbearing or giving day of payment for one whole year above the sum of six dollars for the forbearance of one hundred dollars for a year, and so after that rate for a greater or less sum or for a longer or shorter time, shall forfeit and pay for every such offense the whole of the warrants, part of said contract, and twenty-five per cent interest on the whole sum of said contract, one moiety thereof to the treasury of this Territory, and the other moiety to the person who shall prosecute the same to effect, with costs, before any court proper to try the same, *Provided*, nevertheless, that nothing in this act shall extend to the letting of cattle or other usages of the like nature in practice among farmers, or maritime contracts, bottomry or cause of exchange as hath been heretofore and still is accustomed, the same being adopted from the laws of one of the original States, to wit: The State of Vermont, as far as necessary and suitable to the circumstances of the Territory of Michigan.

Adopted and published at the city of Detroit, in the Territory of Michigan, this twenty-first day of February, one thousand eight hundred and nine.

Attest: WILLIAM HULL,
JOS. WATSON, *Governor of Michigan and President*
Secretary. *of the Legislature.*

No. 60. February 21.

AN ACT concerning district courts. *

No. 61. February 23.

AN ACT concerning attorneys. †

No. 62. February 23.

AN ACT for the limitations of suits on penal statutes, criminal prosecutions, and actions at law.

Limitation for commencement of prosecutions, etc., of suits for forfeiture.

Be it enacted by the Governor and Judges of the Territory of Michigan, That all actions, suits, bills, or informations, which shall hereafter be had, brought, sued, or commenced for any forfeiture upon any penal statute, made or to be made, the benefit whereof is or shall be, by the said statute, limited in whole or in part to the person or persons who shall inform and prosecute in that behalf, shall be had, brought, sued, or commenced by any person or persons who may lawfully pursue the same as aforesaid, within one year from the passing of this act: For past offenses, and for all offenses which shall hereafter be committed within one year from the commission of the same, and not afterwards, and in default of such pursuit, then the same shall be had, brought, or prosecuted by the Territory at any time within two years next after the passing of this act; for past offenses, and for all offenses which shall hereafter be committed within two years

* Printed in full p. 68, vol. 2, Territorial Laws.
† Printed in full p. 79, vol. 2, Territorial Laws.

1809.

from the commission of such offenses, and not afterwards, and any indictment, complaint, or information for any offense against such statute as aforesaid, shall hereafter be found, made, and prosecuted within two years, limited as aforesaid, and not afterwards, any law, usage, or custom to the contrary notwithstanding, excepting in the instance hereinafter provided: *Provided, nevertheless,* and it is hereby further enacted, that where any action, bill, suit, complaint, information, or indictment for any offense against any penal statute already made, or which shall hereafter be made, is or shall be limited by such statute to be brought, had, or prosecuted, within a shorter or longer time than is above mentioned, such action, suit, bill, complaint, information, or indictment, in every such case shall be brought, had, or prosecuted within the time limited by such statute. Proviso.

SEC. 2. *And be it enacted,* That all actions, suits, bills, complaints, informations, or indictments, which at any time hereafter shall be brought, had, commenced, or prosecuted for any crime or misdemeanor (theft, robbery, burglary, forgery, arson, and murder excepted) shall be brought had, commenced, or prosecuted within three years next after the offense was committed, and not after the expiration of the said three years; and all actions, suits, bills, complaints, informations, and indictments which shall be brought, had, commenced, and prosecuted for theft, robbery, burglary, and forgery, shall be brought, had, commenced, and prosecuted within six years after the commission of the offense, and not afterwards; and if any action, suit, bill, complaint, information, or indictment for any crime, or misdemeanor (except arson and murder) shall be brought, had, commenced, or prosecuted after the time hereby limited, that then the same shall be void, and of non-effect, any law, usage, or custom to the contrary notwithstanding: *Provided, always,* That where any information or indictment, or other suit for any crime or misdemeanor is limited by any statute, to be brought, had, commenced, or prosecuted within a shorter or longer time than is hereby limited, then, and in every such case, the information, or other suit, shall be brought, had, commenced, or prosecuted within the time limited by such statute.

Limitation—suits, etc., for crime or misdemeanor.

Exceptions.

For theft, robbery, burglary, and forgery.

If brought after time limited, void, except as to arson and murder.

Proviso.

SEC. 3. *And be it enacted,* That when any bill, complaint, information or indictment shall be exhibited, or any action or suit, brought or commenced, in any of the cases mentioned in the preceding section of this act, the clerk of the court or magistrate to whom such bill, complaint, information, or indictment shall be exhibited, or who shall sign the original writ in such action or suit brought or commenced as aforesaid, shall, at the time of exhibiting or signing as aforesaid, make a minute in writing under his official signature on such bill, complaint, information, indictment, or original writ, of the true, day, month, and year when the same was so exhibited or signed, and every bill, complaint, information, indictment, or original writ on which a minute of the day, month, and year shall not be made as aforesaid shall be void: *Provided always,* That the limitations in this act shall not extend to or effect

All bills, complaints, etc., to have minute made on them of day, year, and month when exhibited, to be void if not.

Proviso.

1809.

any rights, title, or claims to any lands which are or shall hereafter be owned by this Territory, or by the United States within this Territory.

Writ of right, other real action, ejectment, or other possessory action.

SEC. 4. *And be it enacted,* That no writ of right or other real action, no action of ejectment, or other possessory action of whatsoever name or nature shall hereafter be sued, prosecuted, or maintained for the recovery of any lands, tenements or hereditaments if the cause of action shall occur after the passing of this act, but within fifteen years next after the cause of action shall accrue or have accrued to the plaintiff or demandant, or plaintiffs or demandants, or those under whom he, she, or they claim, and that no person having right or title of entry into houses, lands, tenements, or heriditaments shall hereafter thereinto enter but within fifteen years next after such right of entry shall accrue, or have accrued.

Right of entry.

Actions of trespass, trover, or replevin, etc. Account. Debt. Assaults, menace, battery, etc.

SEC. 5. *And be it enacted,* That all actions of trespass, quare clausam fregit, all actions of trespass, detinue, trover, or replevin for goods or chattels, all actions of account and upon the case other than such as concern the trade of merchandise between merchant and merchant, their factors and servants, all actions of debt grounded on any lending or contract without specialty, all actions of debt for arrearages, rent, and all actions of assaults, menance, battery, wounding, and in imprisonment, or any of them which shall be sued and brought after the passing of this act, shall be commenced and sued within the time hereafter limited, and not afterwards, that is to say the said actions of account, the said actions of debt and actions upon the case other than for slander, and the said actions of trespass, detinue and replevin for cattle, and said actions of trespass, quare clausam fregit, within six years next after the cause of such actions or suits shall respectively accrue, and not after, and the said action of assault, menace, battery, wounding, and imprisonment, or any of them within three years next after the cause of such actions or suits respectively shall accrue and not after, and the said actions of the case for slander within two years next after the cause of such actions or suits shall accrue and not afterwards.

Promissory notes, attested.

SEC. 6. *And be it enacted,* That all actions upon promissory notes in writing (attested by one or more witnesses), executive after the passing this act shall be commenced and sued within fourteen years next after the cause of action shall accrue thereon and not after, and all actions on promissory notes in writing, unattested, executed after the passing of this act, shall be commenced and sued within six years next after the cause of action shall accrue thereon and not after, and all actions of debt or scire facias on judgment within eight years next after the rendition of such judgment and not after, and all actions of covenant other than covenants contained in deeds of conveyance of lands for securing the title of said lands, within eight years after the cause of such action shall have accrued and not after, and all actions of covenant brought on any covenant or covenants contained in any deed of conveyance of lands as aforesaid within ten years next after there shall have been a final decision against the debt of the covenanter

Unattested. Scire facias. Covenants, other than contained in title deeds to land. Land covenants.

1809.

on such deed: *Provided always*, and it is hereby further enacted, That if upon any of the said actions or suits judgment shall be rendered for the plaintiff, and the same be reversed by writ of error, or a verdict passed for the plaintiff and for matter alleged in arrest of judgment, the judgment be given against the plaintiff that he take nothing for his plaint, writ, or bill, as also when judgment in any action or suit shall be rendered against the plaintiff on any plea in abatement or in demurrer, and the merits of the cause shall not be tried, that in all such cases the plaintiff, his heirs, executors, or administrators, as the case shall require, may commence a new action or suit from time to time within a year after such judgment reversed or such judgment given in arrest or rendered on plea of abatement or upon demurrer against the plaintiff and not after. Proviso.

SEC. 7. *And be it enacted*, That this act shall not extend to bar any infant, *femme* covert, person imprisoned, or beyond seas, without any of the United States, or parts contiguous thereto, or *non compos mentis*, from bringing either of the actions before mentioned within the time before set, and limitation for bringing such actions, calculating from the time such impediment shall be removed, and if any person against whom there is, or hereafter may be, any cause or suit for any or every species of personal actions before enumerated, who, at the time the same accrued, was without the Territory, and shall not have known property or estate therein, which could by the command or ordinary process of law be attached, that then, and in every such case, the person who was entitled to bring such action or suit shall have liberty to commence the same within the respective periods before limited, after such absent persons coming or return into this Territory. Who not barred. Limitations removed in case of person without the territory, etc.

SEC. 8. *And be it enacted*, That no judgment or proceedings in course of justice, in any real or personal actions, shall, from and after passing of this act, be reversed or avoided for any error or defect therein, unless the writ of error, or suit for reversing such judgment or proceedings in course of justice to be commenced and duly served on the defendant, or defendants in error according to law within one year next after such error or defect shall have intervened; saving always unto infants, *femmes coverts*, persons *non compos mentis*, persons in prison, beyond seas, or without the United States, or parts contiguous, the right of bringing any writ of error, or suit for reversing any judgment or proceeding in the course of justice at any time within one year next after such impediment shall be removed, and not after. Writ of error.

SEC. 9. *And be it enacted*, That all acts and clauses of acts coming within the purview of this act, be and the same are hereby repealed: *Provided, always*, and it is hereby further enacted and expressly declared that this act shall not be construed to extend to or affect any right or rights, action or actions, remedies, fines, forfeitures, privileges, or advantages accruing under any former act or acts, clause or clauses of acts falling within the construction of this act, in any manner whatever, but all proceedings may be had, and advantages therein, in the same man- Repealing. Proviso.

9

1809.

ner as though this act had not been passed, and the former act or acts of limitation, clause, or clauses of acts, which is, are, or were in force at the time of passing this act, shall, for all such purposes be and remain in full force and effect, anything herein contained to the contrary notwithstanding; the same being adopted from the laws of two of the original States, to wit: The States of Massachusetts and Vermont, as far as necessary and suitable to the circumstances of the Territory of Michigan.

Adopted and published at the city of Detroit, in the Territory of Michigan, this twenty-third day of February, one thousand eight hundred and nine.

Attest
JOS. WATSON,
Secretary.

WILLIAM HULL,
Governor of Michigan and President of the Legislature.

No. 63.
February 23.

AN ACT concerning jurors.

Grand jury—number of, and how summoned.

Be it enacted by the Governor and Judges of the Territory of Michigan, That the marshal of the Territory shall, upon every stated sitting of the supreme court, and the district marshals at each session of the district courts, when notified by the attorney general, respectively, summon twenty-four of the most discreet inhabitants, in the case of the supreme court, and of the district in case of the district court, to appear at the court, and the said inhabitants, or any sixteen of them, shall be a grand jury, who shall be sworn to enquire of, and present all offenses and misdemeanor whatever cognizable by the said court.

Oath.

SEC. 2. *And be it enacted,* That an oath in the following words shall be administered to the grand jury: "You shall diligently enquire into and true presentment make of all such matters and things as shall be given you in charge, or otherwise come to your knowledge, touching the present service. The State's counsel, you fellows, and your own, you shall keep secret. You shall present no person through any malice, hatred, or ill-will, nor shall you leave any unrepresented through fear, favor, or affection, or for any reward, hope, or promise thereof, but in all your presentments, you shall present the truth, the whole truth, and nothing but the truth, according to the best of your skill and understanding, so help you God."

Failure to attend upon summon.

SEC. 3. *And be it enacted,* That every person summoned to appear on the grand jury as aforesaid, and failing to attend, not having a reasonable excuse, shall be fined by the courts, respectively, not exceeding twenty dollars, to the use of the territory, or district, as the case may be.

Sickness, death, etc., of juror.

SEC. 4. *And be it enacted,* That in case of sickness, death, or non-attendance of any grand juror who shall have been sworn, it shall be lawful for the court to cause another to be sworn in his stead.

SEC. 5. *And be it enacted,* That for the trial of all causes in the supreme and district courts of this Territory, the marshal shall summon and return as jurors, sober and judicious persons of good reputation, and none other (not being under the age of twenty-one years) to attend the courts, that out of them may empaneled sufficient juries for the trial of causes depending in such courts; which number of jurors shall not be less than sixteen, nor more than forty-four, and if any person so summoned shall fail to attend the courts accordingly, he shall be fined eight dollars, unless he shall offer the court a reasonable excuse for his non-attendance, for the use of the Territory, or district, as the case may be, and no exception against any juror on account of any legal disability, shall be allowed after he is sworn.

Jurors for supreme and district courts—how obtained, qualifications, number, etc.

Penalty, non-attendance.

SEC. 6. *And be it enacted*, That every marshal and vice-marshal, shall, besides the usual oaths or affirmation of office, as required by the laws of the Territory, take the following oath or affirmation according to law: "I, A. B., do swear (or being consciencious1y scrupulous of taking an oath, affirm) that I will use my utmost diligence to prevent any man from being summoned or returned by me, or by any deputy under me, for a juror who, in my judgment, will be influenced by determining any of the matters which shall come before him as a juror, by hatred, malice, or ill-will, fear, or affection, or by any partiality whatsoever."

Oath to be taken by marshal.

SEC. 7. *And be it enacted*, That the marshal, or other returning officer, in every district, shall summon each of the said jurors at least ten days before the sitting of the court, and shall cause a copy of the panel, to be made by him as aforesaid, to be openly and publicly fixed up in his office, and another copy to be in like manner fixed up in the office of the clerk of the proper court seven days, at the least, before the setting of the court, in order that the parties therein concerned may have due and timely notice of the persons who may be called to serve on such jury, and the persons whose names shall be thus fixed up, and no others, shall be returned as jurors to serve in said court as aforesaid.

Mode of summoning jurors by marshal.

SEC. 8. *And be it enacted*, That the marshal, from time to time, enter or register in a book to be kept for that purpose, alphabetically, the surnames of all such persons who shall be summoned and shall attend and serve upon juries in the said courts, with their christian names, additions, and places of abode, and also the times of their respective services; and every person so summoned and attending, or serving as aforesaid, shall, upon application by him made to such marshal, have a certificate testifying such, his attendance or service, which certificate such marshal is hereby directed and required to give without fee or reward; and the said book shall be delivered over by such marshal to his successor and *toties quoties* from time to time.

Record to be kept of jurors serving, etc.

Certificate of service.

SEC. 9. *And be it enacted*, That no person shall be returned to serve on a grand jury, or on a petit jury, in any of the said courts respectively (cases of special juries excepted) who hath served as a juror in any of the same courts within the space of one year preceding, and if any marshal shall willfully trespass herein, the court to which such person shall be summoned con-

Persons serving not to be summoned again within one year.

1809.

Penalty if done.

trary to this act, on examination and proof, in a summary way, of such offense, may set a fine on such offender, as to the court shall seem meet, not exceeding thirty dollars, nor less than ten dollars, for any one offense.

Juries de mediatate linguæ.

SEC. 10. *And be it enacted,* That the juries *de mediatate linquae* may be directed by the courts respectively.

Contempt of court.

SEC. 11. *Be it enacted,* That any juror guilty of contempt to the court, may be fined by such court in any sum not exceeding thirty dollars.

Having knowledge of cause on trial.

SEC. 12. *And be it enacted,* That jurors knowing anything relative to the point or issue shall disclose the same in open court.

No intercourse with jury after they retire.

SEC. 13. *And be it enacted,* That the marshal shall not converse with a juror, but by order of the court, after the jury have retired from the bar, and shall keep them without meat, drink, or candle, unless by permission of the court, until they are with unanimity agreed upon their verdict.

Member of grand jury finding presentment against person shall not serve on trial jury, if challenged.

SEC. 14. *And be it enacted,* That no one of the grand jury by which any person may have been presented for any crime or offense whatsoever, shall be on the jury for the trial of such person, if he be challenged for that cause by the party.

May find special verdict.

SEC. 15. *And be it enacted,* That no jury upon any trial hereafter to be had, shall, on any case, be compelled to give a general verdict, so that they find a special verdict, and shew the truth of the fact; the same being adopted from the laws of five of the original States, to wit: The States of Virginia, New York, Pennsylvania, Massachusetts, and Vermont, as far as necessary and suitable to the circumstances of the Territory of Michigan.

Adopted and published at the city of Detroit, in the Territory of Michigan, this twenty-third day of February, one thousand eight hundred and nine.

Attest:
JOS. WATSON,
Secretary.

WILLIAM HULL,
Governor of Michigan and President of the Legislature.

No. 64.
February 23.

AN ACT concerning forcible entry and detainer.

No person to make forcible entry in lands, etc.

Be it enacted by the Governor and Judges of the Territory of Michigan, That no person or persons shall hereafter make any entry into any lands, tenements, or other possessions, but in cases where entry is given by law, and in such case, not with strong hands, nor with multitude of people, but only in a peaceable and easy manner, and if any person from henceforth do the contrary, and thereof be duly convicted, he shall be punished by fine.

Two justices of peace, one of whom is a judge of district court, and jury to try such entries.

SEC. 2. *And be it enacted,* That two justices of the peace, one of whom shall be a judge of a district court, shall have authority to enquire, by a jury, as hereinafter directed, as well as against those who make unlawful and forcible entry into lands, tenements, or other possessions, and with strong hands detain the same, as against those who having lawful and peaceable entry into lands and tenements, unlawfully, and by force hold the same; and if it

1809.

be found upon such inquiry that an unlawful and forcible entry hath been made, and that the same lands, tenements, or other possessions, are held and detained by force and strong hand, or that the same, after a lawful entry, are held unlawfully, and with force and strong hand, then such justice shall cause the party complaining to have restitution thereof.

Warrant to issue, when.

SEC. 3. *And be it enacted,* That when any complaint shall be formally made in writing, to any two justices of the peace, one of whom shall be a judge as aforesaid, of any such unlawful or forcible entry or detainer, they shall issue a warrant directed to the marshal of the same district, commanding him to apprehend the person against whom such complaint shall be made, and to bring him or her before the said justices, at a day in such warrant named, which shall not be less than six days from the time of issuing the said warrant, and at the place therein mentioned, and they shall also issue a precept to the said marshal, commanding him to cause to come before them twelve freeholders of the vicinity, at a certain time and place in such precept to be mentioned, and at the said time and place appointed for trial, or hearing the said complaint; and if a sufficient number of persons summoned by the marshal do not attend, the said justices may order the marshal to complete the number by returning others forthwith, and the jury empaneled shall be sworn well and truly to try the forcible entry or detainer complained of, and to return a true verdict thereof; and if the jury, after a full hearing, find the person against whom the complaint is made guilty of the forcible entry or detainer complained of, they shall all sign their verdict, and the said justices shall enter up judgment for the complainant to have restitution of the premises, and shall impose such fine, not exceeding ten dollars, considering all the circumstances, as they may think just, and shall tax costs for the complainant, and may commit the person against whom the judgment is so made, until the fine be paid, and the said justices shall also award their writ of restitution; but if the jury find that the person complained against is not guilty, the complaint in their opinion not being supported, the said justices shall tax costs against the complainant, and issue execution accordingly.

Venire.

Verdict.

Judgment.

Warrant, how served.

SEC. 4. *And be it enacted,* That if the marshal cannot find the party against whom the warrant issue, he may, six days before the time appointed for returning the same, leave a true and attested copy of said warrant at the usual place of abode of such person, and if, at the return of the warrant, he shall not be able to find or apprehend the person against whom such warrant issue, he shall make a return of such facts, and that he hath so left a copy as aforesaid, and when the same was done, and if the party doth not appear at the time appointed for hearing the said complaint, the said justices may, in their discretion, adjourn, or proceed *ex parte,* except that in this case they shall not inflict any fine upon him, and in all cases they may, in their writ of restitution, order the costs taxed to be levied, but in every such case, if the jury do not find for the complainant, there shall be no costs taxed for the

Justices may adjourn or proceed ex parte.

Costs, when taxed and levied.

1809.

party complained against, he not having appeared at the empaneling of the jury.

Treble damages, when recoverable.

SEC. 5. *And be it enacted,* That the complainant of any forcible entry and detainer aforesaid, who shall recover against the person complained of, as aforesaid, shall have right to recover treble damages, with cost of suit, by an action of trespass against the offender, or offenders, to be brought for that purpose: *Provided, always,* That nothing in the foregoing part of this act shall be construed to extend to any person or persons who have had the quiet, peaceable, and uninterrupted occupation of any lands, tenements, or other possessions for the space of three whole years next before the entering of such complaint, anything in this act to the contrary notwithstanding.

Proviso, as to three years' occupation.

Refusal of lessee to yield possession, etc.

SEC. 6. *And be it enacted,* That when any person shall willfully and with force hold over any lands, tenements, or other possessions, after the determination of the time for which they are demised or let to him, or to the person under whom he claims, or when any person willfully, and without force, by disseisin shall obtain and continue in possession of any lands, tenements, or other possessions, and after demand made in writing for the delivery of the possession thereof, by the person having the legal right of such possession, his agent or attorney, shall refuse or neglect to quit such possession, upon complaint thereof in writing, to two justices of the peace, one of which shall be a judge of a district court, the said justices shall proceed to hear, try, and determine the same in like manner as in cases of forcible entry and detainer, and issue a writ of execution accordingly: *Provided, always,* That in such case the original process shall be a summons, and the justice shall have no power to assess a fine on the party complained of.

Proviso, as to original process.

Occupants undisturbed for three years not affected.

SEC. 7. *Provided always, and it is hereby further enacted,* That the preceding section shall not extend to any person who has, or shall have continued in possession three years after the determination of the time for which the premises were demised, or let to him, or those under whom he claims, or to any person who continues in possession three years, quietly and peaceably by disseisin, anything herein contained to the contrary notwithstanding.

Damages.

SEC. 8. *And be it enacted,* That the complainant shall have right to action of trespass against the person complained of, and who on trial shall be found guilty, to recover treble damages from the time of notice given to quit the premises, and till that time, damages only.

May appeal to supreme court.

SEC. 9. *And be it enacted,* That if either party in a prosecution on this act, shall think him or herself aggrieved with the determination of the justices aforesaid, he or she shall have liberty to appeal to the next supreme court, giving security in the same manner as provided in the case of appeals from a district court to the supreme court.

When appellee may obtain affirmation of judgment.

SEC. 10. *Provided, nevertheless, and it is hereby further enacted,* That when it shall so happen that the appellant, in any action brought on this statute, shall fail to bring forward his appeal, and enter the same in the court to which said appeal is allowed, the

1809.

appellee shall have the same liberty to obtain an affirmation of the judgment rendered in the court below, as is given by law in cases of appeal from district courts to the supreme court in civil actions; the same being adopted from the laws of one of the original States, to wit: The State of Vermont, as far as necessary and suitable to the circumstances of the Territory of Michigan.

Adopted and published at the city of Detroit, in the Territory of Michigan, this twenty-third day of February, one thousand eight hundred and nine.

Attest: WILLIAM HULL,
JOS. WATSON, *Governor of Michigan and President*
Secretary. *of the Legislature.*

No. 65.
February 23.

AN ACT concerning forms of writs and other process.

Be it enacted by the Governor and Judges of the Territory of Michigan, That the following forms of writs in the several courts within this Territory, and other proceedings, shall, as near as circumstances will admit, be adopted and used:

TERRITORY OF MICHIGAN. } WARRANT BEFORE THE SUPREME COURT.

Warrant before the supreme court.

To the Marshal of the Territory:—GREETING:

[L. S.] In the name of the Territory of Michigan, you are hereby commanded to take the body of A. B., of............, if to be found within your precinct, and him safely keep, so that you have him to appear before the supreme court of the Territory, to be holden at..............on the.... of..............next, then and there to answer to C. D., of ...., in an action of plea of (here insert the cause of action) to the damages of the plaintiff, as he says,............ dollars, to recover which, with just cost, he brings this suit; hereof fail not, but of this writ, with your doings therein, make due return, according to law. ....dated at............this ....day of............, A. D.

..................*Clerk.*

..................recognized to the defendant, in the........ sum of..............as surety for costs of prosecution, in due form of law before me.

..................*Clerk.*

TERRITORY OF MICHIGAN, ...DISTRICT. } WARRANT BEFORE THE DISTRICT COURT.

Warrant before the district court.

To the Marshal of the District of............: GREETING:

In the name of the Territory of Michigan, you are hereby commanded to take the body of.............., of.............., if to be found within your precinct, and him safely keep, so that you have him to appear before the district court to be holden at...... within and for the district of............., in the..........next, there and then to answer to...........of............in an

1809. action or plea of (here insert cause of action) to the damages of the plaintiff, as he says,..........dollars, to recover which, with just costs, he brings this suit; hereof fail not, but of this writ, with your doings thereon make due return, according to law. ....dated at............, this......day of............ A. D.

....................*Clerk.*

..................recognized to the defendant in the sum of ....as surety for costs of prosecution, in due form of law before me.

....................*Clerk.*

Warrant before justice of the peace.

TERRITORY OF MICHIGAN, DISTRICT. } WARRANT BEFORE A JUSTICE OF THE PEACE.

To the Marshal of the District of..............: GREETING:

In the name of the Territory of Michigan, you are hereby commanded to take the body of............, of............, if to be found within your precinct, and him have forthwith (or at a day certain, to be named) before me, at my dwelling house at ...., to answer to............of............in an action or plea (here insert the substance of the case) to the damages of the plaintiff, as he says.........dollars, to recover which, with just costs, he brings this suit; thereof fail not, but of this writ, with your doings therein, make due return according to law. Dated at............this......day of............, A. D.

....................*Justice of the Peace.*

..................recognized to the defendant in the sum of ....as surety for costs of prosecution, in due form of law before me.

....................*Justice of the Peace.*

EXECUTION.

Execution.

TERRITORY OF MICHIGAN. } SS.

To the Marshal of the..............: GREETING:

Whereas, ..., of............, by the consideration of the..........court holden at............within and for............on the day of............recovered judgment against............, of............, for the sum of.......... dollars, and ....cents, debts, damages, &c. (as the case may be) and............dollars, and..........cents costs of suit, as appears of record, whereof execution remains to be done; therefore

In the name of the Territory of Michigan, you are hereby commanded, that of the goods, chattels, or lands of the said........ within your precinct, you cause to be levied, and the same being disposed of as the law directs, paid and satisfied unto the said.... ......the aforesaid sums, being..........dollars, and........ cents, in the whole with..........cents more, for this writ; and thereof also satisfy yourself for your own fees, and for the want

1809.

of goods, chattels, or lands, of the said............to be shown unto you, or found within your precinct, to the acceptance of the said..........to satisfy the sums aforesaid, you are commanded to take the body of the said............., and him commit to the keeper of the jail in the district of............., within the said prison, who is hereby commanded to receive the said............and him safely keep until he pay the full sum above mentioned, with your fees, or that he be discharged by the said............, the creditor, or otherwise by order of law; hereof fail not, but of this writ, with your doings thereon, make due return within........days from the date:

............dated at.............this........day of........, A. D.

...................*Clerk, or Justice of the Peace.*

Execution from a district court, or a justice of the peace to be in the same form, as near as may be, *mutatis mutandis.*

ATTACHMENT.

Attachment.

TERRITORY OF MICHIGAN.

To the Marshal of............:—GREETING:

In the name of the Territory of Michigan, you are hereby commanded to attach the goods and chattels, and for the want thereof the lands of............, to the value of..........dollars, if to be found within your precinct, and him notify thereof, according to law, and also to appear before the............court, to be holden on the............day of............, then and there to answer unto............, of............, in an action of.........., to the damage of the plaintiff, as he says,............dollars, to recover which, with just costs, he brings this suit; hereof fail not, but of this writ, with your doings therein, make due return according to law.

............dated at............this........day of........ A. D.

...................*Clerk, or Justice of the Peace.*

..............recognized to the defendant in the sum of.........for costs of prosecution in due form of law, before me.

...................*Clerk, or Justice of the Peace.*

SUMMON.

Summons.

TERRITORY OF MICHIGAN.

To the Marshal of..............:—GREETING:

In the name of the Territory of Michigan, you are hereby commanded to summon.............., of.............., to appear before the............court, to be holden at............, within and for the............, on the........day of...........next, then and there to answer unto..............., of............, in an action..........to the damages of the plaintiff, as he says,

1809.

............, to recover which, with just cost, he brings this suit; hereof fail not, but of this writ, with your doings therein, make due return according to law.

............dated at............this........day of........ A. D.......

..................*Clerk.*

SUMMON BEFORE A JUSTICE.

Summons before a justice.

TERRITORY OF MICHIGAN, }
DISTRICT OF }

To the Marshal of the District of............:—GREETING:

In the name of the Territory of Michigan, you are hereby commanded to summon............, of..........., to appear before me, at.......dwelling house........, in............, on the ....day of............, then and there to answer unto..... ......of............, in an action............, to the damage of the plaintiff, as he says, ..., to recover which, with just cost, he brings this suit............; hereof fail not, but of this writ, with your doings therein, make due return according to law.

..........dated at........this........day of.........., A. D..

..................*Justice of the Peace.*

WARRANT IN CASE OF FORCIBLE ENTRY AND DETAINER.

Warrant in case of forcible entry and detainer.

TERRITORY OF MICHIGAN, } ss.
DISTRICT OF........ }

To the Marshal of the District of............:—GREETING:

Whereas,............, of............, hath exhibited unto ...., one of the judges of.........., and.........., one of the justices of the peace within and for the district of ...., a complaint against............., of..........,for that the said............, on the....... day of............, at............, aforesaid, with force and arms, and with a strong hand (here insert the substance of the complaint with legal certainty); therefore,

In the name of the Territory of Michigan, you are hereby commanded to apprehend the said............, if to be found in your precinct (or summon the said............, if it be a case proper for a summon) and him have to appear before us, at..... ......, on the.......day of............, at......o'clock in the ....noon, then and there to make answer to and defend against the complaint aforesaid, and further to be dealt with according to law; but if the said............is not to be found within your precinct, you are required to leave a true and attested copy of this warrant, at the usual place of abode of the said.... ...., six days, at least, before the said day of............, and make return of this warrant, with your doings therein, unto us, at............aforesaid, on the........day of..........

Dated at............, this.....day............, A. D.....

..................*Judge of*............

..................*Justice of the Peace.*

PRECEPT FOR JURORS IN CASE OF FORCIBLE ENTRY AND DETAINER. 1809.

Precept for jurors in case of forcible entry and detainer.

TERRITORY OF MICHIGAN, } ss.
DISTRICT........ }

To the Marshal of............:—GREETING:

In the name of the Territory of Michigan, you are hereby commanded to cause to come before us, on the......day of.........., at......o'clock in the ......noon, at..........; twelve men, to be summoned in the same manner as petit jurors, to serve before the supreme or district courts, to try the truth of a complaint exhibited as............, one of the judges of the ...., and............one of the justices of the peace in and for said district of............, by............, of............, against ...., of............, for a forcible entry (or detainer as the case may be) and make return of this writ, with your doings thereon, unto us, at............, on the......day of.......... aforesaid, at........the........day of............, A. D.....

..................*Judge of*............

..................*Justice of the Peace.*

FORM OF THE VERDICT IN FORCIBLE ENTRY AND DETAINER.

Verdict in forcible entry and detainer.

At a court of inquiry held at.........., on the......day of ...., in the year of our Lord........, before.........., one of the judges of.........., and............, one of the justices of the peace in and for the..........of..........aforesaid, ...of..........complainant against..........., of............, respondent, the jury find that the facts alleged in the said............complaint, are true; that the said...... ......is guilty thereof, and that the said............ought to have restitution of the premises therein described, without delay (or in case the jury do not find the allegations of the complaint proven, then the jury find that the said facts alleged in the said ....complaint, are not proven, and that the said........ ....is not guilty).

.... *Foreman.*
....
....
.... *Jurors.*
....
....

FORM OF THE WRIT OF RESTITUTION IN CASE OF FORCIBLE ENTRY AND DETAINER.

Writ of restitution, forcible entry and detainer.

TERRITORY OF MICHIGAN } ss.
DISTRICT OF........ }

To the Marshal of the District of............:—GREETING:

Whereas,............, of............, at a court of enquiry of forcible entry and detainer, holden at............, in the district of............in the............day of............, in the

1809. year of our Lord........., before............., one of the judges of............., and.............one of the justices of the peace in and for the district of............., by the consideration of the said court, recovered judgment against............., of............, to have restitution of (here describe the premises as in the complaint); therefore,

In the name of the Territory of Michigan, you are hereby commanded, that, taking with you the force of the district, if necessary, you cause the said........... to be immediately removed from the premises, and the said.............to have peaceable restitution of the same; you are also hereby commanded, that if the goods, chattels, or lands of the said............., within your precinct, you cause to be levied, and the same being disposed of according to law to be paid and satisfied, the sum of............., being the cost taxed against the said............., for the said ....at the court aforesaid, together with.........cents, for this writ, and thereof also (here follows as in common executions, and must be signed by the judge or justice).

FORM OF A SUBPŒNA ATTESTIFICANDUM.

Subpœna attestificandum. TERRITORY OF MICHIGAN. } ss.

To the Marshal of............., or to............., an indifferent person, as the case may be:—GREETING:

In the name of the Territory of Michigan, you are hereby commanded to summon............., and............., of..........., to appear before (here insert the title of the court, or name of the magistrate, and the time and place of sitting) to give evidence of what they know, relating an action or plea, of this, and there to be heard and tried between............., of............., plaintiff, and............., of............., defendant, and this neither of them may omit, as they will answer their default under the pains and penalty of the law in that behalf made and provided; thereof fail not, and make due return according to law. Dated, &c.

......................*Clerk, or Justice of the Peace.*

SEC. 2. *And be it enacted*, That in all cases in which, by law, a writ of *audita querela* lieth, the same may be sued out in the form of a writ of summon or attachment, under the provisions and restrictions of the first section of an act entitled "An act act concerning attachments," at the election of the complainant, and the form thereof may be as follows:

Writ Audita Querela, how sued out, etc. TERRITORY OF MICHIGAN. } ss.

To the Marshal:—GREETING:

In the name of the Territory of Michigan, you are hereby commanded to summon, or take the body, or attach the goods, chattels, or estate (as the case may be) of............, pursuing the same form as is before prescribed in the common summon warrant or attachment, there and therein the said court to answer unto the grievous complaint of............, of............, who complaineth and saith (here let the declaration, stating the facts with legal certainty, be inserted) by all which the said............, as he sayeth, is greatly injured and aggrieved, and hath suffered damage the sum of........dollars, as shall then and there be made to appear; and have you there this writ, with your doings therein............. Allowed and signed by me (or by us as the case may be) at..........., this......day of............, in the year of our Lord........ 1809

...................*Judge of the Supreme Court.*
...................*Judge of the District Court.*
...................*Judge of the District Court.*

Minute of recognizance to be made and signed as in case of attachment or warrant.

SCIRE FACIAS. Writ scire facias.

TERRITORY OF MICHIGAN. } ss.

To the Marshal of............:—GREETING:

Whereas,............, of............, by the consideration of the............court, holden at............, on the......day of......, A. D......, recovered against..........., of.........., the sum of........dollars, debt, or damages (as the case may be) and also the sum of......dollars, and......cents, costs of suit in that behalf expended, whereof the said............is convict, as appears of record, and, although judgment thereof be rendered, yet the execution of the said debt, or damage and cost, yet remain to be made, whereof the said............hath made application for remedy, to be provided in that behalf; now, to the end that justice be done, you are hereby commanded that you make known to the said............that he, before next to be holden at, within and for the..........., on the......day of..........., A. D. to show cause (if any he hath) wherefore the said.......... ought to have his execution against him, the said............, for his debt (or damages) and costs aforesaid; further to do and receive that which the said court shall consider, and make due return of this writ, with your doings therein, according to law; hereof fail not.

..........Dated at.........., the......day of............, A. D.......

HABEAS CORPUS. Habeas corpus.

TERRITORY OF MICHIGAN, DISTRICT OF } ss.

To the Marshal of............:—GREETING:

In the name of the Territory of Michigan, you are hereby com-

1809. manded that the body of............, of...........in the prison in the district of..........., under your custody (or by you imprisoned and restrained of his liberty, as the case may be), as it is said, together with the day and cause of his commitment (taking and detaining) by whatsoever name the said............shall be called, or charged, you have before the court to be holden........ or before the court now sitting at.......... (or before me at.........) immediately after the receipt of this writ, to do and receive what the said court shall then and there consider concerning him (or her) in this behalf; and have you there this writ, given under our hands (or my hand, as the case may be when signed by the judges, or one judge), and when signed by the clerk, witness, one of the judges of, &c...........A. D.,...... clerk.

Dated at.........., this......day of.........., A. D.

Mittimus, from justice, on conviction of crime.

FORM OF A MITTIMUS, FROM A JUSTICE OF THE PEACE, ON CONVICTION OF A CRIME.

TERRITORY OF MICHIGAN, } ss.
DISTRICT OF }

To the Marshal of the District of............:—GREETING:

Whereas, ..., of the District of..........., on the ......day of........, at.........., in said district, before me, ..., one of the justices of the peace within and for said district, was convicted of the crime (here insert the nature of the crime) and sentenced to pay the treasury of........a fine of...... dollars, costs of prosecution taxed at..........., and to stand committed till sentence be complied with as appears of record; therefore,

In the name of the Territory of Michigan, you are hereby commanded, on his, the said............., neglect or refusal to pay said fine and cost, to commit him, the said............, to the keeper of the jail, in the district of.........., within the said prison, who is hereby commanded to receive the said..........., and him safely keep until he pay the said fine, and costs, and costs of commitment, together with your own fees, or till he be otherwise discharged by order of law; hereof fail not, but of this precept, with your doings therein, make due return. Given under my hand at.........., this......day of.........., A. D.

....................*Justice of the Peace.*

Appeal from decision of justice on suit for book account.

ACTION ON BOOK BEFORE A JUSTICE, WITH AN APPEAL.

TERRITORY OF MICHIGAN, } ss.
DISTRICT OF }

Be it remembered that at a justice court holden at........, in the district of.........., on the......day of..........*Anno Domini*........, before.........., justice of the peace for said district,..........., of..........., was summoned, to answer to........of..........., in an action on book account, whereupon the plaintiff here in court, complains that the defendant is indebted to him, on book, to balance book account, the sum of......dollars, which is to the plaintiff's damage........dollars; now the defendant in court pleads and says he is not indebted to the plaintiff, as is in his said plea set forth, and prays it may be enquired of by the court, whereupon it is adjudged by the court that the plaintiff recover of the defendant the sum of........dollars.... cents debt, to balance the plaintiff and defendant's books, and the sum of........dollars, and......cents, and now the defendant, within...........hours after the rendering the aforesaid judgment, prays that an appeal may be granted him in the matters aforesaid, to the next district court, to be holden at.......... within and for the district of..........on the.....day of........, A. D......, it is thereupon ordered that the defendant be allowed his appeal. The defendant as principal and........... as surety recognized to the plaintiff in the sum of........dollars for the prosecution of said appeal in due form of law.

The foregoing is a true copy from the record, with a minute of the recognizance, examined by

...................*Justice of the Peace.*

A copy of the writ must be annexed.

A RECOGNIZANCE TO BE SENT UP BY A JUSTICE OF THE PEACE IN CRIMINAL PROSECUTIONS.

Recognizance before justice for appearance at higher court.

DISTRICT OF } ss.
....

Be it remembered that on the......day of.........., A. D. ......, before.........., justice of the peace for the district of ...., personally appeared.........., of.........., principal, and.........., and..........of the..........sureties, and acknowledged themselves jointly and severally indebted to the treasurer of.........., in the sum of........dollars, to be levied of their, and each of their goods and chattels, lands and tenements, and for the want thereof, on their bodies, if default be made in the condition following:

The condition of the above recognizance is such that if the above named.........., charged before me with having........ shall make his personal appearance before the..........court, to be holden at.........., in the.........., and answer to the matters and things which shall then and there be objected to him, in this behalf, shall abide the order of the said court, and not depart without leave of the same, then this recognizance to be void, otherwise of effect.

Taken and acknowledged this......day of.........., A. D. ......, before

...................*Justice of the Peace.*

RECOGNIZANCE FOR WITNESS TO APPEAR AND TESTIFY.

Recognizance of witness.

DISTRICT OF } ss.
....

Be it remembered that on the......day of.........., A. D.

1809.

......, before........, justice of the peace for the district of ...., personally appeared..........., of..........., and acknowledged himself indebted to the treasurer of..........., in the sum of.........dollars, to be levied of his goods and chattels, lands and tenements, and for want thereof, on his body, if default be made in the condition following:

The condition of the above recognizance is such that, if the above named...........shall appear before the supreme court to be holden at..........., in the..........., to testify his knowledge in a certain prosecution in behalf of this Territory against ...., and shall not depart without the leave of said court, then this recognizance to be void, otherwise of force.

Taken and acknowledged this......day of..........., A. D. ....

....................*Justice of the Peace.*

Defects in summons, writs, etc., not to be considered, but judgment to be rendered upon the right and equity.

SEC. 3. *And be it enacted,* That no summon, writ, declaration, return, process, judgment, or other proceeding in civil causes in any of the courts of this Territory shall be abated, arrested, quashed, or reversed for any defect or want of forms, but the said courts shall proceed and give judgment according to the right of the case, and matter in law, as shall appear unto them, without regarding any imperfections, defects, or want of form in such writ, declaration, or other pleading, return, process, judgment, or course of proceeding whatsoever, except only those in case of demurrer, which the partydemurring shall specially set down and except, together with his demurrer, as the cause thereof, and the said court, respectively, shall and may by virtue of this act, from time to time, amend all and every such imperfections, defects, and want of forms, other than those only which the party demurring shall express, as aforesaid, and may, at any time, permit either of the parties to amend any defect in the process or pleading, upon such condition as the said courts respectively shall, in their discretion, by their rules prescribe; the same being adopted from the laws of three of the original States, to wit: The States of New York, Vermont, and Massachusetts, as far as necessary and suitable to the circumstances of the Territory of Michigan.

Demurrer, excepted.

Power of court to make corrections, etc.

Adopted and published at the city of Detroit, in the Territory of Michigan, this twenty-third day of February, one thousand eight hundred and nine.

Attest: WILLIAM HULL,
JOS. WATSON, *Governor of Michigan and President*
Secretary. *of the Legislature.*

No. 66.
February 24.

AN ACT regulating enclosures.

Lawful enclosure defined.

Be it enacted by the Governor and Judges of the Territory of Michigan, That all fields and grounds kept for enclosure, shall be well enclosed with fence composed of sufficient posts and rails, posts and palings, palisades, or rails alone, laid out in the manner

1809.

which is commonly called a worm fence, which posts shall be deep set, and strongly fastened in the earth, and all fences composed of posts and rails, posts and palings, or palisades, shall be at least five feet in height, and all fences composed of rails, in the manner which is commonly denominated a worm fence, shall be at least five feet six inches in height, the uppermost rail of each and every panel thereof, supported by strong stakes, strongly set, and fastened in the earth so as to compose what is commonly called staking and riding, otherwise the uppermost rail of every panel of such worm fence shall be braced with two strong rails, poles, or stakes, locking each corner or angle thereof, and in all cases wherein any fence is composed of any of the foregoing materials, the apertures between any of the rails, palings, or palisades, within two feet of the surface of the earth, shall not be more than four inches, and from the distance of two feet from the earth, until the height of three feet six inches from the surface thereof, the apertures between such rails, palings, or palisades shall not be more than six inches, and that in all worm fences, the worm of the same shall be at least one third of the length of the rails which compose the respective panels thereof.

Owner of animal breaking into lawful enclosure liable for damages, amount of, etc.

SEC. 2. *And be it enacted,* That if any horse, gelding, mare, colt, mule, or ass, sheep, lamb, goat, kine, or cattle, shall break into any person's enclosure, the fence being of the aforesaid height and strength, or if an hog, shoat, or pig shall break into any person's enclosure, the fence being of the aforesaid height and sufficiency, and by the view of two persons for that purpose appointed by the district court, found and approved to be such, then the owner of such creature, or creatures, shall be liable to make good all damages to the owner of the enclosure, for the first offense, single damages only, ever after, double the damages sustained.

Partition fences, cost of to be equally borne, when.

SEC. 3. *And be it enacted,* That for the better ascertaining and regulating of partition fences it is hereby directed that when any neighbors shall improve lands adjacent to each other, or where any person shall enclose any land adjoining to another's land already fenced, so that any part of the first person's fence becomes the partition fence between them, in both these cases the charge of such division, so far as enclosed on both sides, shall be equally borne and maintained by both parties; to which, and other ends in this law mentioned, each district court, yearly, and every year in the term ensuing, shall nominate, and hereby is required to nominate and appoint six honest and able men, who must also be freeholders, for each district, who being duly sworn to a faithful discharge of the duties of their appointment, shall, or any three of them, proceed, on the request of any person or persons feeling him, her, or themselves aggrieved, to view all such fence and fences about which any difficulty may happen or arise, and the aforesaid persons, or any two of them, in each district respectively, shall be the sole judges of the charge to be borne by the delinquent, or by both, or either party, and of the sufficiency of all fences, whether partition fences or others, and when they

Fence viewers, appointment of, duties and powers.

1809.

Proceedings in case of refusal to make or repair fence after due notice.

shall judge any fence to be insufficient, they shall give notice thereof to the owners or possessors, and if any one of the owners or possessors, upon request of the other, and due notice given by the said viewers, shall refuse or neglect to make or repair the said fence or fences, or to pay the moiety of the charges of any fence before made, being a division or common fence, within twenty days after notice given, thereupon proof thereof before two justices of the peace of the respective district, it shall be lawful for the said justices to order the person aggrieved and suffering thereby to make or repair the said fence or fences, who shall be reimbursed his costs and charges from the person so refusing or neglecting to make or repair the partition fence or fences aforesaid, or to order the delinquent to pay the moiety of the charge of any fence before made, being a division or common fence, as the case may be, and if the delinquent shall neglect or refuse to pay to the party injured the said moiety of the charge of any fence or fences under the order aforesaid, then the same shall be levied upon the delinquent's goods and chattels under warrant from the said justices of the peace, by distress and sale thereof, the overplus, if any, to be returned to the said delinquents: *Provided,* That nothing herein contained shall be intended to prevent or debar any person or persons from enclosing his or their grounds in any manner they please, with sufficient rails or fences of timber other than those heretofore mentioned or by dykes, hedges, or ditches; all such walls and fences to be in height at least five feet from the ground, and all dykes to be at least three feet in height from the bottom of the ditch, and planted or set with thorn or other quickset, so that such enclosure shall fully answer and serve the several purposes meant to be answered and secured by this law: *Provided, also,* That such walls or fences of timber, other than those heretofore mentioned, and dykes, hedges, and ditches, shall be subject to all provisions, inspections, and restrictions, respectively, to which, by this law, any other enclosure or fence is made liable, according to the true intent and meaning thereof; the same being adopted from the laws of one of the original States, to wit: The State of Vermont, as far as necessary and suitable to the circumstances of the Territory of Michigan.

Penalty.

Proviso.

Proviso.

Adopted and published at the city of Detroit, in the Territory of Michigan, this twenty-fourth day of February, one thousand eight hundred and nine.

Attest: WILLIAM HULL,
JOS. WATSON, *Governor of Michigan and President*
Secretary. *of the Legislature.*

No. 67.
February 24.

AN ACT repealing certain acts therein named.

Be it enacted by the Governor and the Judges of the Territory of Michigan, That the several acts and parts of acts hereinafter mentioned, be and the same are hereby repealed, to wit:

1809.

An act concerning the marshal of the Territory of Michigan, adopted the tenth day of July, one thousand eight hundred and five; Concerning the marshal.

An act concerning the supreme court of the Territory of Michigan, adopted the twenty-fourth day of July, one thousand eight hundred and five; Supreme court.

An act concerning district courts, adopted the twenty-fifth day of July, one thousand eight hundred and five; District courts.

An act concerning the recovery of debts to the value of twenty dollars, adopted the first day of August, one thousand eight hundred and five; Recovery of debts.

An act concerning grand juries, adopted the fourteenth day of August, one thousand eight hundred and five; Grand juries.

An act concerning juries, adopted the seventeenth day of August, one thousand eight hundred and five; Juries.

An act concerning appeals, adopted the twentieth day of August, one thousand eight hundred and five; Appeals.

The fourth section of an act entitled "An act concerning the recording of deeds and other writings," adopted the twenty-ninth day of August, one thousand eight hundred and five; Recording of deeds.

An act concerning ferries, tavern keepers, and retailers of merchandise, adopted the twenty-ninth day of August, one thousand eight hundred and five; Ferries, tavern keepers, etc.

An act concerning auctions, adopted the thirtieth day of August, one thousand eight hundred and five; Auctions.

An act concerning the militia of the Territory of Michigan, adopted the thirtieth day of August, one thousand eight hundred and five; Militia.

An act concerning wills and justices, adopted the thirty-first day of August, one thousand eight hundred and five; Wills and justices.

An act concerning the treasurer of the Territory of Michigan, adopted the fourth day of September, one thousand eight hundred and five; Treasurer.

An act imposing certain taxes, adopted the tenth day of September, one thousand eight hundred and five; Taxes.

An act in addition to an "act concerning the marshal of the Territory of Michigan," adopted the thirteenth September, one thousand eight hundred and five; Marshal.

An act for the relief of the poor, adopted the eighth day of October, one thousand eight hundred and five; Relief of the poor.

An act concerning attachments and absent defendants, adopted the twelfth December, one thousand eight hundred and six; Attachments and absent defendants.

An act concerning the city of Detroit, adopted the thirteenth of September, one thousand eight hundred and six; Detroit, city of.

An additional act concerning district courts, adopted the second day of April, one thousand eight hundred and seven; District courts.

An additional act concerning the recovery of small sums to the amount of twenty dollars, adopted the sixteenth day of April, one thousand eight hundred and seven: Recovery of small sums.

Provided, nevertheless, and it is hereby further enacted and expressly declared, That the aforesaid repealed acts, or laws, shall Proviso.

1809.

be in full force as to all matters and things done or transacted during their existence, to which they relate, to all intents and purposes, as though this act had not been made, and all such matters may be prosecuted, done, and completed at any time hereafter, pursuant to the same laws, and this act shall not be construed to affect any right or rights, remedy or remedies, fines, forfeitures, or penalties incurred or accruing under any former act, or acts, clause, or clauses of acts; anything herein contained to the contrary nothwithstanding.

Acts of the Northwestern or Indiana Territories, to have no further effect.

SEC. 2. *And be it enacted*, That all acts or laws adopted and published by the governor and judges, or by the legislative authority of the Northwestern Territory, or the Indiana Territory, shall, from and after the passing of this act, cease to have any force or operation within this Territory: *Provided, nevertheless*, That the act shall not be construed to defeat or affect any right or rights, fines, forfeitures, or penalties which have already accrued, under any of the laws aforesaid; the same being adopted from the laws of one of the original States, to wit: The State of Vermont, as far as necessary and suitable to the circumstances of the Territory of Michigan.

Proviso.

Adopted and published at the city of Detroit, in the Territory of Michigan, this twenty-fourth day of February, one thousand eight hundred and nine.

Attest;
JOS. WATSON,
Secretary.

WILLIAM HULL,
Governor of Michigan, and President of the Legislature.

No. 68.
February 26.

AN ACT making appropriations for the year one thousand eight hundred eight, and one thousand eight hundred and nine.

Salary of Secretary.

Be it enacted by the Governor and Judges of the Territory of Michigan, That there be and hereby is appropriated as the annual salary of the secretary to the governor and judges of the Territory of Michigan, for the year one thousand eight hundred and nine, the sum of twenty-five dollars; for the services of Jos. Watson rendered for the legislative board, to wit: Forty days, at two dollars per day, is eighty dollars; and for transcribing copies of the laws for the district, sixty-six dollars. For expenses on paupers in one thousand eight hundred and eight, a sum not exceeding four hundred dollars. For expenses on paupers up to the first of March, one thousand eight hundred and nine, a sum not exceeding one hundred and four dollars. For inquisition on dead bodies, a sum not exceeding seventy-five dollars. For the use of a court house, jail, firewood, candles, stoves, &c., a sum not exceeding two hundred and eighty dollars. For the marshal, for attending before magistrates, in criminal cases, a sum not exceeding seventy-five dollars. For James Witherell, John Whipple, and William McD. Scott, as commissioners, for seventeen days' service each, in exploring and superintending the survey of a public road from the foot of the rapids of the river Miami, of Lake Erie, to Detroit,

Jos. Watson.

Paupers.

Inquisitions.

Court house, etc.

Marshal.

Jas. Withrell, John Whipple and Wm. McD. Scott.

1809.

at four dollars per day, each, is two hundred and four dollars. For James McCloskey, in surveying said road, at three dollars per mile, it being sixty-six miles, fifty-two chains, and forty links, is one hundred and ninety-nine dollars and fifty cents. For the hire of two horses and two men, seventeen days, at four dollars per day, is sixty-eight dollars. For eleven days of the service of one man, on the same business, at one dollar per day, eleven dollars. Stationery in the treasury department, ten dollars; and for a contingent fund, to be expended under the direction of the governor, subject to the revision of the legislative power, to meet extraordinary expenses which may occur, a sum not exceeding two hundred dollars.

Jas. McCloskey.

Men and horses.

Stationery.

Contingent fund.

SEC. 2. *And be it enacted,* That the several sums aforesaid and shall be paid out of any money in the Territorial treasury, not otherwise appropriated according to law: *Provided, however,* That the sums of two hundred and four hundred dollars appropriated for the payment of the commissioners, for laying the road as aforesaid, and the sum of one hundred and ninety-nine dollars and fifty cents, for surveying said road, shall not be paid out of the treasury within twelve months from and after the passing of this act, unless it be from moneys which may be in the treasury arising from the sale of lottery tickets, pursuant to an act adopted by the governor and judges of this Territory, the nineteenth day of December, one thousand eight hundred and eight; the same being adopted from the laws of two of the original States, to wit: The States of Pennsylvania and Ohio, as far as necessary and suitable to the circumstances of the Territory of Michigan.

Proviso.

Adopted and published at the city of Detroit, in the Territory of Michigan, this twenty-fourth day of February, one thousand eight hundred and nine.

Attest: WILLIAM HULL,
JOS. WATSON, *Governor of Michigan and President*
Secretary. *of the Legislature.*

No. 69.
February 26.

AN ACT regulating fees.

Be it enacted by the Governor and Judges of the Territory of Michigan, That from and after the passage of this act, the fees for services actually rendered, shall be as is herein specified, viz.:

Fees allowed.

TO THE JUDGES OF THE RESPECTIVE DISTRICT COURTS.

Judges of district courts.

For the entry of each action, whether original or by appeal, one dollar.

For the trial of each action, one dollar.

For the surrender of a principal by his bail, in court, twenty-five cents.

Granting an appeal and taking recognizance, twenty-five cents.

Rendering judgment on the report of auditors or referees, fifty cents.

1809.

Granting a writ of protection, or any other original process, fifty cents.

Granting and serving a writ of *audita querela,* and taking bonds, to each judge signing the same, fifty cents.

For a writ of *habeas corpus,* one dollar.

And to each judge, for every day's attendance in the appointment of district officers, or auditing any district accounts, which by law he is required to do, two dollars.

All the above perquisites to be equally divided among the judges who actually attend to, and perform the services.

Justices of the peace.

TO JUSTICES OF THE PEACE.

For a warrant or attachment, thirty-three and one-third cents.

For a summons, twenty-five cents.

For a subpœna, for one or more witnesses, twelve and one-half cents.

For each judgment on a trial, fifty cents; by confession, defects, or non-suit, twenty-five cents.

Recognizance to prosecute on appeal, seventeen cents; copy of a judgment, and other necessary papers in an appealed cause, fifty cents.

For an execution, twenty-five cents.

For taking and certifying a deposition, thirty-three and one-third cents.

For travel, each way, in taking deposition, thirty-three and one-third cents.

Each oath administered, for private benefit, with certificate, six and one-quarter cents; when certified, twelve and one-half cents.

Recording a complaint and issuing a warrant thereon, in criminal cases, fifty cents.

For the trial of each criminal cause, fifty cents.

For taking and returning a recognizance to the supreme or district court, in a criminal case, fifty cents.

For a mittimus to commit, on a criminal accusation, twenty-five cents.

Clerk of the Supreme Court.

TO THE CLERK OF THE SUPREME COURT.

Entering an indictment, information, or complaint, and all matters relative thereto, fifty cents.

Warrant for a criminal, thirty-three and one-third cents.

Subpœna for one or more witnesses, twelve and one-half cents.

Entering each civil action for trial, twelve and one-half cents.

Recording a verdict, twelve and one-half cents.

Motions for a review, twelve and one-half cents.

Writ of *scire facias,* seventy-five cents.

Entering judgment and taxing costs in a suit, twenty-five cents.

Execution, twenty-five cents.

Writ of *facias habire possessionem,* including entering judgment, and taxing costs, one dollar.

Writ of *habeas corpus,* when signed by the clerk, one dollar; when signed by a judge or judges, twenty-five cents.

Copies of all records or papers containing one hundred words, twelve and one-half cents.

Entering each rule of court, eighteen and three-fourths cents.

Recording a non-suit or default, twenty-five cents.

Entering an appearance, twelve and one-half cents.

Entering satisfaction of judgment on record, thirty-three and one-third cents.

Entering a judgment at large, fifty cents.

Venire for a jury, thirty-three and one-third cents.

For every writ, other than those before mentioned, twenty-five cents.

For each recognizance, including principal and sureties, twelve and one-half cents.

Opening and filing depositions in court, twelve and one-half cents.

Searching records of five years' standing, six and one-fourth cents.

CLERKS OF DISTRICT CORRTS.

Clerks of district courts.

The same as is allowed to the clerk of the supreme court for similar services, except in criminal causes, where it shall be one-eighth part less.

GRAND JURORS.

Grand jurors.

Each grand juror for attending the supreme court, or a district court, for each day, one dollar, and for each mile traveled in coming to court, six and one-fourth cents.

PETIT JURORS.

Petit jurors.

For every verdict returned to the court, to each juror, fifty-cents, and the same mileage as grand jurors.

MARSHAL OF THE TERRITORY.

Marshal of the Territory.

Serving a summons, or citation, by reading, fifty cents; for leaving a copy thereof, twenty-five cents.

Capias, or warrant, and taking the body of one defendant, two dollars, and for each additional defendant, in the same warrant, fifty cents.

Attachments on property, and taking a receipt, two dollars.

Levying execution on property, two dollars.

Levying execution on the body, two dollars.

Collecting an execution, for the first five hundred dollars, six dollars on each hundred, and on each additional hundred dollars, two dollars and one half.

Travel per mile, each way, in all cases, six and one-fourth cents.

Serving a summons on each juror, twenty-five cents.

Each day's attendance on the supreme court, two dollars.

Taking inquisition on dead bodies, per day, three dollars; and for any other actual services rendered, and not herein enumerated, such sums as shall be allowed by the supreme court.

Serving and returning any warrant, execution, summons, or other process, for a justice of the peace, for each person arrested, twenty-five cents.

1809.

Each person summoned, sixteen and and one-fourth cents.

Traveling one or more miles, going only, six and one-fourth cents.

Collecting and paying money on execution from justice of the peace, the same as already provided.

Vice marshal.

VICE MARSHAL.

The same as the marshal.

District marshal.

DISTRICT MARSHAL.

The same fees as is allowed to the marshal of the territory, except that in criminal causes they shall be one-eighth less.

When marshal is party to suit, other person to perform his duty therein.

SEC. 2. *And be it enacted*, That when it shall so happen that the marshal of any district is a party, or interested in any suit, it shall be lawful for the clerk of any district court to deputize some suitable person to perform his duty in such particular case.

Parties.

PARTIES.

For the party recovering, in the supreme court, for his attorney, four dollars.

In all other cases for each judgment recovered, two dollars.

In causes in district court, tried by a jury, three dollars.

In all other cases, for a judgment recovered, one dollar and fifty cents.

For a declaration on a writ, fifty cents.

For each days' attendance before the supreme court or district court, forty cents.

Before a justice of the peace, thirty-three and one-third cents.

Traveling ten miles, within this Territory, to be accounted equal to a day's attendance, but shall in no case be allowed for more than forty miles, unless the party actually performs it by himself, or special agents.

Witnesses.

WITNESSES.

Before the supreme court or district court, in all civil or criminal cases, for each day's attendance, seventy-five cents; for each mile's travel going and coming, four cents.

Before a justice of the peace, referees, or arbitrators, for each day's attendance, thirty-three and one-half cents, and the same traveling fees as allowed in cases of supreme court, or district courts.

Attorney General.

ATTORNEY GENERAL.

For all criminal causes tried by a jury in supreme court, including indictment, information, or complaint, eight dollars.

If by the court, four dollars.

In a district court by a jury, including indictment, information, or complaint, six dollars.

If by the court, four dollars.

And for such other services rendered in criminal prosecutions, as shall be allowed by the court.

JUDGE OF PROBATE.

Judge of probate.

For granting administration, fifty cents.

If litigated, one dollar.

Appointment of a guardian for a minor, or *non compos mentis*, forty cents.

Probate of a will, not litigated, fifty cents.

If litigated, one dollar.

Examining and allowing inventory twenty-five cents.

Administering an oath, if certified, twelve and one-half cents;

If not, six and one-fourth cents.

Examining and allowing any account, if not more that two pages, forty cents.

For each page over two, twelve and one-half cents.

Decree for settling an intestate estate, forty cents.

A citation, seventeen cents.

Summons for a witness, twelve and one-half cents.

Warrant to appraise or divide an estate, thirty-three and one-third cents.

Apponitment of commissioners to examine claims to an insolvent estate, twenty-five cents.

Order of distribution, twenty-five cents.

Granting an appeal, twenty-five cents.

REGISTER OR CLERK OF PROBATE.

Register or clerk of probate.

Writing bond and letter of administration, forty cents.

Bond for guardian, and recording the same, sixty cents.

If for more than one minor, for each additional one, twelve and one-half cents.

Drawing a decree in probate of a will or bond for an execution, thirty-three and one-third cents.

Writing warrant to appraise the estate of a deceased person, entering the account of an administrator, executor, or guardian, twenty-five cents.

Writing a decree of partition or order of distribution, twenty-five cents.

Writing a summons for one or more witnesses, twelve and one-half cents.

Recording or copying, for each hundred words, eight cents.

Writing bond on an appeal to the supreme court, twenty cents.

For searching records, the same as allowed to the clerk of the supreme court.

REGISTER OF DEEDS.

Register of deeds.

For recording each deed, or any other writing, after the rate of, for every hundred words, eight cents.

For copying the record, the same for searching for a record for more than five years standing, six and one-fourth cents.

JAILOR'S FEES.

Jailors.

For turning the key for each person committed or discharged, twenty-five cents.

1809.

For dieting a prisoner, such sum as shall be, from time to time, allowed by the district court.

Costs, criminal prosecutions.

SEC. 3. *And be it enacted,* That all costs arising on criminal prosecutions, shall be paid from the treasury into which the fine by law is made payable, and shall, by the clerks of the courts respectively, be made up in the bill of costs against the respondents, in case of conviction; and the expenses of inquisitions on dead bodies shall be paid from the treasury of the district where they are held.

Inquests.

Penalty for over charging.

SEC. 4. *And be it enacted,* That if any person shall knowingly and wittingly ask, demand, or receive any greater sum for performing any of the services enumerated in this act, than therein is allowed for the same, the person of whom such unlawful asking, demanding or receiving is made or had, shall be entitled to recover of the person so asking, demanding, or receiving as aforesaid, treble the amount, so unlawfully asked, demanded, or received, by action brought on this statute, with costs, before any court of competent jurisdiction; the same being adopted from the laws of one of the original States, to wit: The State of Massachusetts, as far as necessary and suitable to the circumstances of the Territory of Michigan.

Adopted and published at the city of Detroit, in the Territory of Michigan, this twenty-sixth day of February, one thousand eight hundred and nine.

Attest: WILLIAM HULL,
JOS. WATSON, *Governor of Michigan and President*
Secretary. *of the Legislature.*

No. 70.
February 26.

AN ACT concerning schools.

Overseers of the poor to lay out school districts, etc.

Be it enacted by the Governor and Judges of the Territory of Michigan. That it shall be the duty of the overseers of the poor of each judicial district within this Territory, some time in the month of May next, to divide their respective districts into such sections as, in their judgment, will be most convenient for erecting school-houses, and maintaining schools, which sections shall be styled school districts, which may be altered from time to time, as will best accommodate the inhabitants.

Trustees.

SEC. 2. *And be it enacted,* That the said overseers shall be trustees for the said school districts, and shall, on the first Monday of May, in each and every year, make a return to the judges of their respective district courts, of the whole number of children in each school district, as aforesaid, who are between four and eighteen years of age, and the said judges shall annually make an appropriation for a sum not exceeding four dollars, nor less than two dollars, for each child within the age aforesaid, agreeable to the return aforesaid, within their respective districts, which sum shall be collected and paid into the district treasury in the same manner as is directed by law for collecting and paying in other

School census.

Tax, how made, etc.

district taxes, and shall remain in the treasury until drawn out as is hereinafter provided.

District treasurers to report on state of schools, etc.

SEC. 3. *And be it enacted,* That at the end of each year, counting from the first day of May, it shall be the duty of the said treasurers to make a report in writing to the judges of the district court respectively, of the state of the schools kept in the several school districts as aforesaid, wherein shall be stated the number of weeks the school has been kept, and number of scholars, and the wages paid the instructor; and after the said judges have obtained a satisfactory account from all the school districts, within the judicial district, they shall proceed to make an equal distribution of the money collected and paid into the treasury as aforesaid, to each school district, in proportion to the money which the district has actually expended, in erecting a school-house or maintaining a school the preceding year, and draw orders therefor accordingly, in the name of such trustee or trustees as are authorized to represent the district, and the treasurer is directed to pay the same, taking the trustee's receipt therefor, upon such order, which order and receipt shall be good accounting for the said treasurer, in his settlement of accounts with the district, and in case one or more of the said school districts shall neglect to erect a school-house, or to keep a school during one whole year, such district shall not be entitled to receive any part of the money collected for the purpose aforesaid, but it shall be paid to such district or districts as shall keep a school or schools.

Appropriation of tax by the judges.

Compensation allowed trustees.

SEC. 4. *And be it enacted,* That the said trustees shall be allowed a reasonable compensation for their services prescribed by this act, to be allowed by the said judges, and drawn from the district treasury; the same being adopted from one of the original States, to wit: The State of Vermont, as far as necessary and suitable to the circumstances of the Territory of Michigan.

Adopted and published at the city of Detroit, within the Territory of Michigan, this twenty-sixth day of February, one thousand eight hundred and nine.

Attest: WILLIAM HULL,
JOS. WATSON, *Governor of Michigan and President*
Secretary. *of the Legislature.*

No. 71.
May 11.

AN ACT making certain appropriations.

Be it enacted by the Governor and Judges of the Territory of Michigan, That there be and hereby is appropriated, as a compensation for services rendered by Joseph Watson, as secretary to the legislature of this Territory of Michigan, the sum of thirty-one dollars and ninety-three and three-fourths cents; and the sum of sixteen dollars to John Goff, for services rendered in writing military commissions, and copying laws relative to the duty of the marshal of this Territory.

Jos. Watson.

John Goff.

1809. Made and published at the city of Detroit, in the Territory of Michigan, this eleventh day of May, one thousand eight hundred and nine.

Attest: REUBEN ATTWATER,
JOS. WATSON, *Acting Governor of Michigan and President of the Legislature.*
Secretary.

No. 72. May 11.

AN ACT concerning the service of writs.

Be it enacted by the Governor and Judges of the Territory of Michigan, That from and after the fifteenth day of May instant, in all cases, where it is not otherwise specially provided by law, the service of all writs of summon or attachment, made returnable to the supreme court, or to any district court, shall be made at least twelve days before the first day of the session of said courts respectively; and all writs of summon or attachment, issuing from a justice of the peace, in all cases where it is not otherwise specially provided by law, shall be served at least six days before the day of trial named in such writ; the same being adopted from the laws of one of the original States, to wit: The State of Vermont, as far as necessary and suitable to the circumstances of the Territory of Michigan.

Summons and attachment.

Adopted and published at the city of Detroit, in the Territory of Michigan, this eleventh day of May, one thousand eight hundred and nine.

Attest: REUBEN ATTWATER,
JOS. WATSON, *Acting Governor of Michigan and President of the Legislature.*
Secretary.

1810. No. 73. September 1.

AN ACT declaring any and all bills, acts, laws, enactments, or regulations whatever, heretofore existing, or supposed to exist, relating to the manner of authenticating the legislative acts of this government, to be null as to any future operation.*

Be it enacted by the Governor and Judges of the Territory of Michigan, That any and all bills, acts, laws, enactments or regulations whatsoever, heretofore existing, or supposed to exist, relating to the manner of authenticating the legislative acts of this government, shall be null as to any future operation.

Made and published at the city of Detroit, in the Territory of Michigan, this first day of September, one thousand eight hundred and ten.

Attest: WILLIAM HULL,
JOS. WATSON, *Governor of the Territory of Michigan.*
Secretary. A. B. WOODWARD,
One of the Judges of the Territory of Michigan.
JOHN GRIFFIN,
One of the Judges of the Territory of Michigan.
JAMES WITHERELL.

***Title of this act given in Cass Code, p. 210, vol. 1, Territorial Laws.**

AN ACT concerning illegitimate children.* **1810.**

Be it enacted by the Governor and Judges of the Territory of Michigan, That any justice of the peace informed of a female person having an illegitimate child, may issue his warrant to bring such person before him, and may call upon her for security from any public charge that might accrue from such child, and upon any neglect or refusal, may commit her. In case the said person shall discover the father, the justice may discharge her, and call the father before him, and cause him to give security in the sum of eighty dollars, to indemnify the public against any charge for the maintenance of such child; the same being adopted from the laws of one of the original States, to wit: The State of Maryland, as far as necessary and suitable to the circumstances of the Territory of Michigan.

No. 74. September 4.

Mother of illegitimate child may be required to give bond to save the public from charge.

If father be discovered.

SEC. 2. *And be it enacted,* That any justice, upon the application of the mother of an illegitimate child, verifying that she has not received any money from the father, more than credit given, may adjudge such father to pay the mother an adequate sum for the maintenance of the child, not exceeding thirty dollars for one year, until the child shall attain the age of seven years; the same being adopted from the laws of one of the original States, to wit: The State of Maryland, as far as necessary and suitable to the circumstances of the Territory of Michigan.

Father may be compelled to provide for maintenance of child.

Adopted and published at the city of Detroit, within the Territory of Michigan, this fourth day of September, one thousand eight hundred and ten.

Attest: WILLIAM HULL,
JOS. WATSON, *Governor of the Territory of Michigan.*
Secretary. AUGUSTUS B. WOODWARD,
One of the Judges of the Territory of Michigan.
JOHN GRIFFIN,
One of the Judges of the Territory of Michigan.

AN ACT to fix the compensations of counsel and attorneys at law in the supreme court of the Territory of Michigan. †

No. 75. September 7.

Be it enacted by the Governor and the Judges of the Territory of Michigan, That the several laws and regulations now existing on the subject of compensation of counsel and attorneys in the supreme court, be repealed, and the same shall be five dollars; and in cases where the controversy is settled out of the court, one-third of the said sum; the same being in part made under the repealing power, and in part adopted from four of the original States, to wit: The States of Massachusetts, New York, Vermont, and Virginia, as far as necessary and suitable to the circumstances of the Territory of Michigan.

Repealing clause.

New schedule of fees.

Made, adopted, and published at the city of Detroit, within the

* Digest of, Cass Code, p. 180, vol. 1, Territorial Laws.
† Digest of, Cass' Code, p. 139, vol. 1, Territorial Laws.

1810. territory of Michigan, this seventh day of September, one thousand eight hundred and ten.

Attest: WILLIAM HULL,
JOS. WATSON, *Governor of the Territory of Michigan.*
Secretary. AUGUSTUS B. WOODWARD,
One of the Judges of the Territory of Michigan.
JOHN GRIFFIN,
One of the Judges of the Territory of Michigan.

No. 76. September 12.

AN ACT declaring what shall be deemed a lawful enclosure for preventing trespasses, and concerning partition fences and estrays.*

Lawful enclosure defined.

Be it enacted by the Governor and the Judges of the Territory of Michigan, That a fence of strong and sound materials, five feet high and so close that hogs or sheep cannot creep through, or a hedge two feet high upon a ditch three feet deep and three feet broad, or, instead of such hedge, a rail fence of two feet and a half high, the hedge or fence being so close that the animals aforesaid cannot creep through, shall be accounted a lawful fence; the same being adopted from one of the original States, to wit: The State of Virginia, as far as necessary and suitable to the circumstances of the Territory of Michigan.

Animals entering lawful enclosure owners thereof liable for damages.

Double damages, when collectible.

SEC. 2. *And be it enacted,* That if any horse, mare, cattle, hog, sheep, or goat shall break into any grounds, being enclosed with a lawful fence, the owner of the animal shall make reparation to the party injured, to the true value of the damage sustained, for the first trespass committed, and for every trespass afterwards double damages and the costs; the same being adopted from one of the original States, to wit: The State of Virginia, as far as necessary and suitable to the circumstances of the Territory of Michigan.

Legality of enclosure, how ascertained.

SEC. 3. *And be it enacted,* That upon complaint made by the party injured, before a justice of the peace, the justice is hereby empowered and required to issue an order to three honest housekeepers, of the vicinity, not related or interested, requiring them to view the fence where the trespass is alleged to have been committed, and to take memoranda of the same, and their testimony shall be good evidence concerning the legality of the fence; the same being adopted from one of the original States, to wit: The State of Virginia, as far as necessary and suitable to the circumstances of the Territory of Michigan.

Persons not having lawful fence, injuring animals, liable for double damages to owners of animals.

SEC. 4. *And be it enacted,* That if any person injured for want of a sufficient fence, shall hurt, wound, lame, kill, or destroy any animal, the property of another, or shall cause the same to be done, the person offending shall pay, to the owner of the animal, double damages with costs; the same being adopted from one of the original States, to wit: The State of Virginia, as far as necessary and suitable to the circumstances of the Territory of Michigan.

*Digest of, Cass' Code, p. 147, vol. 1, Territorial Laws.

1810.

SEC. 5. *And be it enacted,* That every person who, without leave of the owner, shall take away any boat, canoe, or other vessel, shall pay to the owner, for every offense, ten dollars, and the damage such boat, canoe, or other vessel shall sustain, and the charge of bringing back such boat, canoe, or other vessel, with costs; the same being adopted from one of the original States, to wit: The State of Virginia, as far as necessary and suitable to the circumstances of the Territory of Michigan.

Penalty for taking boats, etc., without leave.

SEC. 6. *And be it enacted,* That the charges of the partition fences shall be equally sustained by both parties, and a justice of the peace, on the request of a person aggrieved, shall nominate and appoint three honest and able men to view any fence about which a difference may exist, and such persons may be the sole judges of the charge to be sustained by the delinquent party, or by both parties, or either of them, and if either of the parties, at the request of the other, shall refuse or neglect to make and repair his fence, or to pay the moiety, or amount in which he is found delinquent, after twenty days' notice, it shall be lawful for a justice of the peace to order the person aggrieved to make or repair the said fence, who shall be reimbursed his costs and charges by the party neglecting, and if the party shall neglect or refuse to reimburse the said costs and charges, or to pay his moiety or amount of any fence, the same shall be levied by execution from a justice of the peace; the same being adopted from one of the original States, to wit: The State of Ohio, as far as necessary and suitable to the circumstances of the Territory of Michigan.

Partition fences, how maintained.

Fence viewers, to apportion charge for.

Penalty for neglect to make or repair after due notice.

SEC. 7. *And be it enacted,* That every person who shall cut or destroy any tree, or sapling, standing or grown upon the land of another, without permission of the owner, shall pay, for every offense, a sum not exceeding ten dollars, recoverable before a justice of the peace, who, if the defendants shall plead title to the land, shall dismiss him on his giving sufficient security to prosecute his claim within one year, and the costs shall, in that case, be made a part of the judgment to be rendered in such action, and if the party fail to bring such action, within one year, a justice of the peace may give judgment and execution against him; the same being adopted from one of the original States, to wit: The State of Ohio, as far as necessary and suitable to the circumstances of the Territory of Michigan.

Penalty for injuring trees, etc., without leave of owner.

When title to land is pleaded.

SEC. 8. *And be it enacted,* That every person taking up a stray animal, or any water craft, gone or going adrift, shall, within five days, cause the same to be viewed by some householder in the vicinity, and shall, with such householder, go before a justice of the peace, and the justice shall take an exact description of the property, and shall issue his warrant to one or more disinterested householders, to appraise the same, and the owner shall pay reasonable costs and charges, if he appear within one year to reclaim his property; and if he appear after one year, and the property be not a horse, or otherwise be not above the value of twenty dollars, he shall take the property, or the appraised value, at the option of

Estrays, boats, etc.

Appraisal of.

Owner, rights and duties.

1810. the party in possession; the same being adopted from one of the original States, to wit: The State of Ohio, as far as necessary and suitable to the circumstances of the Territory of Michigan.

Adopted and published at the city of Detroit, within the Territory of Michigan, this twelfth day of September, one thousand eight hundred and ten.

Attest: WILLIAM HULL,
JOS. WATSON, *Governor of the Territory of Michigan.*
Secretary. AUGUSTUS B. WOODWARD,
One of the Judges of the Territory of Michigan.
JOHN GRIFFIN,
One of the Judges of the Territory of Michigan.
JAMES WITHERELL.

No. 77. September 14.

AN ACT to regulate the internal government and police of the several districts in the Territory of Michigan.*

Electors, who are.

Be it enacted by the Governor and the Judges of the Territory of Michigan, That the free male adult citizens of the United States of America, within the several districts of the Territory of Michigan, who have resided one year within the district, shall, on the second Tuesday of October, annually, elect five councilors, selectmen, or commissioners, of integrity and knowledge for the internal government and police of the district; the elections to be notified, held, conducted, and certified by the marshal of the district; the same being adopted from the laws of three of the original States, to wit: The States of Connecticut, Ohio, and Pennsylvania, as far as necessary and suitable to the circumstances of the Territory of Michigan.

Council elected and vested with internal government, etc.

Election, how conducted.

Quorum.

SEC. 2. *And be it enacted,* That a majority of the council shall be a quorum for the transaction of business, and a majority of such quorum shall determine a question. The council shall have power to determine contested elections of their own members, and when vacancies accrue within the year, to provide for an election to supply such vacancy. The council shall provide for the support of the poor, for the maintenance and repair of roads and bridges, and generally for the internal government and police of the district, for the education of youth, and for those and other purposes shall levy and collect rates and taxes, and make and enact all laws and regulations necessary to give effect to their powers, not contravening the constitution and laws of the United States, or the laws of the Territory, and shall appoint all officers necessary to carry into execution such powers, laws, and regulations, and shall have succession, and may use a seal, and may sue and be sued, and may acquire, hold, and alien property, real and personal, and all courts and ministers of justice shall be aiding to the execution of their powers; the same being adopted from the laws of four of the original States, to wit: The States of Con-

Powers and duties of councel.

* For act repealing, see Cass' Code, p. 211, vol. 1, Territorial Laws.

1810.

necticut, Ohio, Pennsylvania, and Vermont, as far as necessary and suitable to the circumstances of the Territory of Michigan.

Adopted and published at the city of Detroit, within the Territory of Michigan, this fourteenth day of September, one thousand eight hundred and ten.

Attest: WILLIAM HULL,
JOS. WATSON, *Governor of the Territory of Michigan.*
Secretary. AUGUSTUS B. WOODWARD.
One of the Judges of the Territory of Michigan.
JOHN GRIFFIN,
One of the Judges of the Territory of Michigan.

AN ACT to repeal all acts of the Parliament of England, and of the Parliament of Great Britain, within the Territory of Michigan, in the United States, and for other purposes.* No. 78. September 16.

AN ACT rendering territorial offices incompatible with offices under the general government.† No. 79. September 16.

Be it enacted by the Governor and the Judges of the Territory of Michigan, That a Territorial office shall be incompatible with an office under the general government, excepting justices of the peace, and officers of the militia: *Provided,* That justices of the peace, holding any commission under the general government, shall not take cognizance of any matter, civil or criminal, and that officers of the militia shall not exercise a territorial office when in the actual service of the United States, and receiving, or entitled to receive pay; The same being adopted from the laws of two of the original States, to wit: The States of Pennsylvania and Virginia, as far as necessary and suitable to the circumstances of the Territory of Michigan. Justices of the peace and militia officers excepted. Proviso.

SEC. 2. *And be it enacted,* That this act shall commence from the first day of January, one thousand eight hundred and fifteen; the same being adopted from the laws of one of the original States, to wit: The State of Virginia, as far as necessary and suitable to the circumstances of the Territory of Michigan. When to take effect.

Adopted and published at the City of Detroit, within the Territory of Michigan, this sixteenth day of September, one thousand eight hundred and ten.

Attest: WILLIAM HULL,
JOS. WATSON, *Governor of the Territory of Michigan.*
Secretary. AUGUSTUS B. WOODWARD,
One of the Judges of the Territory of Michigan.
JOHN GRIFFIN,
One of the Judges of the Territory of Michigan.

---

* Printed in full, p. 900, vol. 1, Territorial Laws.
Digest of, Cass Code, p. 210, vol. 2, Territorial Laws.
Sec. 4 of this act is important, as by it all laws passed between June 2nd, 1807, and September 1st, 1810, were repealed, being most of those contained in this volume. A note in the manuscript would lead one to infer that it had been contested. It repeals repealing acts, and thus reinstates the acts repealed(?)

† Repealing act, Cass Code, p. 211, vol. 1, Territorial Laws.

1810. No. 80. September 16.

AN ACT to abolish the courts of districts, and to define and regulate the powers, duties, and jurisdiction of justices in matters civil and criminal.*

Repealing clause.

Be it enacted by the Governor and the Judges of the Territory of Michigan, That all acts and parts of acts, relating to the courts of districts, and to the judges thereof, be repealed.

Justices of the peace, jurisdiction of.

SEC. 2. *And be it enacted,* That every justice, within his district, shall have power to hear, and where the matter exceeds not twenty dollars, to try; and where the matter exceeds twenty dollars, by the consent of the parties, to try, and after trial by such consent, or by jury, to render judgment upon all pleas and matters of a criminal or penal nature, where the fine or penalty exceeds not twenty dollars, or the imprisonment twenty days, and all pleas and matters of a civil nature where the debt or sum, or balance due, or damages, or thing or matter demanded, or in controversy exceed not the amount or value of one hundred dollars. He shall have power to apprehend, commit, and recognize all offenders whose offenses surpass his jurisdiction; he shall make fair and accurate entries of his proceedings, in all cases, and his proceedings, signed by him, shall be records; the same being adopted from the laws of four of the original States, to wit: The States of New York, Ohio, Pennsylvania, and Vermont, as far as necessary and suitable to the circumstances of the Territory of Michigan.

Jury trial, when.

SEC. 3. *And be it enacted,* That where the matter exceeds twenty dollars, either party shall be entitled to a trial by jury; the same being adopted from the laws of one of the original States, to wit: The State of Vermont, as far as necessary and suitable to the circumstances of the Territory of Michigan.

Arbitrators.

Judgment on their award.

SEC. 4. *And be it enacted,* That the parties consenting, the case shall be submitted to any disinterested person, or persons, and on the return of their award, signed by them, judgment shall be rendered thereon; the same being adopted from the laws of one of the original States, to wit: The State of Ohio, as far as necessary and suitable to the circumstances of the Territory of Michigan.

Appeal to Supreme Court.

Trial may be by jury or court.

Bond.

Whole case to be heard.

SEC. 5. *And be it enacted,* That where any party shall conceive themselves aggrieved by the judgment or sentence of a justice, in any plea, action, matter, or conduct whatsoever, such party may appeal to the supreme court of the Territory of Michigan. Either party may demand, in the supreme court, trial by jury, or submit the matter to be determined by the court, at their election. Before granting any appeal, the party praying the appeal, or some person for him, shall enter into bond, with sufficient security, in a penalty to be fixed by the justice granting the same, conditioned to pay the amount of the recovery and all costs, interest, and damages awarded, in case the judgment be affirmed. On the trial of the appeal the whole case shall be heard and determined according to the law, equity, and right of the matter. If the judgment

*Digest of, Cass Code, p. 186, Territorial Laws.

1810.

be reversed, in whole or in part, the supreme court shall render such judgment as ought to have been originally rendered. If the defendant appeals, and the judgment be affirmed, there shall be added ten dollars damages. The appeal shall be entered within twenty days from the rendition of the judgment; the appellant shall produce the record. If the record be not filed within the three first days of the succeeding term, it shall not be afterwards received, without the consent of the appellee, unless good cause be shown to the court to the contrary. The appellee, after the expiration of the said three days, and during the same term, may produce the record, and judgment shall be rendered; or he may have execution on the original judgment. In criminal or penal matters, the bond or recognizance shall be to prosecute the appeal, and to abide the judgment of the supreme court thereupon, and, in the mean time, to be of good behavior; the same being adopted from the laws of seven of the original States, to wit: The States of Maryland, Massachusetts, Ohio, Pennsylvania, New York, Vermont, and Virginia, as far as necessary and suitable to the circumstances of the Territory of Michigan.

Decision to be according to law, equity, and right.

If judgment be affirmed.

Time for appeal.

Rights of appellee.

Bond in criminal or penal cases.

SEC. 6. *And be it enacted*, That the proceedings, duties, and powers of justices, shall, as nearly as may be, conform to the law, duties, powers, proceedings, and practices of the supreme court of the Territory of Michigan; and the said supreme court, or any two judges of the same, or any one judge of the same, in case the other two be absent from the Territory, shall direct the forms of process, from time to time, in such manner as shall seem advisable; the same being adopted from the laws of one of the original States, to wit: The State of Virginia, as far as necessary and suitable to the circumstances of the Territory of Michigan.

Proceedure of justices to conform to that of Supreme Court.

Forms of process.

SEC. 7. *And be it enacted*, That the original process against a freeholder, or housekeeper, shall be by summons, and in other cases, or if in the case of a freeholder or housekeeper, the plaintiff shall satisfy the justice he is in danger of losing his claim, the process shall be by capias; original process shall be returnable in five days; intermediate process, when the justice shall direct, and final process in sixty days. If the justice originally issuing the process shall be unable to hear and determine the case, any other justice of the same district may take cognizance of and determine the same. Any case may be continued for sufficient cause, witnesses refusing to appear or give evidence, and any party or person guilty of contempt, may be fined not exceeding ten dollars, and imprisoned for non-payment of the same. Judgment may be given in favor of the defendant against the plaintiff, if the plaintiff be found culpable, or indebted. Executions shall first command the amount to be levied of the property, and shall further command, if sufficient property cannot be found, to take the body; one cow, one sheep, one hog, the apparel, bedding, and tools of the party shall be exempt from execution. At least five days' notice shall be given of sales. On giving good security a stay of execution for three months shall be allowed, for sums not exceeding twenty-five dollars, of six months for sums not exceeding fifty

Form of original process.

When returnable.

Who may hear.

May be continued.

Penalty, witnesses refusing to appear, etc.

Judgment.

Executions.

Exemption.

Notice of sale.

Stay of Execution.

1810.

dollars; of nine months for sums not exceeding seventy-five dollars; and of one year for sums not exceeding one hundred dollars. If the amount be not paid, the execution shall be against both principal and security. Officers detaining money levied by execution, shall pay twenty-five per centum, per annum, interest. If a justice die, or if in any other case his judgment remain unsatisfied, any other justice, of the same district, may issue a writ of *duces tecum* for the record, and grant a *scire facias* against the party, and render judgment thereon. If a justice remove from the district, he shall deliver his records to another justice, and his legal representatives shall do the same in case of his death. After two years such records shall be deposited with the clerk of the supreme court. The parties may plead and set off their mutual debts and demands, and shall be precluded for neglect, unless the amount exceed one hundred dollars. In criminal and penal matters, the justice shall recognize the necessary witnesses, and commit for refusal. Judgment may be confessed without process. No justice shall determine a matter where he is of kin to either of the parties, or interested; nor be of counsel in a matter in which he has acted as justice. Justices may celebrate the rites of matrimony; justices may apprehend for escapes; justices shall take acknowledgments and proof of deeds, and other writings; justices shall hear and determine complaints between masters and apprentices, or servants, and disputes relating to indentures, contracts, and wages, and controversies between inhabitants and Indians; justices shall hear and determine forcible entries and detainers; justices shall bind out unprotected minors; the same being adopted from the laws of seven of the original States, to wit: The States of Connecticut, Massachusetts, Maryland, New York, Ohio, Pennsylvania, and Vermont, as far as necessary and suitable to the circumstances of the Territory of Michigan.

Penalty, retention of levies. Judgment unsatisfied on death of justice, etc. Removal of justice, disposition of records. Set-offs allowed. Recognizance of witnesses. Confession of judgment. Justices, what forbidden. Justices may celebrate the rites of matrimony, etc.

SEC. 8. *And be it enacted,* That the ministerial officers of justices shall be the marshal and his deputies, and when no person is found to serve process, the justice shall appoint a person for that purpose, who shall be entitled to the same fees, and liable to the same penalties; the same being adopted from the laws of one of the original States, to wit: The State of Ohio, as far as necessary and suitable to the circumstances of the Territory of Michigan.

Marshal, etc., ministerial officers of justices. May appoint person to serve process, etc.

SEC. 9. *And be it enacted,* That every justice shall, before he execute his office, take and subscribe the following oaths of office: "I (here repeating and inserting the name of the person) do solemnly swear that I will support the constitution of the United States of America. I (here repeating and inserting the name of the person) do solemnly swear that I will take no reward for doing of justice, or any fee or gift of gold, silver, or any other thing, by myself or any other, privately or openly, directly or indirectly, of any person or persons, great or small, for any matter done, or to be done, by virtue of my office, other than such salary, fees, or compensation as are or shall be allowed by law. I will deny no one right, but in all things execute the laws. I will administer justice and execute my office according to law, and without respect to persons.

Oath.

1810.

I will do equal right to all, and all manner of people, great and small, high and low, ignorant and learned, rich and poor. I will not maintain any quarrel, but endeavor with mercy and justice to quiet the same. I will not spare any one, for any gift, fee, or reward, or for any other cause. If any letter or request come to me, contrary to the law, I will do nothing for such letter or request, but will proceed to do the law, any such letter or request notwithstanding. I will faithfully and honestly discharge and perform all the duties incumbent upon me as one of the justices of the district of (repeating and inserting here the name of the district) in the Territory of Michigan, and in all things belonging to my said office, during my continuance therein, I will, according to the best of my skill and judgment, do full, equal, and effectual justice, without fraud, favor, affection, or the smallest partiality, agreeably to the constitution of the United States of America, the laws of the United States, and the laws of the Territory of Michigan, in defense of the freedom and independence thereof, and for the maintenance of liberty and the distribution of justice among the good citizens, inhabitants, and people of the said United States of America, and Territory of Michigan; the same being adopted from the laws of two of the original States, to wit: The States of New York and Virginia, as far as necessary and suitable to the circumstances of the Territory of Michigan.

Liable to indictment, etc.

SEC. 10. *And be it enacted,* That justices shall be liable to be indicted, tried, and punished, in the supreme court of the Territory of Michigan; the same being adopted from the laws of one of the original States, to wit: The State of Maryland, as far as necessary and suitable to the circumstances of the Territory of Michigan.

Fees allowed.

SEC. 11. *And be it enacted,* That there shall be allowed to every justice the following compensation for his services, to be paid by the parties requiring the services respectively, on the same being rendered: that is to say, for issuing original process, twenty-five cents; for making an entry relating to the case, six and one-quarter cents; for a summons for a witness, or witnesses, including in one summons all witnesses applied for at one time, six and one-quarter cents; for a judgment, twenty-five cents; for an execution or any other process, twelve and one-half cents; for filing any paper, six and one-fourth cents; for swearing a witness, or administering any other oath, not of a public nature, six and one-fourth cents; for writing or recording any matter distinct from entries in suits, or for a copy, transcript, or exemplification of any matter, or for a certificate of any matter, for every one hundred words, six and one-fourth cents; for a marriage, one dollar; the same being adopted from the laws of three of the original States, to wit: The States of Maryland, Massachusetts, and Pennsylvania, as far as necessary and suitable to the circumstances of the Territory of Michigan.

Limitation of suits, etc.

SEC. 12. *And be it enacted,* That all suits or matters, and all recognizances, rights, remedies, and privileges in such suits and matters depending before the courts of districts, and not brought

1810. to a termination on or before the seventeenth day of September, one thousand eight hundred and ten, where the matter does not exceed one hundred dollars, shall be brought to a termination by such justice, as the plaintiff shall bring the record thereof before, with the costs of the said court; and where the matter exceeds one hundred dollars, before the supreme court, in like manner, in which cases the court or justice shall notify the opposite party, their counselor or agent, if within the Territory; and the court and justice respectively, shall have the same power to bring such matters to a termination, as the district court would originally have had, and all rights and remedies which the parties had before the district courts in any actions transferred, shall be the same as they would have been had they been finally determined in the district courts, and process returnable shall be returned to the supreme court at the first term after the passing of this law, and before a justice, within sixty days from the passing of this law, and the original jurisdiction of the supreme court shall extend to all matters above the value of one hundred dollars, and to the probate of wills, and the judges of the district courts shall settle, adjust, and determine all matters of public accounts arising previous to the seventeenth day of September, one thousand eight hundred and ten, at any time thereafter in the same manner as if this act had never been made; the same being adopted from the laws of two of the original States, to wit: The States of Maryland and Ohio, as far as necessary and suitable to the circumstances of the Territory of Michigan.

Jurisdiction of Supreme Court.

Settlement of public accounts, etc.

Made, adopted, and published at the city of Detroit, within the Territory of Michigan, this sixteenth day of September, one thousand eight hundred and ten.

Attest: WILLIAM HULL,
JOS. WATSON, *Governor of the Territory of Michigan.*
Secretary. AUGUSTUS B. WOODWARD,
One of the Judges of the Territory of Michigan.
JOHN GRIFFIN,
One of the Judges of the Territory of Michigan.

No. 81.
September 22.

AN ACT concerning forcible entry and detainer.*

Entry in lands, by force, forbidden.

Be it enacted by the Governor and Judges of the Territory of Michigan, That no person or persons shall hereafter make any entry into any lands, tenements, or other possessions, but in cases where entry is given by law, and in such case, not with strong hand, nor with multitude of people, but only in a peaceable and easy manner; and if any person from henceforth do to the contrary, and thereof be duly convicted, he shall be punished by fine.

Two justices and a jury to try such entries.

SEC. 2. *And be it enacted,* That two justices of the peace shall have authority to enquire by a jury, as hereinafter directed, as well against those who make unlawful and forcible entry into

* Digest of, Cass' Code, p. 149, vol. 1, Territorial Laws, dated October 22, which is error.

1810.

lands, tenements, or other possessions, and with strong hand detain the same as against those who, having lawful and peaceable entry into lands and tenements, unlawfully and by force hold the same, and if it be found, upon such inquiry, that an unlawful and forcible entry hath been made, and that the same lands, tenements, or other possessions are held and detained by force and strong hand, or that the same, after a lawful entry, are held unlawfully, and with force and strong hand, then such justices shall cause the party complaining to have restitution thereof.

Issue of warrant.

SEC. 3. *And be it enacted,* That when any complaint shall be formally made, in writing, to any two justices of the peace, of any such unlawful or forcible entry or detainer, they shall issue a warrant, directed to the marshal of the same district, commanding him to apprehend the person against whom such complaint shall be made, and to bring him or her before the said justices, at a day in such warrant named, which shall not be less than six days from the time of issuing the said warrant, and at the place therein mentioned, and they shall also issue a precept to the said marshal, commanding him to cause to come before them twelve discreet citizens, of lawful age, of the vicinity, at a certain time and place in such precept to be mentioned, and at the said time and place appointed for trial or hearing the said complaint, and if a sufficient number of persons summoned by the marshal, do not attend, the said justices may order the marshal to complete the number by returning others forthwith, and the jury impaneled shall be sworn well and truly to try the forcible entry or detainer complained of, and to return a true verdict thereof, and if the jury, after a full hearing, find the person against whom the complaint is made guilty, of the forcible entry or detainer complained of, they shall all sign their verdict, and the said justices shall enter up judgment for the complainant to have restitution of the premises, and shall impose such fine, not exceeding ten dollars, considering all the circumstances, as they may think just, and shall tax cost for the complainant, and may commit the person against whom judgment is so made, until the fine be paid, and the said justices shall also award their writ of restitution; but if the jury find that the person complained against is not guilty, the complaint, in their opinion, not being supported, the said justices shall tax costs against the complainant, and issue execution accordingly.

Venire.

Verdict.

Judgment.

Service of warrant.

SEC. 4. *And be it enacted,* That if the marshal cannot find the party against whom the warrant issued, he may, six days before the time appointed for returning the same, leave a true and attested copy of said warrant at the usual place of abode of such person, and if, at the return of the warrant, he shall not be able to find or apprehend the person against whom such warrant issued, he shall make a return of such facts, and that he hath so left a copy as aforesaid, and when the same was done, and if the party doth not appear at the time appointed for hearing said complaint, the said justices may, in their discretion, adjourn or proceed *ex parte*, except that in this case they shall not inflict any

May adjourn or proceed ex parte

1810.

Costs.

fine upon him, and in all cases they may, in their writ of restitution, order the costs taxed to be levied, but in every such case, if the jury do not find for the complainant, there shall be no costs taxed for the party complained against, he not having appeared at the empaneling of the jury.

Treble damages.

SEC. 5. *And be it enacted,* That the complainant of any forcible entry and detainer as aforesaid, who shall recover against the person complained of as aforesaid, shall have right to recover treble damages, with costs of suit, by an action of trespass against the offender or offenders, to be brought for that purpose: *Provided, always,* That nothing in the foregoing part of this act shall be construed to extend to any person or persons who have had the quiet, peaceable, and uninterrupted occupation of any lands, tenements, or other possession for the space of three whole years next before the entering of such complaint, anything in this act to the contrary notwithstanding.

Proviso, quiet possession for three years.

Lessee refusing to quit, etc.

SEC. 6. *And be it enacted,* That when any person shall willfully, and with force hold over any lands, tenements, or other possessions, after the determination of the time for which they are demised or let to him, or to the person under whom he claims, or where any person wrongfully and without force, by disseisin shall obtain and continue in possession of any lands, tenements, or other possession, and after demand made in writing for the delivery of the possession thereof, by the person having the legal right of such possession, his agent or attorney, shall refuse or neglect to quit such possession, upon complaint thereof in writing, to two justices of the peace, the said justices shall proceed to hear, try, and determine the same in like manner as in cases of forcible entry and detainer, and issue a writ of execution accordingly: *Provided, always,* That in such case the original process shall be a summons, and the justices shall have no power to assess a fine on the party complained of.

Proviso.

Quiet possession for three years not affected.

SEC. 7. *Provided always, and it is hereby further enacted,* That the preceding section shall not extend to any person who has or shall have continued in possession three years after the determination of the time for which the premises were demised or let to him, or those under whom he claims, or to any person who continues in possession three years, quietly and peaceably by disseisin, anything herein contained to the contrary notwithstanding.

Treble damages.

SEC. 8. *And be it enacted,* That the complainant shall have right to action of trespass against the person complained of, and who on trial shall be found guilty, to recover treble damages from the time of notice given to quit the premises, and till that time damages only.

May appeal to Supreme Court.

SEC. 9. *And be it enacted,* That if either party in a prosecution on this act shall think him or herself aggrieved with the determination of the justices aforesaid, he or she shall have liberty to appeal to the next supreme court.

Neglect to enter appeal, etc.

SEC. 10. *And be it enacted,* That when it shall so happen that the appellant in any action brought on this statute shall fail to bring forward his appeal and enter the same in the court to

1810.

which said appeal is allowed, the appellee shall have liberty to obtain, on producing the copies, an affirmation of the judgment rendered by the justices.

Affirmation of judgment.

SEC. 11. *And be it enacted*, That the following forms, as near as circumstances will admit, shall be adopted and used in proceedings under this statute, viz.:

WARRANT.

Form of warrant.

TERRITORY OF MICHIGAN, } ss.
DISTRICT OF............

To the Marshal of the District of............:

Whereas, ..., of............, hath exhibited unto ...., and............, justices of the peace within and for the district of............, a complaint against............, of............, for that the said............, on the......day of............, at............, with force and arms, and with a strong hand (here insert the substance of the complaint with legal certainty) therefore: In the name of the Territory of Michigan, you are hereby commanded to apprehend the said.........., if he be found in your precinct, and him have to appear before us at.........., on the ......day of.........., at......o'clock in the......noon, then and there to make answer to, and defend against the complaint aforesaid, and further to be dealt with according to law, but if the said..........is not to be found within your precinct, you are hereby required to leave a true and attested copy of this warrant at the usual place of abode of the said............, six days at least, before the said day of.........., and make return of this warrant, with your doings therein, unto us at ....aforesaid, on the......day of..........

Dated at.........., this......day.

} *Justices.*

PRECEPT FOR JURORS.

Precept.

TERRITORY OF MICHIGAN, } ss.
DISTRICT OF

To the Marshal of the District of............: GREETING:

In the name of the Territory of Michigan, you are hereby commanded to cause to come before us on the......day of.......... at......o'clock in the......noon, at.........., twelve men to be summoned in the same manner as petit jurors to serve before the supreme court, to try the truth of a complaint exhibited to us.........., and.........., justices of the peace in and for said district of........, by........., of........., against ...., of.........., for a forcible entry (or detainer, as the case may be), and make return of this writ, with your doings thereon, unto us at........, on the.....day of........aforesaid...........

Dated at.........., the......day of..........

} *Justices.*

1810.

VERDICT.

Verdict.

At a court of inquiry held at..........on the......day of..........., in the year of our Lord........, before.........., and.........., justices of the peace in and for the district of......., of.........., complainant, against.........., respondent, the jury find that the facts alleged in the said........complaint, are true; that the said..........is guilty thereof, and that said..........ought to have restitution of the premises therein described, without delay (or in case the jury do not find the allegations of the complaint proved, then the jury find that the said facts alleged in the said..........complaint, are not proven, and that the said..........is not guilty.

................*Foreman.*

....
....
.... *Jurors.*
....
....
....

Writ of restitution.

WRIT OF RESTITUTION.

TERRITORY OF MICHIGAN, } ss.
DISTRICT OF }

To the Marshal of the District of..............:—GREETING:

Whereas, ..., of.........., at a court of inquiry of forcible entry and detainer, holden at.........., in the district of.........., on the.....day of.........., in the year of our Lord........, before............, and............, justices of the peace in and for the district of.........., by the consideration of the said court, recovered judgment against..........., of.........., to have restitution of (here describe the premises as in the complaint) therefore: In the name of the Territory of Michigan, you are hereby commanded that, taking with you the force of the district, if necessary, you cause the said .... to be immediately removed from the premises, and the said..........to have peaceable restitution of the same; you are also hereby commanded that of the goods, chattels, or lands of the said............., within your precinct, you cause to be levied, and the same being disposed of according to law, to be paid and satisfied the sum of.........., being the cost taxed against the said.............for the said............, at the court aforesaid, together with......cents for this writ, and thereof (here follow as in common executions).

.... } *Justices.*
.... }

The same being adopted from the laws of three of the original States, to wit: The States of New York, Vermont, and Massachusetts, as far as necessary and suitable to the circumstances of the Territory of Michigan.

Adopted and published at the city of Detroit, within the Territory of Michigan, this twenty-second day of October, one thousand eight hundred and ten. 1810.

Attest:
Jos. Watson,
Secretary.

William Hull,
Governor of the Territory of Michigan.
John Griffin,
One of the Judges of the Territory of Michigan.
James Witherell.

1811.

AN ACT to amend an act entitled "An act concerning the supreme court of the Territory of Michigan."* No. 82. January 14.

---

* Printed in full p. 80, vol. 2, Territorial Laws.

ACTS

PASSED AT THE SPECIAL SESSION

OF THE

SIXTH LEGISLATIVE COUNCIL

OF THE

TERRITORY OF MICHIGAN,

BEGUN AND HELD

AT THE CAPITOL, IN THE CITY OF DETROIT,

ON

Monday, 17th August, 1835.

BY AUTHORITY.

LANSING:
W. S. GEORGE & CO., STATE PRINTERS AND BINDERS.
1884.

LAWS OF MICHIGAN.

1835.

AN ACT to authorize the sale of certain lands.

SECTION 1. *Be it enacted by the Legislative Council of the Territory of Michgan,* That Moses Robert, of the county of Monroe, a minor, under the age of twenty-one years, be, and he is hereby authorized and empowered to make sale of all his right, title, interest, and claim of, in, and to the following described parcel of land, lying and being in the township of Monroe, in the county of Monroe aforesaid, bounded and described as follows, viz.: "Beginning at a post standing on the south border of the River Raisin, between this tract and a tract claimed by Meldrum and Park; thence south, twenty-nine degrees west, thirty-nine chains seventy-nine links, to a post standing on the north border of a bay formed by Navarre's Mill Creek; thence along the border of said bay, up stream, north, seventy-five degrees west, seventy-one chains twenty-five links, to a post standing on the east line of a tract confirmed to Baptiste Reaume; thence on said line north, twenty-nine degrees east, sixty-nine chains, to a post standing on the border of the River Raisin; thence along the border of said river, down stream, south fifty-eight degrees east, twenty-two chains seventy-five links; thence south, eighty-one degrees east, twenty-one chains seventy-five links; thence south, fifty-seven degrees east, nine chains seventy-five links; thence south twenty-two degrees east, twenty-one chains sixty-two links, to the place of beginning;" and to make such deed or deeds as may be necessary for a complete conveyance of all his right and title to the above described premises: *Provided,* That Antoine Robert, executor of the last will and testament of Francis Robert, deceased, and guardian of said minor, shall consent to the said sale, and shall endorse his consent on such deed or deeds; which deed or deeds so executed and endorsed, shall be good and valid deed or deeds in law, to convey all the right and title of said minor in the said lands, to the purchaser, his heirs and assigns forever.

Authority to sell.

Description of land.

To make deed.

Guardian shall consent.

SEC. 2. That Mary Levoix, for herself and children, Lambert Levoix, Paul Levoix, David Levoix, Fabien Levoix, and Francois Levoix, minors under the age of twenty-one years, be, and they are hereby authorized and empowered to make sale of all their right, title, interest, and claim of, in, and to the following described parcel of land, lying and being in the township of Port Lawrence, in the county of Monroe, bounded and described as follows, viz.: Being the fraction of section number twenty, of

Mary Lavoix for herself and children authorized to sell land.

1835. township number nine south, in range number eight east, in the district of Detroit, Michigan Territory, containing seventy-seven acres and sixty eight-hundredths of an acre; and to make such deed or deeds as may be necessary for a complete conveyance of all their right and title to the above described premises; which deed or deeds, so executed, shall be good and valid deed or deeds in law, to convey all the right and title of the said Mary Lavoix and children in the said lands, to the purchaser or purchasers, their heirs and assigns forever.

To make valid deed.

Approved August 20, 1835.

AN ACT to incorporate the River Raisin and Grand River railroad company, and for other purposes.

Commissioners appointed.

SEC. 1. *Be it enacted by the Legislative Council of the Territory of Michigan*, That S. Blanchard, S. Fargo, J. J. Godfrey, O. Wilder, Edward D. Ellis, Edwin Smith, Reynolds Gillet, Isaac E. Crary, and Geo. Ketchum, be, and they are hereby appointed commissioners, under the direction of a majority of whom, subscriptions may be received to the capital stock of the River Raisin and Grand River railroad company, hereby incorporated, and they may cause books to be opened, at such times and places as they shall direct for the purpose of receiving subscriptions to the capital stock of said company, first giving reasonable notice of the times and places of taking such subscriptions.

Books to be opened and subscriptions received. Notice to be given.

Capital stock, shares $50 each.

SEC. 2. The capital stock of said River Raisin and Grand River railroad company, shall be one and a half million of dollars, in shares of fifty dollars each; and that as soon as one thousand shares of said stock shall be subscribed, the subscribers of said stock, with such other persons as shall associate with them for that purpose, their successors and assigns shall be, and they are hereby created a body corporate and politic, by the name and style of the "River Raisin and Grand River Railroad Company," with perpetual succession, and by that name shall be capable in law of purchasing, selling, leasing, and conveying estate, either real or personal, or mixed, as far as the same may be necessary for the purposes hereinafter mentioned, and no further; and in their corporate name may sue and be sued, may have a common seal, which they may alter and renew at pleasure, and shall have, enjoy, and may exercise all the powers, rights, and privileges which appertain to corporate bodies, for the purpose mentioned in this act.

Created a body politic and corporate.

May hold and sell property, etc.

May sue and be sued, and have corporate seal.

Power to construct and use railroad.

SEC. 3. Said corporation hereby created shall have power to construct a single or double railroad, commencing at the head of ship navigation, on the River Raisin; and said corporation are hereby required to make or construct a single or double track in each bank of said river at the starting point, and to unite the same at any point above the limits of the village of Monroe, to the rapids of Grand River, or to such point below on said river as said corporation shall see fit, passing through the villages of Tecumseh,

1835.

Clinton and Marshall, on or near the route recently surveyed from Monroe to Marshall by Lieut. J. M. Berrien, with power to transport, take, and carry property or persons upon the same, by the power and force of steam, of animals, or of any mechanical or other power, or of any combination of them.

When certain parts and the whole of said road to be finished.

SEC. 4. If said corporation shall not, within two years from the passage of this act, commence the construction of said railroad, and shall not, within six years from the passage of this act, construct, finish, and put in operation thirty miles in distance of said railroad, and shall not, within fifteen years from the passage of this act, construct, finish, complete, and put in operation, one-half of the said railroad, and shall not, within thirty years from the passage of this act, complete and put in operation, the whole of said railroad, or in the event of a failure of the company to construct the parts of the said railroad within either of the times above mentioned, then the rights, privileges, and powers of the said corporation, under this act, shall be null and void; as to said parts of the said road which are not finished within the times limited by this act, and to them only, the said company shall make return to the governor, to be laid before the legislature annually, by the president, and on the oath of the president or treasurers, with the statement of the receipts and expenditures upon the said railroad, together with the costs thereof; and if at any time on such return, the amount divided from the part of said railroad completed, over and above all repairs, shall exceed fourteen per cent on the capital stock paid in, and equal interest from the time of payment, then it shall be the duty of said company to complete the next adjoining section within five years after making such return, or, on failure thereof, to pay all surplus moneys arising from the road so completed, over and above the fourteen per cent, into the treasury of the Territory.

When to be void.

Company to make returns to the governor, etc.

If dividend exceed 14 per cent.

When nine directors to be chosen.

SEC. 5. Whenever one thousand shares of the aforesaid stock shall have been subscribed, if within two years after the passage of this act, the commissioners shall call a general meeting of the subscribers, to such time and place as they may appoint, by giving sixty days' public notice of such meeting; and at such meeting the commissioners shall lay the subscription books before the subscribers then and there present, and thereupon the subscribers or stockholders, or a majority of them, shall elect nine directors by ballot, a majority of whom shall be competent to manage the affairs of said company; they shall have the power of electing a president of said company, either from amongst the directors, or the stockholders; and in said election, and on every occasion wherein a vote of the stockholders is to be taken, every share shall entitle the holder thereof to one vote, and every stockholder may vote himself or by proxy.

Election of president.

When president and directors to be chosen.

SEC. 6. To continue the succession of the president and directors of said company, nine directors shall be chosen annually, on the first Monday of October, at such place as may be appointed by the directors; and if any vacancy shall occur by death, resignation, or otherwise, of any president or director, before the year

1835.

for which he was elected shall have expired, a person to fill such vacant place for the residue of the year, may be appointed by the directors of said company or a majority of them. The directors of said company shall hold and exercise their offices until a new election of president and directors. All elections which are by this act, or by the by-laws of the company, to be made on any particular day, if not made on such day, may be made at any time within thirty days thereafter.

If elections be not held on the day appointed.

Meetings to be held annually.

SEC. 7. A general meeting of the stockholders of said company, shall be held annually at the time and place appointed for the appointment of president and directors; and a meeting may be called at any time during the interval between said annual meetings, by the president and directors, or by the stockholders owning not less than one-fourth of the whole stock, by giving thirty days' public notice of the time and place of meeting; and when any such meetings are called, by the stockholders, the notice shall specify the particular object of the call; and if at any meetings thus called, a majority, in value, of the stockholders are not present in person, or by proxy, such meeting shall be adjourned from day to day not exceeding three days, without transacting any business; and if within said three days, stockholders having a majority of the stock do not attend such meeting, then the same shall be dissolved.

Of extra meetings.

When meeting dissolved.

When president and directors to account.

SEC. 8. At the regular annual meetings of the stockholders of said company, it shall be the duty of the president and directors in office for the preceding year, to exhibit a clear and distinct statement of the affairs of the company and at any called meeting of the stockholders, a majority of those present in person or by proxy, may require similar statements from the president and directors, whose duty it shall be to furnish them when thus required; and at all general meetings of the stockholders, a majority in value of all the stockholders in said company, may remove from office any president or any of the directors of said company, and may appoint others in their stead.

When president and directors may be removed

Oath of president and directors.

SEC. 9. Any president or director of said company, before he acts as such shall swear or affirm that he will well and truly discharge the duties of his office to the best of his skill and judgment.

May appoint and remove officers, etc.

SEC. 10. The president and directors, or a majority of them, shall have power to appoint, contract with, and determine the compensation of all such officers, engineers, agents, or servants whatsoever, as they may deem necessary for the transaction of the business of the company and remove them at pleasure: and the said president and directors, or a majority of them, shall have power to determine the manner of adjusting and settling all accounts against the company; also the manner and evidence of transfers of stock in said company, and they shall have power to pass all by-laws which they may deem necessary for carrying into execution all the powers vested in the company hereby incorporated: *Provided*, such by-laws shall not be contrary to the laws of this territory, or of the constitution or laws of the United States.

Power to settle accounts, make by-laws, etc.

Proviso.

1835.

Power to construct and repair said road.

SEC. 11. The president and directors of said company shall be, and they are hereby invested with all the privileges, rights and powers necessary for the location, construction and keeping in repair said railroad not exceeding one hundred feet in width; and the said president and directors, or their agents, or those with whom they may contract for making said road, or any part of it, may enter upon, use, and excavate any land which may be wanted for the site of said railroad, or any other purpose which is necessary in the construction or repair of said road, or its works, so soon as the amount is ascertained, and tendered as hereinafter provided.

Power to contract for, use, or excavate any land, etc.

May agree for materials for said road.

SEC. 12. The president and directors of said company may agree with the owner or owners of any land, earth, timber, gravel, stone, or other materials, or any articles whatsoever, which may be wanted in the construction or repair of said road, or any of its works, for the purchase or occupation of the same; and if such materials (not previously taken or appropriated by the owner to any particular use) as may be necessary for the construction or repair of said railroad, be found on any unimproved land adjoining to or near the same, and if the parties cannot agree, or if the owner or owners of any of them be a *femme covert*, under age, *non compos mentis*, or out of the county in which the property wanted may lie, application may be made to any of the justices of the peace of such county, who shall thereupon issue his warrant under his hand and seal directed to the sheriff of said county, or if the sheriff be interested, to some disinterested person, requiring him to summon a jury of twelve freeholders in the county, not in any way interested in the matter, or related to the parties, to meet on or near the property or materials to be valued, on a day named in said warrant, not less than five or more than ten days after issuing the same; and if, at the same time and place, any of the persons summoned do not attend, the said sheriff, or summoner, shall immediately summon as many as may be necessary, with the persons in attendance as jurors, to furnish a panel of twelve jurors, and from them each party, or his, or her, or their agent or attorney, or if either be not present in person or by agent, the sheriff, or summoner for him, her, or them, may strike off three jurors, and the remaining shall sit as a jury of inquest of damages; and before they act as such, the sheriff, or summoner shall administer to each of them an oath or affirmation, that they will justly and impartially value the damages which the owner or owners will sustain by the use or occupation of the land, materials, or property required by said company; and the said jury shall reduce their inquisition to writing, and shall sign and seal the same, and it shall then be sent to the clerk of the circuit court of said county, and by said clerk filed in his office, and shall be confirmed by said court at its next session, if no sufficient cause to the contrary be shown, and when confirmed the same shall be recorded by said clerk, at the expense of said company; but if set aside, said court may direct another inquisition to be taken in manner above prescribed; said inquisition shall describe the property taken, or the

If parties cannot agree jury to be summoned.

Jury to assess damages.

Inquisition to be reduced to writing, etc.

Sent to circuit court.

1835.

Valuation tendered, property to vest in the company.

bounds of the land condemned. Such valuation, when paid or tendered to the owner or owners of said property, his, her, or their legal representatives, shall entitle said company to the estate, and interest in the same thus valued, as fully as if it had been conveyed by the owner or owners of the same, for such term of time as said company shall occupy the same as a railroad; and if valuation be not received, when tendered, it may, at any time thereafter, be received from the company, without cost; and the sheriff, summoner, and jurors, shall be allowed the ordinary fees for like services, to be taxed by the court.

When company to make wagon ways, etc.

SEC. 13. Whenever in the construction of said railroad, it shall be necessary to cross or intersect any established road, it shall be the duty of said president and directors so to construct said railroad across such established road as not to impede the passage or transportation of persons or property along the same, or when it shall be necessary to construct it through the land of any individual, it shall be their duty to provide for such individual, proper wagon ways across said road, from one part of his land to another.

Neglect to make wagon ways, liable for damages.

SEC. 14. If said company shall neglect to provide proper wagon ways across said road, as required by the preceding section of this act, it shall be lawful for any individual to sue said company, and shall be entitled to such damages as a jury may think him or her entitled to, for such neglect or refusal on the part of said company.

May contract for the use of any other road.

SEC. 15. If it shall be necessary for the said railroad company, in the selection of the route, or the construction of the said road, to be by them laid out and constructed, or any part of it, to connect the same with any turnpike, road, or bridge, made or erected by any incorporated company, or authorized by any law of this Territory, it shall, and may be lawful for said president and directors to contract with any other corporation for the right to such road or bridge, or for transfer of any of the corporate or other rights and privileges of such corporation, to the said company hereby incorporated; and every such other incorporation, acting under the laws of this Territory, is hereby authorized to make such contract, or transfer, by and through the agency of the person authorized by the respective acts of incorporation, to exercise their corporate powers, or by any persons who are by any law of this Territory entrusted with the management and direction of such turnpike, road, or bridge, or any of the rights or privileges aforesaid. Every contract or transfer, made in pursuance of the power and authority hereby granted, when executed by the several parties, under their respective corporate seals, shall vest in the company hereby incorporated, all such rights and privileges, and the right to use and enjoy the same, as fully as they are now used by the said corporations in which they are now vested.

Other corporations may contract.

Such contract to be valid.

Power to purchase machines, etc.

SEC. 16. The said president and directors shall have power to purchase with the funds of the company, and place on any railroad constructed by them under this act, all machines, wagons, carriages, or vehicles of any description which they may deem necessary or proper for the purpose of transportation on said road;

1835.

and that they shall have power to charge for tolls and transportation, such sums as shall be established by the by-laws of the company hereby incorporated, and it shall not be lawful for any other company, or any person or persons to transport any passengers or property, of any description whatever, along said road, or any part of it, without license or permission of the said president and directors of said company; and the said road, with all their improvements, works, and profits, and all machinery used on said road for transportation, are hereby vested in said company incorporated by this act, and their successors forever; and the shares of the capital stock of said company shall be considered personal property, and shall be transferable agreeably to the by-laws of said company, and subject to be taken on execution agreeably to such laws as are or may thereafter be in force.

Power to transport property, etc., and charge tolls.

Property vested in the company.

Shares considered personal property and liable for debts.

SEC. 17. The said president and directors shall annually, or semi-annually, declare and make such dividend as they may deem proper, of the net profits from the resources of said company, deducting the necessary current expenses; and they shall make the dividend among the stockholders of said company, in proper proportions to their respective shares.

Of dividends.

SEC. 18. If any person or persons shall willfully and knowingly and maliciously, by any means whatever, injure, impair, or destroy any part of the railroad constructed by said company, under this act, or any of the necessary works, buildings, or machinery of said company, such person or persons so offending, shall each of them, for every such offense, forfeit and pay to the said company, a sum not exceeding three times the amount of damages caused by such offense, which may be recovered in the name of said company, by an action of debt in any court having competent jurisdiction in the county wherein the offense shall be committed, and shall also be subject to an indictment; and upon conviction of such offense, shall be punished by fine and imprisonment, at the discretion of the court.

Persons injuring the road, liable for damages and punishment.

SEC. 19. The right and privilege are hereby reserved to the Territory or State, to connect with the road hereby provided for, any other railroads, leading from the main route to any part or parts of the Territory: *Provided*, That in forming such connection, no injury shall be done to the works of the company hereby incorporated: *Provided, further*, That the said company, or companies so connecting, may have the free use of said road by paying such a tariff of tolls as may be established by the legislature, and this shall be entitled to the same rights and privileges of any and all roads hereafter connected.

Right reserved to connect any other railroad with this road.

Proviso.

SEC. 20. The Territory or State shall have the right, at any time after the expiration of twenty years from the completion of said railroad, to purchase and hold the same for the use of the Territory or State, at a price not exceeding the original cost of said road, and fourteen per cent thereon, of which cost an accurate account shall be kept and submitted to the legislature duly attested by the officers of said company, whenever, and as often as said legislature shall require the same.

Right of Territory or State to purchase said road.

Account to be kept of cost.

1835.

Authority to establish a bank.

Capital stock to be $100,000.

Of subscription to capital stock.

SEC. 21. The stockholders of the River Raisin and Grand River railroad company, be, and they are hereby authorized to establish a bank at the village of Tecumseh, the capital stock whereof shall, for the present, be one hundred thousand dollars, to be divided into two thousand shares, each being fifty dollars; and the subscriptions towards constituting said stock, shall be open at such times and places, under the superintendence of the president and directors of said company as they may designate, giving at least three weeks' public notice thereof, in one or more newspapers published in said Territory or State, and the subscription aforesaid shall continue open until the whole number of shares are subscribed, and if the subscriptions to said capital stock shall, within six days after the same are opened, exceed the amount authorized by this section, it shall be the duty of the directors to deduct such excess, in a proportional manner, from the largest number of shares subscribed, in such a manner that each person subscribing shall be entitled to at least five shares, if he subscribe so many.

When and how installments to be paid.

Notice to be given, etc.

SEC. 22. One tenth part of the amount of each share shall be paid to the said president and directors, in specie, at the time of subscribing, and the balance shall be paid in such installments, and at such time as the directors for the time being may require; *Provided,* That whenever the payment of any installment is required by the directors, they shall give at least sixty days' notice thereof, in a newspaper printed in this Territory or State, but no one installment shall exceed five dollars on a share: *Provided, further,* That no note or evidence of debt shall be discounted, or received by the directors, in payment of any installment called in or required to be paid, with intent of providing the means of furnishing such payment, or with intent of enabling any stockholder to withdraw any part of the money paid in by him on his stock.

Stockholders to be a body corporate and politic.

Their privileges as a body corporate.

SEC. 23. All persons who shall become stockholders of said bank, shall be, and they are hereby constituted, ordained, and declared to be a body corporate and politic, in fact and in name, by the name of "the president, directors, and company of the bank of Tecumseh;" that by that name they and their successors shall, and may have continual succession, and shall be persons in law capable of suing and being sued, pleading and being impleaded, answering and being answered, defending and being defended, in all courts and places whatsoever, and in all manner of actions, suits, complaints, matters, and causes whatsoever; and that they and their successors may have a common seal, and may change and alter the same at their pleasure; and they and their successors by the name of "the president, directors, and company of the bank of Tecumseh," shall be in law capable of purchasing, holding, and conveying any estate, real or personal, for the use of said corporation.

Who shall be managers.

SEC. 24. The stock, property, affairs, and concerns of the said bank shall be managed by the president and directors of said railroad company.

SEC. 25. The directors for the time being, or a majority of them,

1835.

shall have power to make and prescribe such by-laws, rules, and regulations, as to them shall appear needful and proper, touching the arrangement and disposition of the stock, property, estate, and effects of said corporation, the duties and conduct of the officers, clerks, and servants employed therein, and all such other matters as appertain to the business of a bank; and shall also have power to appoint so many officers, clerks, and servants, for carrying on said business, and with such salaries and allowances as to them shall seem meet: *Provided,* That such by-laws, rules, and regulations be not repugnant to the constitution or laws of the United States, or to the laws of this Territory or State; and it shall be the duty of the president and cashier, whenever thereto required, to furnish to the legislature, or governor, a statement, under oath or affirmation, of the condition of the bank, stating the amount of deposits, the profits on hand, the amount of bills in circulation, the amount of debts due from the directors, the amount due from the stockholders, the amount of debts due from all other persons, or corporations, not, however, naming them; the amount of specie in bank, the amount of all bills of other banks, the amount of their deposits in other banks, the amount of their real estate, and all their other property not herein specified, and shall contain a true exhibit of the state of said bank.

Powers of the directors to make by-laws, etc.

Proviso.

When to render a statement of affairs, etc.

SEC. 26. This Territory or State shall have a right to subscribe any number of shares in said bank, not exceeding in the whole, the number of five hundred at any time, when by law they shall authorize any person or persons for that purpose, and the Territory or State shall have a right to increase the number of shares and stock which the said corporation may hold, to the amount of the sum to be subscribed.

Territory or State may subscribe for shares.

SEC. 27. The amount of debts, which the said corporation shall at any time owe, whether by bond, bill, note, or other contract, over and above the specie then actually deposited in the bank, shall not exceed three times the amount of capital stock subscribed and actually paid into said bank; and in case of such excess, the directors under whose administration it shall happen, shall be liable for the same in their separate and private capacities; but this shall not be construed to exempt the said corporation on any estate real or personal, which they may hold as a body corporate, from being also liable for, and chargeable with such excess; but such of the directors as have been absent when the said excess was contracted, or may have dissented from the resolution or act, whereby the same was contracted, shall not be so liable. No loan or discount shall be made to the directors of such corporation, or upon paper which such directors, or any of them, shall be responsible, to any amount exceeding the capital stock actually paid in and possessed by the corporation.

The debts of the bank shall not exceed three times the amount of stock paid in.

When directors liable.

When loans shall not be made to directors.

SEC. 28. The lands, tenements, and hereditaments which it shall be lawful for the said corporation to purchase and hold, shall be only such as shall be required for its accommodation in relation to the convenient transaction of its business, or such as shall have been bona fide mortgaged to it by way of security, or conveyed to

When and how corporation may hold land, etc.

1835.

it in satisfaction of debts, previously contracted in the course of its dealings, or purchased at sales upon judgments which shall have been obtained for such debts: *And further,* The said corporation shall not, directly nor indirectly, deal or trade in buying or selling any goods, wares, or merchandise, or commodities whatsoever, unless in selling the same when truly pledged by way of security for debts due the said corporation, or purchasing the same at sale on judgments, which shall have been obtained for any debts previously contracted in the course of its dealings, and afterwards selling the same.

Not to trade in goods, etc., except in certain cases.

Bills under seal to be assignable by endorsement.

SEC. 29. The bills obligatory and of credit, under the seal of the said corporation, which shall be made to any person or persons, shall be assignable by endorsement thereupon, under the hand or hands of such person or persons, his, her, or their assignee or assignees respectively, and to enable such assignee or assignees to bring and maintain an action thereupon, in his, her, or their own name or names; and bills or notes which may be issued by order of said corporation, promising the payment to any person or persons, his, her, or their order, or to bearer, though not under the seal of the said corporation, shall be binding and obligatory upon the same in like manner, and with like force and effect as upon any private person or persons, if issued by him, her, or them, in his, her, or their private or natural capacities, and shall be assignable and negotiable in like manner as if they were so issued by such private person or persons; and if such bills obligatory and of credit, and such bills and notes issued as aforesaid, are not paid when the same are due and demanded at the banking house of the said bank, and within usual banking hours, in legal money of the United States, the said corporation shall be dissolved, subject to the benefits and provisions of the act relative to banking institutions, approved April twenty-third, one thousand eight hundred and thirty-three.

Of bill or notes not under seal.

If bills or notes are not paid on demand, corporation to be dissolved.

Dividends to be made half yearly.

SEC. 30. The directors shall make half yearly dividends, commencing in six months after the said bank shall have gone into operation, of so much of the profits of the said bank as to them, or a majority of them, shall seem advisable; and the directors shall also, after ten thousand dollars shall have been paid in, provide a convenient place for the transaction of the business of said bank, and commence operations; and every cashier and clerk, before they enter upon the duties of their offices, shall give bond, with two or more securities, to the satisfaction of the directors, conditioned for the faithful discharge of their duties: *Provided,* That no dividend shall be paid, except from the surplus profits arising from the business of the corporation, and it shall not be lawful to divide, withdraw, or in any way reduce the capital stock, or any part thereof, without the consent of the legislature.

When they may commence operation.

Cashier and clerk to give bond.

Proviso.

Compensation of officers.

SEC. 31. No president, or other officer, shall be entitled to any emoluments for their services, unless the same shall have been allowed by the stockholders at a general meeting. Four directors shall constitute a board for the transaction of business, of whom the president shall be one, except in case of necessary

Four directors to constitute a board.

absence, when he shall, in writing, appoint one of the directors to act as president *pro tempore*; but for making ordinary discounts, such a number of directors shall constitute a board as shall be required by the laws of said corporation.

President pro tem.

SEC. 32. The stock of said corporation shall be assignable according to such rules as shall be made in that behalf by the by-laws of the said corporation, but no assignment or transfer shall be valid or effectual, until such assignment shall be entered or registered in a book to be kept for that purpose; nor shall any stockholder be capable of assigning or transferring his or her stock in said bank, until all notes, dues, and debts, of whatever nature, due to said corporation from such stockholder, either as drawer or endorser, on any note or bill, or otherwise, shall be first paid and discharged.

The stock shall be assignable when debts due the bank are paid.

SEC. 33. The stockholders may at any time augment the capital stock of the said bank, at any special meeting called for that purpose, a majority of all the votes being given thereupon, under such regulations, restrictions, and conditions as the said stockholders shall, at such meeting judge proper, to any amount not exceeding five hundred thousand dollars.

The stockholders may augment the capital stock.

SEC. 34. The property of every individual member of the said corporation, vested in said corporate funds, shall be liable in the same manner as other personal property is liable by the laws of the Territory or State, to the payment and satisfaction of his just debts to any of his bona fide creditors; and when any execution shall issue against the personal property of any such individual member, and the creditor is desirous that the same should be levied upon the property of such debtor, in the said corporate funds, the officer to whom such execution may be directed, shall levy the same, by leaving with the cashier of said bank an attested copy of such execution, and a written notice that the said execution is levied upon the property of said debtor in said corporate funds; and such property thus levied upon, shall be sold in the same manner as is, or shall by law, be provided for the sale of personal property taken in execution; and such corporate funds, thus levied upon and sold, shall be transferred to the purchaser by entering in the proper book of such corporation, a copy of the said execution, and a statement of the sale of such property by virtue thereof, which entry the officer serving such execution, shall be permitted to make: *Provided*, That no property vested in the corporate funds, shall be thus taken and sold, until all debts due to the said bank by such debtor, either as drawer and endorser of any note, or otherwise, shall be fully discharged and paid; and upon any execution being levied on any shares in said bank, it shall be the duty of the cashier of said bank, to expose the proper book of the officer, and to furnish him with a certificate, under his hand in his official capacity, stating the number of shares the debtor holds in the said bank, and the amount of dividends thereon due.

Property vested in said corporation to be liable for debts.

How it may be levied upon and sold.

Provided debts due the corporation be first satisfied.

SEC. 35. The said corporation shall not take more than six per centum per annum in advance, on its loans or discounts.

Rate of interest on discounts.

1835.

No note less than $1.

SEC. 36. No note shall be issued by said bank less than one dollar.

When to take effect.

If $10,000 be not paid in two years and unless 10 miles of said railroad be finished this act to be void.

Before the bank shall go in operation, the railroad company to give security.

SEC. 37. This act shall take effect from and after its passage, and so much of this act as confers banking privileges upon the said corporation, shall continue in force for the term of thirty years from said time: *Provided, however,* That unless the sum of ten thousand dollars in specie shall be paid in said bank within two years from the first Monday of September next, and unless ten miles of the said railroad be made and put in operation within three years thereafter, this act shall become void and of no effect: *And provided further,* That before the bank shall be permitted to issue its bills under its charter, the directors of the River Raisin and Grand River railroad company shall each give good and sufficient security, to the satisfaction of the treasurer, with the approbation of the auditor of this territory or State, in the sum of ten thousand dollars, to be by him held as collateral security for the redemption of all issues, until ten miles of said railroad shall have been completed.

President and directors to report annually to legislature.

When the road to become the property of the State or Territory and be a free road.

SEC. 38. It shall be the duty of the president and directors to report annually to the legislature of the Territory or State of Michigan, the true state and condition of said railroad, and whenever the net proceeds of said road shall have paid the cost of erecting the same, and all expenses in keeping the same in repair and operation, and fourteen per cent on all moneys so expended as aforesaid, the said road shall become the property of the Territory or State, and be subject to the control of the legislature of the said Territory or State, and shall become a free road, except sufficient toll to keep the same in repair, and after such period said bank shall be a separate and distinct institution.

Railroad company to convey to the bank all its stock.

SEC. 39. Before the said bank shall commence operation under the provisions of this act, the said River Raisin and Grand River railroad company shall convey by such instrument and form as as shall be approved by the governor of this Territory or State, to said bank, the entire stock of said railroad company, which shall stand as a security for the redemption of all notes and debts of said bank, which may be levied upon and sold for such debts, in the manner provided for in the thirty-fourth section of this act.

How this act to be construed.

SEC. 40. This act is, and the same is hereby declared to be a public act, and the same shall be construed in all courts and places benignly, and favorably for every beneficial purpose therein mentioned.

Approved August 22, 1835.

AN ACT to provide for the payment of expenses incurred in sustaining the supremacy of the laws of Michigan in the disputed territory.

Five thousand dollars appropriated to carry into effect certain laws of the territory.

SECTION 1. *Be it enacted by the Legislative Council of the Territory of Michigan,* That the sum of five thousand dollars be, and the same is hereby appropriated, and placed at the disposal of Stevens T.

1835.

Mason, acting governor of the Territory, to be used at his discretion in carrying into effect the laws of the Territory, which may be drawn by him from the territorial treasury, in the mode and manner now directed by law; and that an account of the disbursements and expenditures of all moneys drawn from the treasury of the Territory, under the preceding provision, shall be kept by him, and furnished to the legislature whenever required.

Approved August 24, 1835.

AN ACT to authorize a certain loan upon the credit of the Territory of Michigan.

Acting Governor authorized to borrow $310,000.

SECTION 1. *Be it enacted by the Legislative Council of the Territory of Michigan,* That Stevens T. Mason, acting governor of this Territory, be, and he is hereby authorized, if he should deem it necessary, to borrow, on the credit of the Territory of Michigan, any sum of money not exceeding three hundred and ten thousand dollars, for any period of time not exceeding one year from the first day of January next, at a rate of interest not exceeding six per cent per annum; and to issue scrip therefor, redeemable as aforesaid.

Approved August 24, 1835.

AN ACT in addition to an act to amend the several acts now in force, regulating the election of a delegate to the Congress of the United States, and the election of members of the legislative council of this Territory, and for other purposes.

When elections to be held.

SECTION 1. *Be it enacted by the Legislative Council of the Territory of Michigan,* That the election of a delegate to the Congress of the United States, and the election of members of the the legislative council, to be held on the first Monday of October next, according to the several acts now in force regulating such elections.

When inhabitants of Milwaukee to hold elections.

SEC. 2. That the inhabitants of the township of Milwaukee may assemble and hold the said elections at the following places, to wit:—At the house of Solomon Juneau, in the village of Milwaukee—at See's dwelling house, on the Rapids of Root river—at Knapp's store, at the mouth of Root river—and at Griffin's dwelling house at forks of Pickerel river, in the county of Milwaukee, and at such places in the county of Demoine as the judges of the county court of said county may appoint. The said election shall be held by three persons, at each place above mentioned, elected to perform such service, by a majority of the inhabitants then present at each of said places, between the hours of nine and twelve of the said day, which said persons, so elected, shall proceed to hold said elections according to the mode prescribed by law for holding township elections, and make returns thereof, upon oath, to the justices of the county court of each of said

How election shall be held and conducted.

1835.

counties respectively, who shall canvass the votes given at the several polls within their counties, and declare the names of the persons who shall have been duly elected at such election.

Clerks of certain counties to certify the number of votes given to the clerk of Brown county.

SEC. 3. That the clerks of the counties of Crawford, Iowa, Dubuque, and Demoine, shall each certify, under the seal of their respective counties, the number of votes given for every person in their several counties, to the clerk of the county of Brown, who shall make return thereof to the clerk of the supreme court of the said Territory, at Detroit; and all other returns of the said elections shall be made to the clerk of the supreme court, who shall give a certificate, under the seal of the said court, of the whole number of votes given at said elections, in all of the counties of this Territory, for every person voted for thereat.

Approved August 24, 1835.

AN ACT to incorporate the Macomb and Saginaw railroad company, and for other purposes.

Commissioners appointed.

SECTION 1. *Be it enacted by the Legislative Council of the Territory of Michigan,* That Christian Clemens, John S. Axford, Neil Gray, Azariah Prentiss, James Brown, Rodney C. Cooley, and Lansing B. Mesner, be, and they are hereby appointed commissioners, under the direction of a majority of whom subscriptions may be received to the capital stock of the Macomb and Saginaw railroad company, hereby incorporated, and they may cause books to be opened, at such times and places as they shall direct, for the purpose of receiving subscriptions to the capital stock of said company, first giving reasonable notice of the times and places of taking said subscriptions.

Capital stock $1,000,000, in shares of $50.

SEC. 2. That the capital stock of said Macomb and Saginaw railroad company, shall be one million of dollars, in shares of fifty dollars each; and that as soon as one thousand shares of said stock shall be subscribed, the subscribers of said stock, with such other persons as shall associate with them for that purpose, their successors and assigns, shall be, and they are hereby created a body corporate and politic, by the name and style of the "Macomb and Saginaw railroad company," with perpetual succession; and by that name shall be capable in law of purchasing, holding, selling, leasing, and conveying estate, either real, personal, or mixed, so far as the same may be necessary for the purposes hereinafter mentioned, and no further; and in their corporate names may sue and be sued, may have a common seal, which they may alter and renew at pleasure; and shall have, enjoy, and may exercise all the powers, rights, and privileges which appertain to corporate bodies, for the purposes mentioned in this act.

Created a body corporate and politic.

May hold and sell property.

Powers, rights, and privileges enjoyed.

Power to construct and use railroad.

SEC. 3. Said corporation, hereby created, shall have power to construct a single or double railroad from Mount Clemens, on the most eligible route, to Lapeer, thence to the seat of justice of the county of Saginaw; to be located under the direction of Israel Curtis, Jacob Tucker, and Charles C. Hascall (who are hereby

Commissioners to locate said road.

1835.

appointed commissioners for that purpose), with power to transport, take and carry property and persons upon the same, by the power and force of steam, of animals, or of any mechanical or other power, or of any combination of them.

Power to transport property and persons.

SEC. 4. If said corporation shall not, within four years from the passage of this act, commence the construction of said railroad, and shall not, within eight years from the passage of this act, construct, finish, and put in operation, ten miles in distance of said railroad, and shall not, within fifteen years from the passage of this act, construct, finish, and put in operation, one-half of said railroad, and shall not, within forty years from the passage of this act, complete and put in operation the whole of the said railroad, or in the event of a failure of the company to construct the parts of the said railroad, within either of the times above mentioned, then the rights, privileges, and powers of the said corporation, under this act, shall be null and void, as to said parts of the said road which are not finished within the times limited by this act, and to them only; the said company shall make return to the governor, to be laid before the legislsture annually, by the president and on oath of the president or treasurer, with the statement of the receipts and expenditures upon the said railroad, together with the costs thereof; and if at any time on such return, the amount divided from the part of said railroad completed, over and above all repairs, shall exceed fourteen per cent on the capital stock paid in, and equal interest from the time of payment, then it shall be the duty of said company to complete the next adjoining section within five years after making such return, or on failure thereof, to pay all the surplus moneys arising from the road so completed, over and above the said fourteen per cent, into the treasury of the Territory.

Within what time certain parts and the whole of said road to be finished.

To make retnrn of the receipts and expenditures on said road and the cost thereof.

If the amount of dividend exceed 14 per cent the adjoining section to be completed in five years.

SEC. 5. That whenever one thousand shares of the aforesaid stock shall have been subscribed, if within two years after the passage of this act, the commissioners shall call a general meeting of the subscribers, at such time and place as they may appoint, by giving sixty days' public notice of such meeting, and at such meeting the commissioners shall lay the subscription book before the subscribers then and there present, and thereupon, the subscribers or stockholders, or a majority of them, shall elect nine directors by ballot, a majority of whom shall be competent to manage the affairs of said company; they shall have power of electing a president of said company, either from amongst the directors or the stockholders, and in said election, and on every occasion wherein a vote of the stockholders is to be taken, every share shall entitle the holder thereof to one vote, and every stockholder may vote himself or by proxy.

Election of directors.

Election of president.

How stockholders may vote.

SEC. 6. That to continue the succession of president and directors of said company, nine directors shall be chosen annually, on the first Monday of October, at such place as may be appointed by the directors; and if any vacancy shall occur by death, resignation, or otherwise, of any president or director, before the year for which he was elected shall have expired, a person to fill

When president and directors to be chosen.

1835.

such vacant place for the residue of the year, may be appointed by the directors of said company, or a majority of them; the directors of said company shall hold and exercise their offices until a new election of president and directors. All elections which are by this act, by the by-laws of the company, to be made on any particular day, if not made on such day, may be made at any time within thirty days thereafter.

If elections be not held on the day appointed.

Meeting to be held annually.

SEC. 7. That a general meeting of the stockholders of said company shall be held annually, at the time and place appointed for the appointment of president and directors; and a meeting may be called at any time during the interval between said annual meetings, by the president and directors, or by the stockholders owning not less than one-fourth of the whole stock, by giving thirty days' public notice of the time and place of meeting; and when any such meetings are called by the stockholders, the notice shall specify the particular object of the call; and if, at any meetings thus called, a majority in value of the stockholders are not present, in person or by proxy, such meeting shall be adjourned from day to day, not exceeding three days, without transacting any business; and if within three days, stockholders having a majority of the stock do not attend such meeting, then the same shall be dissolved.

Of extra meetings.

When meeting dissolved.

When president and directors to account.

SEC. 8. That at the regular annual meetings of the stockholders of said company, it shall be the duty of the president and directors in office for the preceding year, to exhibit a clear and distinct statement of the affairs of the company; and at any called meeting of the stockholders, a majority of those present in person, or by proxy, may require similar statements from the president and directors, whose duty it shall be to furnish them when thus required; and at all general meetings of the stockholders, a majority in value of all the stockholders in said company, may remove from office any president, or any of the directors of said company, and may appoint others in their stead.

President and directors may be removed.

Oath of president and directors.

SEC. 9. That every president and director of said company, before he acts as such, shall swear or affirm, that he will well and truly discharge the duties of his office to the best of his skill and judgment.

May appoint and remove officers, etc.

SEC. 10. That the president and directors, or a majority of them, shall have power to appoint, contract with, and determine the compensation of all such officers, engineers, agents, or servants whatsoever, as they may deem necessary for the transaction of the business of the company, and remove them at pleasure; and the said president and directors, or a majority of them, shall have power to determine the manner of adjusting and settling all accounts against the company; also the manner and evidence of transfers of stock in said company; and they shall have power to pass all by-laws which they may deem necessary for carrying into execution all the power vested in the company hereby incorporated: *Provided* Such by-laws shall not be contrary to the laws of this Territory, or the constitution, or laws of the United States.

To settle accounts, make by-laws, etc.

SEC. 11. That the president and directors of said company

1835.

shall be, and they are hereby invested with all the privileges, rights, and powers necessary for the location, construction, and keeping in repair said railroad, not exceeding one hundred feet in width; and the said president and directors, or their agents, or those with whom they may contract for making said road, or any part of it, may enter upon, use, and excavate any land which may be wanted for the site of said railroad, or any other purpose which is necessary in the construction or repair of said road, or its works, so soon as the amount is ascertained and tendered as hereinafter provided.

To construct and keep said road in repair.

May contract for, use, and excavate any land, etc.

SEC. 12. That the president and directors of said company may agree with the owner or owners of any land, earth, timber, gravel, stone, or other materials, or any articles whatsoever, which may be wanted in the construction or repair of said road, or any of its works, for the purchase or occupation of the same; and if such materials (not previously taken or appropriated by the owner to any particular use) as may be necessary for the construction or repair of said railroad, be found on any unimproved land adjoining to or near the same, and if the parties cannot agree, or if the owner or owners of any of them be a *femme covert*, under age, *non compos mentis*, or out of the county in which the property wanted may lie, application may be made to any justice of the peace of such county, who shall thereupon issue his warrant, under his hand and seal, directed to the sheriff of said county, or, if the sheriff be interested, to some disinterested person, requiring him to summon a jury of twelve freeholders in the county, not in any way interested in the matter, or related to the parties, to meet on or near the property or materials to be valued, on a day named in said warrant, not less than five nor more than ten days after the issuing of the same; and if at the said time and place any of the persons summoned do not attend, the said sheriff or summoner shall immediately summon as many as may be necessary, with the persons in attendance as jurors, to furnish a panel of twelve jurors, and from each party, or his, or her, or their agent or attorney, or if either be not present in person or by agent, the sheriff or summoner for him, her, or them, may strike off three jurors, and the remaining shall set as a jury of inquest of damages, and before they act as such, the sheriff or summoner shall administer to each of them an oath or affirmation, that they will justly and impartially value the damage which the owner or owners will sustain by the use or occupation of the land, materials, or other property required by said company; and the said jury shall reduce their inquisition to writing, and shall sign and seal the same, and it shall thence be sent to the clerk of the circuit court of said county, and by said clerk filed in his office, and shall be confirmed by said court at its next session, if no sufficient cause to the contrary be shown; and when confirmed, the same shall be recorded by said clerk, at the expense of said company; but if set aside, said court may direct another inquisition, to be taken in the manner above prescribed; said inquisition shall describe the property taken, or the bounds of the land condemned. Such valuation, when paid

May agree for materials, etc.

How to proceed when parties cannot agree.

Jury to be summoned, etc.

Inquisition to be in writing and sent to circuit court.

1835.

Valuation tendered, property to vest in company, etc.

or tendered to the owner or owners of said property, his, her, or their legal representatives, shall entitle said company to the estate and interest in the same, thus valued, as fully as if it had been conveyed by the owner or owners of the same, for such term of time as the said company shall occupy the same as a railroad; and if valuation be not received when tendered, it may, at any time thereafter be received from the company without cost; and the sheriff, and summoners, and jurors shall be allowed the ordinary fees for like services, to be taxed by the court.

When company to make wagon ways, etc.

SEC. 13. That whenever in the construction of said railroad, it shall be necessary to cross or intersect any established road, it shall be the duty of the said president and directors so to construct the said railroad across such established road as not to impede the passage or transportation of persons or property along the same; or when it shall be necessary to construct it through the land of any individual, it shall be their duty to provide for such individual, proper wagon ways across said road from one part of his land to another.

Neglect to make wagon ways, liable for damages.

SEC. 14. That if said company shall neglect to provide proper wagon ways across said road, required by the preceding section of this act, it shall be lawful for any individual to sue said company, and shall be entitled to such damages as a jury may think him or her entitled to, for such neglect or refusal on the part of said company.

May contract with any other company for the use of any road, bridge, etc.

SEC. 15. That if it shall be necessary for the said railroad company, in the selection of the route, or the construction of the said road, to be by them laid out and constructed, or any part of it, to connect the same with any turnpike road or bridge, made or erected by any incorporated company, or authorized by any law of this Territory, it shall be lawful for said president and directors to contract with any other corporation for the right to use such road or bridge, or for transfer of any of the corporate or other rights and privileges of such corporation to the said company hereby incorporated; and every such other incorporation, acting under the laws of this Territory, is hereby authorized to make such contract or transfer, by and through the agency of the persons authorized by the respective acts of incorporation, to exercise their corporate power, or by any persons which are, by any law of this Territory entrusted with the management and direction of such turnpike, road, or bridge, or any of the rights or privileges aforesaid.

Such contract to be valid.

Every contract or transfer, made in pursuance of the power and authority hereby granted, when executed by the several parties under the irrespective corporate seals, shall vest in the company hereby incorporated, all such rights and privileges, and the right to use and enjoy the same, as fully as they are used and enjoyed by the said corporation in whom they are now vested.

May purchase machines, etc.

SEC. 16. That the said president and directors shall have power to purchase, with the funds of the company, and place on any railroad constructed by them under this act, all machines, wagons, carriages, or vehicles of any description, which they may deem necessary or proper for the purpose of transportation on said road;

1835.

and that they shall have power to charge, for tolls and transportation, such sums as shall be established by the by-laws of the company hereby incorporated; and it shall not be lawful for any other company, or any person or persons, to transport any passengers or merchandize, or property of any description whatever, along said road, or any part of it, without the license or permission of the said president and directors of said company; and the said road, with all its improvements, works, and profits, and all machinery used on said road for transportation, are hereby vested in said company incorporated by this act, and their successors forever; and the shares of the capital stock of said company, shall be considered personal property, and shall be transferable agreeably to the by-laws of said company, and subject to be taken on execution agreeably to such laws as are or may thereafter be in force.

May transport property and persons, and receive tolls.

Property vested in the company.

Shares considered personal property, and liable for debts.

SEC. 17. That the said president and directors shall, annually, or semi-annually, declare and make such dividend as they may deem proper, of the net profits from the resources of said company, deducting the necessary current expenses; and they shall make the dividend among the stockholders of said company, in proper proportions to their respective shares.

Of dividends.

SEC. 18. That if any person or persons shall willfully, knowingly, and maliciously, by any means whatever, injure, impair, or destroy any part of the railroad constructed by said company under this act, or any of the necessary works, buildings, or machinery of said company, such person or persons so offending, shall, each of them, for every such offense, forfeit and pay to the said company, a sum not exceeding three times the amount of damages caused by such offense, which may be recovered in the name of said company, by an action of debt, in any court having competent jurisdiction, in the county wherein the offense shall be committed; and shall also be subject to an indictment; and upon conviction of such offense, shall be punished by fine and imprisonment, at the discretion of the court.

Persons injuring said road liable for damages, etc.

SEC. 19. That the right and privilege is hereby reserved to the Macomb and Saginaw railroad company, to connect with the road hereby provided for, any other railroads leading from the main route to any part or parts of the Territory: *Provided,* That in forming such connection, no injury shall be done to the works of the company hereby incorporated: *Provided, further,* That the said company or companies so connecting, may have free use of said road by paying such a tariff of tolls as may be established by the legislature; and this company shall be entitled to the same rights and privileges to any and all roads hereafter connected.

Right reserved to connect other railroad with this road.

Proviso.

SEC. 20. That this act shall be favorably construed to effect the purposes thereby intended; and the same is hereby declared to be a public act, and copies thereof, printed by authority of the Territory, shall be received as evidence thereof.

Construction.

SEC. 21. That the stockholders of the Macomb and Saginaw railroad company be, and they are hereby authorized to establish a bank at the village of Mount Clemens, the capital stock whereof

Authority to establish a bank.

1835.

shall, for the present, be one hundred thousand dollars, to be divided into two thousand shares, each being fifty dollars; and the subscriptions towards constituting said stock, shall be open at such times and places, under the superintendence of the president and directors of said company, as they may designate, giving at least three weeks' public notice thereof, in one or more newspapers published in said Territory; and the subscription aforesaid shall continue open until the whole number of shares are subscribed, and if the subscriptions to the said capital stock shall, within six days after the same are opened, exceed the amount authorized by this section, it shall be the duty of the directors to deduct such excess, in a proportional manner, from the largest number of shares subscribed, in such a manner that each person subscribing shall be entitled to at least five shares, if he subscribe so many.

Of subscriptions for capital stock.

When and how installments to be paid.

SEC. 22. One-tenth part of the amount of each share, shall be paid to the said president and directors, in specie, at the time of subscribing, and the balance shall be paid in such installments, and at such times as the directors for the time being may require: *Provided,* That whenever the payment of any installment is required by the directors, they shall give at least sixty days' notice thereof, in a newspaper printed in this Territory; but no one installment shall exceed five dollars on a share: *Provided, further,* That no note or evidence of debt shall be discounted or received by the directors in payment of any installment called in or required to be paid, with intent of providing the means of furnishing such payment, or with intent of enabling any stockholder to withdraw any part of the money paid in by him on his stock.

Notice to be given.

Proviso.

Stockholders to be a body politic and corporate.

SEC. 23. All persons who shall become stockholders of said bank, shall be, and they are hereby constituted, ordained, and declared to be a body corporate and politic, in fact and in name, by the name of "the President, Directors, and Company of the Bank of Macomb County;" that by that name they and their successors shall and may have continual succession, and shall be persons in law capable of suing and being sued, pleading and being impleaded, answering and being answered, defending and being defended, in all courts and places whatsoever, and in all mannner of actions, suits, complaints, matters, and causes whatsoever, and that they and their successors may have a common seal, and may change and alter the same at their pleasure; and they and their successors, by the name of "the President, Directors, and Company of the Bank of Macomb County," shall be, in law, capable of purchasing, holding, and conveying any estate, real or personal, for the use of said corporation.

Its style and powers.

Who to manage.

SEC. 24. The stock, property, affairs, and concerns of the said bank shall be managed by the president and directors of the said railroad company.

Directors to make by-laws, rules, etc.

SEC. 25. The directors for the time being, or a majority of them, shall have power to make and prescribe such by-laws, rules, and regulations, as to them shall appear needful and proper, touching the arrangement and disposition of the stock, property, estate, and effects of said corporation, the duties and conduct of the

1835.

officers, clerks, and servants employed therein, and all such other matters as appertain to the business of a bank; and shall also have power to appoint so many officers, clerks, and servants, for carrying on said business, and with such salaries and allowances as to them shall seem meet: *Provided,* That such by-laws, rules, and regulations be not repugnant to the constitution or laws of the United States, or to the laws of this Territory; and it shall be the duty of the said directors, whenever thereto required, to furnish to the legislature or governor, a statement, under oath or affirmation, of the condition of the bank, stating the amount of deposits, the profits on hand, the amount of bills in circulation, the amount of debts due from the directors, the amount due from the stockholders, the amount of debts due from all other persons or corporations, not, however, naming them, the amount of specie in bank, the amount of all bills of other banks, the amount of their deposits in other banks, the amount of their real estate, and all their other property not herein specified, and shall contain a true exhibit of the state of said bank.

Their powers, duty, etc.

Statement of affairs.

SEC. 26. This Territory shall have a right to subscribe any number of shares in said bank, not exceeding in the whole the number of five hundred, at any time when by law they shall authorize any person or persons for that purpose; and the Territory shall have a right to increase the number of shares and stock which the said corporation may hold, to the amount of the sum to be subscribed.

Right of territory to take stock.

SEC. 27. The total amount of debts which the said corporation shall at any time owe, whether by bond, bill, note, or other contract, over and above the specie then actually deposited in the bank, shall not exceed three times the amount of capital stock subscribed and actually paid into said bank; and in case of such excess, the directors under whose administration it shall happen, shall be liable for the same in their separate and private capacities; but this shall not be construed to exempt the said corporation, or any estate, real or personal, which they may hold as a body corporate, from being also liable for, and chargeable with such excess; but such of the directors who have been absent when the said excess was contracted, or who may have dissented from the resolution or act whereby the same was contracted, shall not be so liable. No loan or discount shall be made to the directors of such corporation, or upon paper on which such directors, or any of them, shall be responsible, to any amount exceeding the capital stock actually paid in and possessed by the corporation.

Amount of debts which bank shall not exceed.

Liable in case of excess.

Loans to directors.

SEC. 28. The lands, tenements, and hereditaments which it shall be lawful for the said corporation to purchase and hold, shall be only such as shall be required for its accommodation in relation to the convenient transaction of its business, or such as shall have been *bona fide* mortgaged to it by way of security, or conveyed to it in satisfaction of debts previously contracted, in the course of its dealings, or purchased at sales upon judgments which shall have been obtained for such debts; and further, the said corporation shall not, directly or indirectly, deal or trade in buying or selling any goods, wares, or merchandize, or commodities whatso-

Lands and tenements which bank may hold.

Not to trade in merchandise.

1835. ever, unless in selling the same when truly pledged by way of security for debts due the said corporation, or purchasing the same at sale on judgments which shall have been obtained for any debts previously contracted in the course of its dealings, and afterwards selling the same.

Bills to be assignable, etc.

SEC. 29. The bills, obligatory and of credit, under the seal of the said corporation, which shall be made to any person or persons, shall be assignable by endorsement thereupon, under the hand or hands of such person or persons, his, her, or their assignee or assignees, so as absolutely to transfer and vest the property thereof in each and every assignee or assignees respectively, and to enable such assignee or assignees to bring and maintain an action thereupon, in his, her, or their own name or names; and bills or notes which may be issued by order of said corporation, promising the payment to any person or persons, his, her, or their order, or to bearers, though not under the seal of the said corporation, shall be binding and obligatory upon the same in like manner, and with like force and effect as upon any private person or persons, if issued by him, her, or them, in his, her, or their private or natural capacities, and shall be assignable and negotiable in like manner as if they were so issued by such private person or persons; and if such bills, obligatory and of credit, and such bills and notes issued as aforesaid, are not paid when the same are due and demanded at the banking house of the said bank, and within the usual banking hours, in the legal money of the United States, the said corporation shall be dissolved, subject to the benefits and provisions of the act entitled an act relative to banking institutions, approved April twentty-three, one thousand eight hundred and thirty-three.

Bills to be paid when demanded or corporation dissolved.

Of dividends.

SEC. 30. The directors shall make half yearly dividends, commencing in six months after the said bank shall have gone into operation, of so much of the profits of the said bank as to them, or a majority of them, shall seem advisable; and the directors shall also, after ten thousand dollars shall have been paid in, provide a convenient place for the transaction of the business of said bank, and commence operation; and every cashier and clerk, before they enter upon the duties of their offices, shall give bond, with two or more sureties, to the satisfaction of the directors, conditioned for the faithful discharge of their duties: *Provided,* That no dividend shall be paid except from the surplus profits arising from the business of the corporation; and it shall not be lawful to divide, withdraw, or in any way reduce the capital stock, or any part thereof, without the consent of the legislature.

When bank may commence business.

Cashier and clerks to give bond.

Salary of officers.

SEC. 31. No president, or other officer, shall be entitled to any emoluments for their services, unless the same shall have been allowed by the stockholders at a general meeting. Four directors shall constitute a board for the transaction of business, of whom the president shall be one, except in case of necessary absence, when he shall in writing, appoint one of the directors to act as president *pro tempore*; but for making ordinary discounts, such a number of directors shall constitute a board as shall be required by the laws of said corporation.

Board for business.

1835.

SEC. 32. The stock of the said corporation shall be assignable according to such rules as shall be made in that behalf by the by-laws of the said corporation; but no assignment or transfer shall be valid or effectual until such assignment or transfer shall be entered or registered in a book to be kept for that purpose; nor shall any stockholder be capable of assigning or transferring his or her stock in said bank, until all notes, dues, and debts, of whatsoever nature, due to said corporation from such stockholder, either as drawer, or endorser, on any note or bill, or otherwise, shall be first paid and discharged.

Assignment of stock.

SEC. 33. The stockholders may, at any time, augment the capital stock of the said bank, at any special meeting called for that purpose, a majority of all the votes being given thereupon, under such regulations, resolutions, and conditions as the said stockholders shall at such meeting judge proper, to any amount not exceeding five hundred thousand dollars.

Stockholders may augment capital stock.

SEC. 34. The property of every individual member of the said corporation, vested in said corporate funds, shall be liable in the same manner as other personal property is liable by the laws of the Territory, to the payment and satisfaction of his just debts, to any of his *bona fide* creditors; and when any execution shall issue against the personal property of any such individual member, and the creditor is desirous that the same shall be levied upon the property of such debtor in the said corporate funds, the officer to whom such execution may be directed, shall levy the same, by leaving with the cashier of said bank, an attested copy of such execution, and a written notice that the said execution is levied upon the property of the said debtor in said corporate funds; and such property, thus levied upon, shall be sold in the same manner as is or shall by law be provided for the sale of personal property taken in execution; and such corporate funds, thus levied upon and sold, shall be transferred to the purchaser, by entering in the proper book of such corporation, a copy of the said execution, and a statement of the sale of such property by virtue thereof, which entry the officer serving such execution shall be permitted to make: *Provided*, That no property vested in the said corporate funds shall be thus taken and sold, until all debts due to the said bank by such debtor, either as drawer or endorser of any note or otherwise, shall be fully paid and discharged; and upon any execution being levied on any shares in said bank, it shall be the duty of the cashier of said bank to expose the proper book of the corporation to the officer, and to furnish him with a certificate, under his hand and in his official capacity, stating the number of shares the debtor holds in the said bank, and the amount of dividends thereon due.

Property vested in the bank to be liable for debts.

How levied upon and sold.

Provided debts due the bank be first paid.

SEC. 35. The said corporation shall not take more than seven per centum per annum in advance on its loans or discounts.

Rate of interest.

SEC. 36. No note shall be issued by said bank less than one dollar.

No note less than $1.

SEC. 37. This act shall take effect from and after its passage, and shall continue in force for the term of forty years from said

Term of charter.

1835.

In what case charter to be void.

time: *Provided, however,* That unless the sum of ten thousand dollars in specie shall be paid in said bank within two years from the first Monday of July next, and unless ten miles of the said railroad, commencing at Mount Clemens, be made and put in operation within six years thereafter, this act shall become void and of no effect.

Territory to have the right to purchase said road.

SEC. 38. That the Territory or State may, at any time after the expiration of twenty-five years from the completion of said railroad, have the right to purchase and hold the same for the use of said Territory or State, at a price not exceeding the original cost of said road and the expenses in keeping the same in repair and operation, and seven per cent on all moneys so expended, together with fourteen per cent thereon; and after such period, the said bank shall become a separate and distinct institution.

Road company to convey the stock to the bank.

SEC. 39. Before the said bank shall commence operation under the provisions of this act, the said Macomb and Saginaw railroad company shall convey, by such instrument and form as shall be approved by the governor of this Territory, to said bank, the entire stock of said railroad company, which shall stand as a security for the redemption of all notes and debts of said bank, which may be levied upon and sold for such debts, in the manner provided for in the fourteenth section of this act.

Directors of this company to give security.

SEC. 40. That the directors of the said company, shall, before they issue bills under this charter, give good and sufficient security, to the satisfaction of the treasurer, with the approbation of the auditor of this Territory or State, in the sum of fifty thousand dollars, to the said Territory or State, to be held by him as a collateral security for the redemption of all bills emitted by said bank, until ten miles of the said railroad shall have been completed.

Construction.

SEC. 41. This act is, and the same is hereby declared to be a public act, and that the same be construed in all courts and places benignly and favorably for every beneficial purpose therein mentioned.

Approved August 24, 1835.

AN ACT to authorize the building a dam across the Manitoowoc river, in the county of Brown.

Who authorized to build a dam, erect mills, etc.

SECTION 1. *Be it enacted by the Legislative Council of the Territory of Michigan, as follows:* John P. Arndt, Lewis Rouse, Albert G. Ellis, and Lewis Morris, and their heirs and assigns are hereby authorized and empowered to build a dam across the Manitoowoc river, at the lowest rapid in said river, on sections twenty-three and twenty-four, township nineteen north, range twenty-three east, in the county of Brown, to erect mills or other machinery, as they may deem proper, or in any other manner to make use of the water power created thereby; to build wharves, and to erect ware houses, or such other buildings as may be deemed necessary and useful for commercial purposes, either above or below said

To build wharves, erect ware houses, etc.

1835.

dam, and for the accomplishment thereof, to collect and use any materials which may be supplied from the bed of said river.

How dam and lock to be constructed.

SEC. 2. The dam shall not exceed four feet rise above the surface of the said stream at high water, and shall contain a convenient lock for the passage of boats, barges, canoes, rafts, or other water craft, not less than one hundred feet in length, and twenty feet in width, so constructed as to receive boats below said dam in slack water of sufficient depth for the ordinary purposes of navigation upon said river, and pass them to slack water of sufficient depth as aforesaid, above said dam.

If land flowed, no action of trespass.

SEC. 3. If by the erection of said dam, any lands shall be flowed to the injury thereof, the owner of said lands shall be entitled to damages, to be ascertained as herein prescribed, but no action of trespass shall be had or maintained by any owner or proprietor as aforesaid.

If land be flowed, how damage assessed.

SEC. 4. Whenever application shall be made, in writing, to any judge of the circuit court, by or on behalf of any owner or proprietor whose lands are flowed by reason of said dam, the said judge shall forthwith appoint five disinterested persons to enquire and ascertain the damages by a view of the premises, and report their opinion, together with the amount of damages, if any, which ought to be allowed for the injury occasioned as aforesaid; which amount shall be paid by the owner or owners of said dam.

When and how appeal to be taken from decision of the appraisers.

SEC. 5. From the decision of the appraisers there shall be an appeal to the county court of the county in which said dam is situated: *Provided*, Said appeal be entered by the party aggrieved, in the clerk's office, within twenty days after the award may be made; and if an appeal shall not be taken, within the time herein limited, and either party refusing to pay the amount rendered against him, he shall be liable to an action of debt for the recovery thereof, with twelve per cent damages and costs, before any court having cognizance thereof; the trial of an appeal from the award of the appraisers, shall be conducted in the same manner as those from justices of the peace.

To be kept in repair.

SEC. 6. It shall be the duty of the owners of said dam, at all times, to keep the said lock in repair, and to pass any water craft, which can be admitted through the same, free of toll, without any unnecessary delay.

Liability of persons injuring lock or dam.

SEC. 7. Any person who shall destroy, or in any wise injure said lock, or dam, shall be deemed to have committed a trespass upon the owner or owners thereof, and liable accordingly; and any person willfully and maliciously doing damage to said lock, or dam, shall be deemed guilty of a misdemeanor and punishable by fine and imprisonment, in the discretion of the court: *Provided*, That the imprisonment shall not exceed the term of one year.

This act may be amended.

SEC. 8. The legislature may, at any time, so alter or amend this act, as to provide for the further improvement of the navigation of said Manitoowoc river.

Approved August 25, 1835.

1835.

AN ACT to organize the counties of Allegan and Milwaukee.

County of Allegan to be organized.

SECTION 1. *Be it enacted by the Legislative Council of the Territory of Michigan*, That the county of Allegan shall be organized from and after the passage of this act, and the inhabitants thereof entitled to all the rights and privileges to which by law the inhabitants of other counties in this territory are entitled.

Of suits, etc., pending in Kalamazoo county.

SEC. 2. That all suits, prosecutions, and other matters now pending before the courts of record of Kalamazoo county, or before any justice of the peace of said county, shall be prosecuted to final judgment and execution, and all taxes heretofore levied and now due, shall be collected in the same manner as though the said county of Allegan had not been organized.

Bonds of justices.

SEC. 3. That the bonds of justices of the peace for the county of Allegan shall be approved and received by the clerk of said county, and be subject to the penalties and liabilities prescribed by law, until a treasurer is elected and qualified.

Of justices in commission.

SEC. 4. That the justices of the peace, now in commission in said county, shall continue to perform their judicial functions until their successors are elected and qualified.

When circuit court to be holden.

SEC. 5. That the circuit court for the county of Allegan shall be holden on the second Thursdays next after the fourth Mondays of April and October, annually, at such place as shall be provided by law.

Of matters pending before circuit court.

SEC. 6. That all causes, writs, process, and other matters whatsoever, pending in, or issued, or to be issued before or on the third Tuesday next after the fourth Monday in April, next, and returnable into the said court on any day in any term thereof heretofore fixed by law, shall be continued and proceeded in, and be returned into the said court, to, and at the respective and proper terms of the said court hereby established, as fully and effectually as though such causes, writs, process, and other matters had been regularly continued to, and made returnable at the respective and proper terms of said court, as hereby established.

Duty of sheriff.

SEC. 7. It shall be the duty of the sheriff of the county of Allegan, until public buildings are erected in said county, to provide a convenient place at or near the county site for said county, for the holding of said court.

When circuit court to be holden.

SEC. 8. The circuit court for the county of Allegan shall be held on the———Thursdays next after the fourth Mondays of April and October, in each year.

County of Milwaukee organized.

SEC. 9. That the county of Milwaukee shall be, and the same is hereby declared to be organized, and the inhabitants thereof entitled to the same rights and privileges, in all respects whatever, with the inhabitants of other organized counties within the said Territory.

Of the county court.

SEC. 10. There shall be a county court established in the said county, which court shall hold one term on the first Monday of May, and one term on the first Monday of October, in each and every year, at the village of Milwaukee, which is hereby declared to be the county seat of said county.

1835.

SEC. 11. The county clerks of said counties of Allegan and Milwaukee shall be *ex officio* register of deeds in and for said counties, until a register shall be elected according to law. County clerk.

SEC. 12. The provisions of the act entitled "An act to prescribe the mode of holding elections in the county of Iowa," approved April twenty, one thousand eight hundred and thirty-three, are hereby declared applicable to said county of Milwaukee, and said act shall be in force in said county, anything in any law to the contrary notwithstanding. Of elections.

SEC. 13. That all that part of the county of Milwaukee lying north of a line drawn due west from a point on Lake Michigan, six miles south of the mouth of the Milwaukee river, to the western boundary of said county, shall be a township, and be called Root River, and the first township meeting shall be held on the first Monday of October next, at Gee's Mills, in said township. Of townships, etc. Town meeting.

SEC. 14. This act shall take effect and be in force on and after the first Monday of September, next. When to take effect.

Approved August 25, 1835.

AN ACT making certain appropriations out of the territorial treasury.

SECTION 1. *Be it enacted by the Legislative Council of the Territory of Michigan,* That the following sums be allowed and paid out of any moneys in the territorial treasury, in full for their services rendered said Territory in taking the census: *Provided,* That no payment shall be made to any person hereinafter named, until said person shall forward to the auditor of the Territory, a certified account, showing that the services hereinafter named have been performed by said person, and that said person has received no compensation therefor. Appropriation.

SEC. 2. To Thomas Fitzuel, clerk of the county of Berrien, for copying the returns of the sheriff of said county, and of his assistants, containing one thousand seven hundred and eighty-seven inhabitants, at three dollars per thousand, five dollars and thirty-six cents. Thos. Fitzuel.

SEC. 3. To Stephen Vickery, clerk of Kalamazoo county, for copying the returns of the sheriff of said county, and of his assistants, containing three thousand one hundred and twenty-six inhabitants, at three dollars per thousand, nine dollars and thirty-seven cents. S. Vickery.

SEC. 4. To Wales Adams, clerk of the county of Branch, for copying the returns of the sheriff of said county, and his assistants, containing seven hundred and sixty-four inhabitants, at three dollars per thousand, two dollars and twenty-nine cents. W. Adams.

SEC. 5. To Stephen Truesdell, clerk of the county of St. Joseph, for copying the returns of the sheriff of said county, and of his assistants, containing three thousand one hundred and sixty-six inhabitants, at three dollars per thousand, nine dollars and fifty cents. S. Truesdell.

1835.

L. Le Barren. SEC. 6. To Levi Le Barron, clerk of the county of Lenawee, for copying the returns of the sheriff of said county, and of his assistants, containing seven thousand four hundred and seventy-six inhabitants, at three dollars per thousand, twenty-two dollars and forty-three cents.

H. James. SEC. 7. To Horace James, clerk of the county of St. Clair, for copying the returns of the sheriff of said county, and of his assistants, containing two thousand two hundred and forty-four inhabitants, at three dollars per thousand, six dollars and seventy-three cents.

M. C. Whitman. SEC. 8. To Martin C. Whitman, clerk of the county of Cass, for copying the returns of the sheriff of said county, and his assistants, containing three thousand two hundred and eighty inhabitants, at three dollars per thousand, nine dollars and eighty-four cents.

Approved August 25, 1835.

AN ACT to incorporate the Wisconsin internal improvement company.

First directors. SECTION 1. *Be it enacted by the Legislative Council of the Territory of Michigan*, That Daniel Jackson, Ramsay Crooks, James Boyd, jun., Richard Suydam, Ferd. Suydam, D. R. Campbell, F. R. Tillson, Ben. Clapp, John Lawe, Wm. B. Slaughter, Samuel W. Beall, Morgan L. Martin, John D. Ashley, Michael Dousman, Robert Stuart, Albert G. Ellis, and James D. Doty, and such other persons as shall associate with them, for the purpose of opening a communication, by land or water, between Green Bay and the Mississippi river, by removing the obstructions in the bed of the Fox river, or by creating a slack water navigation over its rapids, and cutting a canal from the Fox to the Wisconsin or Rock rivers, or from Winnebago lake; or by constructing a rail or mcadamized road around the rapids of the Fox and Rock rivers, from and to such points as shall be deemed most expedient, shall be, and they are hereby constituted a body politic and corporate, by the name and style of the "Wisconsin Internal Improvement Company," and by that name they and their successors shall and may have continued succession, and be persons in law capable of suing and being sued, pleading and being impleaded, answering and being answered unto, defending and being defended in all courts and places whatsoever, and in all manner of actions, complaints, matters, and causes; and by the same name and style shall be in law capable of purchasing, holding, and enjoying any estate, real or personal, for the use of said corporation.

Power to open communication between Green Bay and Mississippi River.

Constituted a body politic, etc.

May sue and be sued, etc.

Capital stock $500,000—the shares $150 each. SEC. 2. That the capital stock of said company shall be five hundred thousand dollars, with the privilege of increasing the same one hundred and fifty thousand dollars, and to be divided into shares of one hundred and fifty dollars each, which shall be considered personal property, and transferable according to the by-laws of the corporation. Ramsey Crooks, Dan'l. Jackson, Wil-

1835.

liam B. Slaughter, John D. Ansley, and James D. Doty, be, and they are hereby appointed commissioners to receive subscriptions for said stock; each of the said persons shall furnish himself with a book, which shall be kept open for the purpose of receiving subscriptions for two years, unless one-tenth of the whole number of shares now created shall be sooner subscribed. Each subscriber shall pay to the commissioner receiving his subscription, one-tenth of the amount of one share per each share which he shall subscribe, and the residue to the president and directors to be elected, at such time and place as they shall, from time to time, require. As soon as ten thousand dollars shall have been subscribed, the said commissioners shall, by advertisement, to be published in two of the newspapers printed in said Territory, give at least thirty days' notice of the time and place when and where the subscribers shall meet to choose directors. At the election so appointed the commissioners present shall preside; and the subscribers present, or their proxies, by a plurality of votes, shall choose, by ballot, nine stockholders, to be directors of said corporation during the ensuing year. The commissioners shall deliver their respective subscription books to the directors so to be chosen, at their first meeting, and shall then pay over to such directors the money received by them respectively, on such subscriptions. An election for directors shall be annually held on the same day on which the first was held, and at each election, including the first, the stockholders present, by a plurality of votes, shall elect by ballot three persons to preside at the next succeeding election; and the persons presiding at any election shall, immediately after receiving the ballots, openly estimate the votes, and thereupon make and subscribe a certificate of the result of such election, and after the first election make return thereof to the president and directors, at their next meeting after such election. Every stockholder, in person or by proxy, shall, at each election, be entitled, on the shares then held by him, to one vote for each share. If an annual election shall not be held on the day fixed by law, the corporation shall not cease, but the election shall be held in the same manner, and with like effect, on some early day, to be appointed by the directors then in office, who shall give and publish the same notice thereof as is required in respect to the first election; and who, after the day on which such election ought to have been held, shall be incapacitated from doing any act as directors, other than such as may be necessary to give effect to such election. Five directors shall be a board for the transaction of business, and the acts of a majority of the board shall bind the corporation.

Commissioners to receive subscriptions.

Of subscriptions for stock, etc.

Of elections, etc.

Five directors to make a board.

SEC. 3. The directors at their first meeting after their election, shall, by ballot, elect one of their number for president. The president and directors shall have power, and it shall be their duty to meet from time to time, at such place as they may deem expedient, to make such by-laws, rules, and regulations, not inconsistent with the laws of the United States, and of this Territory, as, in their judgment, the affairs of the corporation shall require; to appoint subordinate officers, artists, and workmen, as they shall

Election of president.

Power of president and directors.

1835.

Of subscriptions for stock—money due on shares, etc.

deem necessary to execute the business of the corporation; to continue to receive subscriptions of shares until the whole capital stock shall be subscribed; and to demand at such time, and in such proportion as they shall see fit, from the respective stockholders, the sums of money due on their respective shares, under pain of forfeiture of such shares, and of all previous payments thereon, to the corporation; or to sue the delinquent stockholder for the amount due on his shares, in an action of assumpsit, in any court having cognizance thereof.

Power of corporation to make improvements.

SEC. 4. The corporation, hereby created, shall have power to make, construct, and maintain a canal of suitable width and dimensions, or railroad, to be determined by the directors of said company, from the Fox to the Mississippi river; to erect dams on the rapids of said Fox and Rock rivers, so as to produce a slack-water navigation of said streams, or locks to pass said rapids; to remove the stone and logs from the bed of said Fox and Rock rivers; and to make a road or canal around said rapids from and to such points on the Fox river and Winnebago lake as shall be deemed most expedient; to regulate the time and manner, size, and order, in which all boats, craft, carriages, and property shall pass the said canal, roads, or river, where the same is improved, and to establish the amount of tolls, or transit duties upon such boats, craft, carriages, packets, and all animals passing the said roads, as soon as any or either of them shall be completed and in a situation to be used; to lease, alien, and convey any lands and real estate belonging to the said company, which they may deem unnecessary to retain for the purposes of said corporation, whether the same was vested in them by purchase, mortgage, or voluntary donation, to erect piers, wharves, warehouses, and other necessary buildings and improvements in and about said canal, rivers, and roads, for commercial purposes; to hold and convey such real estate as shall be requisite for its immediate accommodation in the convenient transaction of its business, or such as shall have been mortgaged to it in good faith, by way of security, for loans previously contracted, or for moneys due, or such as shall have been conveyed to it in satisfaction of debts previously contracted in the course of its dealings, or such as shall have been purchased at sales upon judgments, decrees, or mortgages obtained or made for such debts, or acquired in any other manner whatsoever; to enter upon and take possession of such lands, by consent of the owners thereof, as may be necessary for the construction of said canals, locks, roads, and other works.

Power to regulate the passage of boats, carriages, etc.

Power to hold, lease, sell, etc. real estate.

When this act to be void.

SEC. 5. If the construction of the said works shall not be commenced within two years, and completed within six years from the time when the same is approved by Congress, the privileges herein conferred shall cease, and this act shall become null and void.

When to take effect.

SEC. 6. This act shall not take effect until the same is approved by Congress.

Approved August 25, 1835.

1835.

AN ACT to authorize the granting of administration on the estate of Daperon Baby, deceased.

Be it enacted by the Legislative Council of the Territory of Michigan, That the judge of the probate of Wayne county, in said Territory, be, and he is hereby authorized to grant administration on the estate of said Daperon Baby, deceased, to Jean Bt. Baby, his son, or to any other person legally entitled thereto, which shall be as valid and effectual as if granted within twenty years from the death of the deceased, any law or usage to the contrary thereof notwithstanding: *Provided,* That such administration shall give bail, and in all other respects conform to, and comply with the existing probate law in their behalf made.

Judge of probate authorized to grant letters of administration.

Approved August 25, 1835.

AN ACT to amend an act entitled "An act to incorporate the village of Monroe," approved April 12, 1827.

SECTION 1. *Be it enacted by the Legislative Council of the Territory of Michigan,* That the president and trustees of the village of Monroe, with the approbation of the citizens of said village, in legal meeting assembled, shall have power, and are hereby authorized to improve the navigation of the River Raisin, from the present head of navigation to such point within the limits of said village as they shall see fit.

Power to improve the navigation of the River Raisin.

SEC. 2. It shall be competent for the said president and trustees of said village to remove from the bed of said river, or the margin, or any of the bayous near the said river, earth, gravel, or stone, and to sell or convert the same to their use, for the benefit of the said village: *Provided,* That the improvement, when completed, shall be and remain a public highway: *And provided, further,* That the course of said river shall not be changed or diverted from its natural bed or channel.

May remove obstructions, etc.

SEC. 3. It shall be competent for the said president and trustees to take and receive subscriptions towards the completion of said work.

Of subscriptions.

SEC. 4. That the rights conferred by this act, to receive subscriptions and to make improvements in the said river, shall not be construed to enlarge the powers of the corporation, so as to authorize the laying any tax upon the citizens of said village beyond what the said corporation, by previously existing laws, were authorized to levy.

How the right to receive subscriptions construed.

SEC. 5. The said president and trustees of said village may agree with the owner or owners of land which may be wanted in excavating and improving said navigation, for the purchase or occupation of the same, or if the owner or owners of any of them be a *femme covert,* under age, *non compos mentis,* or out of the county, application may be made to any justice of the peace of such county, who shall thereupon issue his warrant, under his hand and seal, directed to the sheriff of said county; or if the

President and trustees may agree for land, etc.

How to proceed when parties cannot agree.

1835.

sheriff be interested, to some disinterested person, requiring him to summon a jury of eighteen freeholders of said county, not in any way interested in the matter, or related to the parties, to meet on or near the property to be valued, on a day to be named in said warrant, not less than five nor more than ten days after the issuing of the same: and if at the said time and place, any of the persons summoned do not attend, the said sheriff or summoner shall immediately summon as many as may be necessary, with the persons in attendance as jurors, to furnish a panel of eighteen jurors; and from them each party, or his, or her, or their agent or attorney, or if either be not present, in person or by agent, the sheriff or summoner, for him, her, or them, may strike off three jurors, and the remaining shall act as a jury of inquest of damages; and before they act as such, the sheriff or summoner shall administer to each of them an oath or affirmation that they will justly and impartially value the damages which the owner or owners will sustain by the use or occupation of the land required by the said president and trustees; and the said jurors shall reduce their inquisition to writing, and sign and seal the same, and it shall be sent to the circuit court of said county, and by said clerk filed in his office, and shall be confirmed by said court at its next session, if no sufficient cause to the contrary be shown; and when confirmed, the same shall be recorded by said clerk, at the expense of said president and trustees; but if set aside, said court may direct another inquisition, to be taken in the manner above prescribed; said inquisition shall describe the property taken, or the boundaries of the land condemned; such valuation when paid or tendered to the owner or owners of said property, his, her, or their legal representatives, shall entitle said president and trustees to the estate and interest in the same thus valued, as fully as if it had been conveyed by the owner or owners for such term of time as the said improvement shall be occupied by the public; and if the valuation be not received, when tendered, it may at any time thereafter be received without cost; and the said sheriff or summoner, and jurors, shall be allowed the ordinary fees.

Jury to be summoned.

Inquisition of jury to be in writing and sent to circuit court.

Valuation tendered, property to vest in company.

When to take effect.

SEC. 6. This act to take effect and to be in force from and after its passage, and not to continue in force more than two years unless said work be commenced within that period.

Approved August 25, 1835.

AN ACT to amend an act entitled an act to incorporate the Detroit and St. Joseph railroad company.

Authority to establish a bank, capital $100,000.

SECTION 1. *Be it enacted by the Legislative Council of the Territory of Michigan,* That the stockholders of the Detroit and St. Joseph railroad company be, and they are hereby authorized to establish a bank at the village of Ypsilanti, the capital stock whereof shall, for the present, be one hundred thousand dollars, to be divided into two thousand shares, each being fifty dollars; and the subscriptions towards constituting said stock, shall be

1835.

open at such times and places, under the superintendence of the president and directors of said company, as they may designate, giving at least three weeks' public notice thereof, in one or more newspapers published in said Territory; and the subscription aforesaid shall continue open until the whole number of shares are subscribed, and if the subscriptions to the said capital stock shall, within six days after the same be opened, exceed the amount authorized by this section, it shall be the duty of the directors to deduct such excess in a proportional manner from the largest number of shares subscribed, in such a manner that each person subscribing shall be entitled to at least five shares, if he subscribe so many.

How subscriptions received and proportioned.

Sec. 2. One-tenth part of the amount of each share shall be paid to the said president and directors in specie, at the time of subscribing, and the balance shall be paid in such installments, at such time, as the directors for the time being may require: *Provided,* That whenever the payment of any installment is required by the directors, they shall give at least sixty days' notice thereof, in a newspaper printed in this Territory; but no one installment shall exceed five dollars on each share: *Provided, further,* That no note or evidence of debt shall be discounted or received by the directors, in payment of any installment called in or required to be paid, with intent of providing the means of furnishing such payment, or with intent of enabling any stockholder to withdraw any part of the money paid in by him on his stock.

Amount to be paid on subscribing, and when balance to be paid.

Notice to be given when installments to be paid.

Proviso.

Sec. 3. All persons who shall become stockholders of said bank, shall be, and they are hereby constituted, ordained, and declared to be a body corporate and politic, in fact and in name, by the name of "the President, Directors, and Company of the Bank of Ypsilanti;" that by that name they and their successors shall and may have continued succession, and shall be persons in law capable of suing and being sued, pleading and being impleaded, answering and being answered, defending and being defended, in all courts and places whatsoever, and in all manner of actions, suits, complaints, matters, and causes whatsoever; and that they and their successors may have a common seal, and may change and alter the same at their pleasure; and that they and their successors, by the name of "the President, Directors, and Company of the Bank of Ypsilanti," shall be in law capable of purchasing, holding, and conveying any estate, real or personal, for the use of said corporation.

Stockholders to be a body corporate and politic.

Its style, powers, etc.

Sec. 4. The stock, property, affairs, and concerns of the said bank shall be managed by the president and directors of the said railroad company.

Who shall manage.

Sec. 5. The directors for the time being, or a majority of them, shall have power to make and prescribe such by-laws, rules, and regulations, as to them shall appear needful and proper, touching the arrangement and disposition of the stock, property, estate, and effects of said corporation; the duties and conduct of the officers, clerks, and servants employed therein, and all such other matters as appertain to the business of a bank; and shall also

Directors to make rules, by-laws, etc.

1835.

Their powers, duties, etc.

have power to appoint so many officers, clerks, and servants, for carrying on said business, and with such salaries and allowances as to them shall seem meet: *Provided*, That such by-laws, rules, and regulations be not repugnant to the constitution or laws of the United States, or to the laws of this Territory; and it shall be the duty of the said directors, whenever thereto required, to furnish to the legislature or governor, a statement, under oath or affirmation, of the condition of the bank, stating the amount of deposits, the profits on hand, the amount of bills in circulation, the amount of debts due from the directors, the amount due from the stockholders, the amount of debts due from all other persons, or corporations, not, however, naming them; the amount of specie in bank, the amount of all bills of other banks, the amount of their deposits in other banks, the amount of their real estate, and all their other property not herein specified, and shall contain a true exhibit of the state of said bank.

Statement of affairs, etc.

Right of territory to take stock.

SEC. 6. The Territory shall have a right to subscribe any number of shares in said bank, not exceeding in the whole, the number of five hundred at any time, when by law they shall authorize any person or persons for that purpose, and the Territory shall have a right to increase the number of shares and stock which the said corporation may hold, to the amount of the sum to be subscribed.

Amount of debts which the bank shall not exceed.

SEC. 7. The total amount of debts, which the said corporation shall at any time owe, whether by bond, bill, note, or other contract, over and above the specie then actually deposited in the bank, shall not exceed three times the amount of capital stock subscribed and actually paid into said bank; and in case of such excess, the directors under whose administration it shall happen, shall be liable for the same in their separate and private capacities; but this shall not be construed to exempt the said corporation, or any estate, real or personal, which they may hold as a body corporate, from being also liable for, and chargeable with such excess; but such of the directors who have been absent when said excess was contracted, or who may have dissented from the resolution or act whereby the same was contracted, shall not be so liable; no loan or discount shall be made to the directors of such corporation, or upon paper on which such directors, or any of them, shall be responsible, to any amount exceeding the capital stock actually paid in and possessed by the corporation.

Directors liable in case of excess.

Of loans to directors.

Lands and tenements which bank may hold.

SEC. 8. The lands, tenements, and hereditaments which it shall be lawful for the said corporation to purchase and hold, shall be only such as shall be required for its accommodation in relation to the convenient transaction of its business, or such as shall have been *bona fide* mortgaged to it by way of security, or conveyed to it in satisfaction of debts previously contracted in the course of its dealings, or purchased at sales upon judgments which shall have been obtained for such debts; and further, the said corporation shall not directly, nor indirectly, deal or trade in buying or selling any goods, wares, or merchandize, or commodities whatsoever, unless in selling the same when truly pledged by

Not to trade in merchandise.

1835.

way of security for debts due the said corporation, or purchasing the same at sale on judgments which shall have been obtained for any debts previously contracted in the course of its dealings, and afterwards selling the same.

Bills to be assignable, etc.

SEC. 9. The bills, obligatory and of credit, under the seal of the said corporation, which shall be made to any person or persons, shall be assignable by endorsement thereupon, under the hand or hands of such person or persons, his, her, or their assignee or assignees, so as absolutely to transfer and vest the property thereof in each and every assignee or assignees respectively, and to enable such assignee or assingees to bring and maintain an action thereupon, in his, her, or their own name or names; and the bills or notes which may be issued by order of said corporation, promising the payment to any person or persons, his, her, or their order, or to bearer, though not under the seal of the said corporation, shall be binding and obligatory upon the same in like manner and with like force and effect, as upon any private person or persons, if issued by him, her, or them, in his, her, or their private or natural capacities, and shall be assignable and negotiable in like manner as if they were so issued by such person or persons; and if such bills, obligatory and of credit, and such bills and notes issued as aforesaid, are not paid when the same are due and demanded at the banking house of the said bank, and within usual banking hours, in the legal money of the United States, the said corporation shall be dissolved, subject to the benefits and provisions of the act entitled an act relative to banking institutions, approved April twenty-three, one thousand eight hundred and thirty-three.

Bills to be paid when demanded or corporation dissolved.

Of dividends.

SEC. 10. The directors shall make half yearly dividends, commencing six months after the said bank shall have gone into operation, of so much of the profits of the said bank as to them, or a majority of them, shall seem advisable; and the directors shall also, after ten thousand dollars shall have been paid in, provide a convenient place for the transaction of the business of the said bank, and commence operations, and every cashier and clerk, before they enter upon the duties of their offices, shall give bond, with two or more securities, to the satisfaction of the directors, conditioned for the faithful discharge of their duties: *Provided*, That no dividend shall be paid except from the surplus profits arising from the business of the corporation; and it shall not be lawful to divide, withdraw, or in any way reduce the capital stock, or any part thereof, without the consent of the legislature.

When bank may commence business.

Cashier and clerks to give bonds.

Salary of officers.

SEC. 11. No president, or other officer, shall be entitled to any emoluments for their services, unless the same shall have been allowed by the stockholders at a general meeting. Four directors shall constitute a board for the transaction of business, of whom the president shall be one, except in case of necessary absence, when he shall in writing appoint one of the directors to act as president *pro tempore*, but for making ordinary discounts, such a number of the directors shall constitutie a board as shall be required by the laws of said corporation.

Board for business.

1835.

Assignment of stock.

SEC. 12. The stock of said corporation shall be assignable according to such rules as shall be made in that behalf by the by-laws of the said corporation; but no assignment or transfer shall be valid or effectual, until such assignment or transfer shall be entered or registered in a book to be kept for that purpose; nor shall any stockholder be capable of assigning or transferring his or her stock in said bank, until all notes, dues, and debts, of whatever nature, due to said corporation from such stockholder, either as drawer or endorser, on any note or bill, or otherwise, shall be first paid and discharged.

Stockholders may augment the capital stock.

SEC. 13. The stockholders may, at any time, augment the capital stock of the said bank, at any special meeting called for that purpose, a majority of all the votes being given thereupon, under such regulations, restrictions, and conditions as the said stockholders shall, at such meeting, judge proper, to any amount not exceeding five hundred thousand dollars.

Property vested in the bank to be liable for debts, etc.

How levied upon and sold.

Provided debts due the bank be first paid.

SEC. 14. The property of every individual member of said corporation, vested in said corporate funds, shall be liable in the same manner as other personal property is liable by the laws of the Territory, to the payment and satisfaction of his just debts, to any of his *bona fide* creditors; and when any execution shall issue against the personal property of any such individual member, and the creditor is desirous that the same should be levied upon the property of such debtor in the said corporate funds, the officer to whom such execution may be directed, shall levy the same, by leaving with the cashier of said bank, an attested copy of such execution, and a written notice that the said execution levied upon the property of the said debtor in said corporate funds; and such property thus levied upon, shall be sold in the same manner as is, or shall by law be provided for the sale of personal property taken in execution, and such corporate funds thus levied upon and sold, shall be transferred to the purchaser by entering in the proper book of such corporation a copy of the said execution, and a statement of the sale of such property by virtue thereof, which entry the officer serving such execution shall be permitted to make: *Provided*, That no property vested in the said corporate funds shall be thus taken and sold, until all debts due to the said bank by such debtor, either as drawer or endorser of any note, or otherwise, shall be fully paid and discharged, and upon any execution being levied on any shares in said bank, it shall be the duty of the cashier of said bank, to expose the proper book of the corporation to the officer, and to furnish him with a certificate, under his hand, in his official capacity, stating the number of shares the debtor holds in the said bank, and the amount of dividends thereon due.

Rate of interest.

SEC. 15. The said corporation shall not take more than six per centum per annum in advance on its loans or discounts.

No note less than $1.

SEC. 16. No note shall be issued by said bank less than one dollar.

Term of charter.

SEC. 17. This act shall take effect from and after its passage, and shall continue in force for the term of thirty years from said

1835.

time: *Provided, however*, That unless the sum of ten thousand dollars in specie shall be paid in said bank within two years from the first Monday in September next, and unless ten miles of the said railroad, commencing at or near the United States arsenal, at Dearbonville, and running west, be made and put in operation within two years from the passage of this act, the same shall become void and of no effect: *And provided, further*, That before the bank shall be permitted to issue its bills under this charter, the directors of the Detroit and St. Joseph railroad company shall each give good and sufficient security, to the satisfaction of the treasurer, with the approbation of the auditor of this Territory or State, in the sum of ten thousand dollars, to be by him held as a collateral security for the redemption of all issues, until ten miles of said railroad shall have been completed.

In what case charter to be void.

Security to be given before bank goes into operation.

SEC. 18. It shall be the duty of the president and directors to report annually to the legislature of the Territory or State of Michigan, the true state and condition of said railroad, and whenever the net proceeds of said road shall have paid the cost of erecting of the same, and all expenses in keeping the same in repair and operation, and fourteen per cent on all moneys so expended as aforesaid, the said road shall become the property of the Territory or State, and be subject to the control of the legislature of said Territory or State, and shall become a free road, except sufficient toll to keep the same in repair, and after such period said bank shall be a separate and distinct institution.

President and directors to report to the legislature the state of the road, etc.

When said road to be free.

SEC. 19. Before the said bank shall commence operation under the provisions of this act, the said Detroit and St. Joseph railroad company shall convey, by such instrument and form as shall be approved by the governor of this Territory, to said bank, the entire stock of said railroad company, which shall stand as a security for the redemption of all notes and debts of said bank, which may be levied upon and sold for such debts in the manner provided for in the fourteenth section of this act.

Railroad company to convey the stock to the bank.

SEC. 20. That the Territory shall have the right, at any time, after the expiration of twenty years from the completion of said railroad, to purchase and hold the same for the use of the Territory or State of Michigan, at a price not exceeding the original cost and expenses, and all fixtures and property connected with or attached to said railroad, and fourteen per centum thereon, of which cost an accurate account shall be kept, attested by the oath of the president, or some officer of said company, whenever and as often as the legislature shall require the same.

Territory to have the right to purchase said road.

Account to be kept of the cost of said road.

SEC. 21. This act is, and the same is hereby declared to be a public act, and that the same be construed in all courts and places benignly and favorably for every beneficial purpose therein mentioned.

How this act to be construed.

Approved August 25, 1835.

1835.

AN ACT to incorporate the Detroit and Maumee railroad company.

Commissioners appointed.

SECTION 1. *Be it enacted by the Legislative Council of the Territory of Michigan*, That John R. Williams, Austin E. Wing, Levi Cook, James J. Godfroy, John Anderson, Salmon Keeney, John Biddle, John M'Donell, and Dan B. Miller, with authority to fill such vacancies as may occur in their own body, be, and they are hereby appointed commissioners, under the direction of a majority of whom subscriptions may be received to the capital stock of the Detroit and Maumee railroad company, hereby incorporated, and they may cause books to be opened at such times and places as they shall direct, for the purpose of receiving subscriptions to the capital stock of said company, first giving reasonable notice of the times and places of taking said subscriptions.

Books to be opened and subscriptions received.

Capital stock $500,000, in shares of $50.

SEC. 2. That the capital stock of said Detroit and Maumee railroad company shall be five hundred thousand dollars, in shares of fifty dollars each; and that as soon as five hundred shares of said stock shall be subscribed, the subscribers of said stock, with such other persons as shall associate with them for that purpose, their successors and assigns, shall be, and they are hereby created a body corporate and politic, by the name of "the Detroit and Maumee Railroad Company" with perpetual successsion, and by that name shall be capable in law of purchasing, holding, selling, leasing, and conveying estate, either real, personal, or mixed, so far as the same may be necessary for the purposes hereinafter mentioned, and no further; and in their corporate name may sue and be sued, may have a common seal, which they may alter and renew at pleasure, and shall have, enjoy, and may exercise all the powers, rights, and privileges which appertain to corporate bodies for the purposes mentioned in this act.

Created a body corporate and politic.

May hold and sell property, etc.

May sue and be sued, and have common seal.

Power to construct and use railroad.

SEC. 3. Said corporation hereby created, shall have power to construct a single or double railroad from, at, or near the city of Detroit, in the county of Wayne, and from thence on the territorial road, selecting the most eligible route through the village of Monroe, to the Maumee Bay in the county of Monroe, and with power to transport, take, and carry property and persons upon the same, by the power and force of steam, of animals, or of any mechanical or other power, or any combination of them.

When this act to be void.

SEC. 4. If said corporation shall not, within three years from the passage of this act, commence the construction of said railroad, and shall not, within seven years from the passage of this act, construct, finish, and put in operation said railroad, within the time above mentioned, then the rights, privileges, and powers of the said corporation under this act, shall be null and void.

Election of directors.

SEC. 5. That whenever one hundred shares of the aforesaid stock shall have been subscribed, if within two years after the passage of this act, the commissioners shall call a general meeting of the subscribers, at such time and place as they may appoint by giving sixty days' public notice of such meeting; and at such meeting the commissioners shall lay the subscription books before the subscribers then and there present, and thereupon the subscribers or stockholders or a majority of them, shall elect nine directors by ballot, a majority of whom shall be competent to manage the affairs of said company; they shall have the power of electing a president of said company, either from amongst the directors or the stockholders, and in said election, and on every occasion wherein a vote of the stockholders is to be taken, every share shall entitle the holder thereof to one vote, and every stockholder may vote himself or by proxy.

Election of president.

How stockholders may vote.

SEC. 6. That to continue the succession of president and directors of said company, nine directors shall be chosen annually, on the first Monday of October, at such place as may be appointed by the directors, and if any vacancy shall occur, by death or otherwise, of any president or director, before the year for which he was elected shall have expired, a person to fill such vacant place for the residue of the year may be appointed by the directors of said company, or a majority of them. The directors of said company shall hold and exercise their office until a new election of president and directors. All elections which are by this act, or by the by-laws of the company to be made on any particular day, if not made on such day, may be made at any time within thirty days thereafter.

When president and directors to be chosen.

If election be not held on day appointed.

SEC. 7. That a general meeting of the stockholders of said company shall be held annually, at the time and place appointed for the appointment of president and directors; and a meeting may be called at any time during the interval between said annual meetings, by the president and directors, or by the stockholders owning not less than one-fourth of the whole stock, by giving thirty days' public notice of the time and place of meeting; and when any such meetings are called by the stockholders, the notice shall specify the particular object of the call; and if, at any meeting thus called, a majority in value of the stockholders are not present in person or by proxy, such meeting shall be adjourned from day to day, not exceeding three days, without transacting any business; and if, within said three days, stockholders having a majority of the stock do not attend such meeting, then the same shall be dissolved.

Meetings to be held annually.

Of extra meetings.

When meeting dissolved.

SEC. 8. That at the regular annual meetings of the stockholders of said company, it shall be the duty of the president and directors in office for the preceding year, to exhibit a clear and distinct statement of the affairs of the company. And to any called meeting of the stockholders, a majority of those present in person or by proxy may require similar statements from the president and directors, whose duty it shall be to furnish them when thus required; and at all general meetings of the stockholders, a majority in value of all the stockholders in said company may remove from office any president, or any of the directors of said company, and may appoint others in their stead.

When president and directors to account.

President or directors may be removed.

SEC. 9. That every president and director of said company, before he acts, as such, shall swear or affirm that he will well and truly discharge the duties of his office to the best of his skill and judgment.

Oath of president and directors.

1835.

May appoint and remove officers, agents, etc.

SEC. 10. That the said president and directors, or a majority of them, shall have power to appoint, contract with, and determine the compensation of all such officers, engineers, agents, or servants whatsoever, as they may deem necessary for the transaction of the business of the company, and remove them at pleasure; and the said president and directors, or a majority of them, shall have power to determine the manner of adjusting and settling all accounts against the company; also the manner and evidence of transfers of stock in said company, and they shall have power to pass all by-laws which they may deem necessary for carrying into execution all the power vested in the company hereby incorporated: *Provided*, Such by-laws shall not be contrary to the laws of this Territory, or to the constitution or laws of the United States.

Power to settle accounts, make by-laws, etc.

Power to construct and keep road in repair.

SEC. 11. That the president and directors of said company shall be, and they are hereby invested with all the privileges, rights, and powers necessary for the location, construction, and keeping in repair of said railroad, not exceeding one hundred feet in width; and the said president and directors, or their agents, or those with whom they may contract for making said road, or any part of it, may enter upon, use, and excavate any land which may be wanted for the site of said railroad, or any other purpose which is necessary in the construction or repair of said road, or its works, so soon as the amount is ascertained and tendered as hereinafter providod.

Power to contract, to use, and excavate any land, etc.

May agree for materials for said road.

SEC. 12. That the president and directors of said company may agree with the owner or owners of any land, earth, timber, gravel, stone, or other materials, or any article whatsoever, which may be wanted in the construction or repair of said road, or any of its works, for the purchase or occupation of the same; and if such materials (not previously taken or appropriated by the owner to any particular use) as may be necessary for the construction or repair of said railroad, be found on any unimproved land, adjoining to or near the same, and if the parties cannot agree, or if the owner or owners of any of them be a *femme covert*, under age, *non compos mentis*, or out of the county in which the property wanted may lie, application may be made to any justice of the peace of such county, who shall thereupon issue his warrant under his hand and seal, directed to the sheriff of said county, or if the sheriff be interested, to some disinterested person, requiring him to summon a jury of twelve freeholders in the county, not in any way interested in the matter, or related to the parties, to meet on or near the property or materials to be valued, on a day named in said warrant, not less than five nor more than ten days after the issuing of the same, and if, at the same time and place, any of the persons summoned do not attend, the said sheriff, or summoner, shall immediately summon as many as may be necessary, with the persons in attendance as jurors, to furnish a panel of twelve jurors, and from them, each party, or his, or her, or their agent or attorney, or if either be not present in person or by agent, the sheriff or summoner for him, her, or them may strike off three jurors, and the remaining shall act as a jury of inquest of damages, and before they act as such, the sheriff, or summoner,

How to proceed when parties cannot agree.

Jury to be summoned, etc.

1835.

shall administer to each of them an oath or affirmation, that they will justly and impartially value the damages which the owner or owners will sustain by the use or occupation of the land, materials, or property required by said company; and the said jury shall reduce their inquisition to writing, and shall sign and seal the same, and it shall then be sent to the clerk of the circuit court of said county, and by the said clerk filed in his office, and shall be confirmed by said court at its next session, if no sufficient cause to the contrary be shown, and when confirmed, the same shall be recorded by said clerk, at the expense of said company; but if set aside, said court may direct another inquisition to be taken in the manner above prescribed; said inquisition shall describe the property taken, or the bounds of the land condemned; such valuation, when paid or tendered to the owner or owners of said property, his, her, or their legal representatives, shall entitle said company to the estate and interest in the same thus valued as fully as if it had been conveyed by the owner or owners of the same, for such term of time as said company shall occupy the same as a railroad; and if the valuation be not received when tendered, it may, at any time thereafter, be received from the company without cost, and the sheriff or summoner and jurors shall be allowed the ordinary fees for like services, to be taxed by the court.

Inquisition to be in writing and sent to circuit court.

Valuation tendered, property to vest in company, etc.

SEC. 13. That whenever in the construction of said railroad, it shall be necessary to cross or intersect any established road, it shall be the duty of the president and directors so to construct the said railroad across the established road as not to impede the passage or transportation of persons or property along the same, or where it shall be necessary to construct it through the lands of any individual it shall be their duty to provide for such individual proper wagon ways across said road from one part of his land to another.

When said road shall cross any road or land, company to make wagon ways, etc.

SEC. 14. That if said company shall neglect to provide proper wagon ways across said road, as required by the preceding section of this act, it shall be lawful for any individual to sue said company, and shall be entitled to such damages as a jury may think him or her entitled to for such neglect or refusal on the part of the company.

Neglect to make wagon ways liable for damages.

SEC. 15. That it shall be necessary for the said railroad company, in the selection of the route, or the construction of the said railroad, to be by them laid out and constructed, or any part of it, to connect the same with any turnpike, road, or bridge made or erected by any incorporated company, or authorized by any law of this territory, it shall be lawful for said president and directors to contract with any other corporation for the right to use such road, or bridge, or for transfer of any of the corporate or other rights and privileges of such corporation, to the said company hereby incorporated; and every such other corporation, acting under the laws of this Territory, is hereby authorized to make such contract or transfer, by and through the agency of the person authorized by the respective acts of incorporation to exercise their corporate powers, or by any persons which are by any

May contract with any other company for the use of any road, bridge, etc.

Such contracts to be valid.

1835.

law of this Territory entrusted with the management and direction of such turnpike, road, or bridge, or any of the rights or privileges aforesaid; every contract or transfer made in pursuance of the power and authority hereby granted, when executed by the several parties, under their respective corporate seals, shall vest in the company hereby incorporated, all such rights and privileges, and the right to use and enjoy the same as fully as they are now used and enjoyed by said corporations in whom they are now vested.

Power to purchase machines, etc.

SEC. 16. That the said president and directors shall have power to purchase with the funds of the company, and place on any railroad constructed by them under this act, all machines, wagons, carriages, or vehicles of any description which they may deem necessary or proper for the purpose of transportation on said road; and that they shall have power to charge for tolls and transportation, such sums as shall be established by the laws of the company. hereby incorporated; and it shall not be lawful for any other company, or person, or persons, to transport any passengers, merchandise, or property of any description whatever, along said road, or any part of it, without the license or permission of the said president and directors of said company; and the said road, with all their improvements, works, and profits, and all machinery used on said road for transportation, are hereby vested in said company incorporated by this act, and their successors forever; and the shares of the capital stock of said company shall be considered personal property and shall be transferable agreeably to the laws of said company, and subject to be taken on execution agreeably to such laws as are or may hereafter be in force.

Power to transport property and persons, receive toll, etc.

Property vested in the company.

Shares considered personal property and liable for debts.

Of dividends.

SEC. 17. That the said president and directors shall, annually, or semi-annually, declare and make such dividend as they may deem proper, of the net profits from the resources of said company, deducting the necessary current expenses; and they shall make the dividend among the stockholders of said company in proper proportions to their respective shares.

Persons injuring said road liable for damages.

SEC. 18. That if any person or persons shall willfully, knowingly, and maliciously, by any means whatever, injure, impair, or destroy any part of the railroad constructed by said company under this act, or any of the necessary works, buildings, or machinery of said company, such person or persons so offending, shall, each of them, for every such offense, forfeit and pay to the company, a sum not exceeding three times the amount of damage caused by such offense, which may be recovered in the name of said company, by an action of debt in any court having competent jurisdiction in the county wherein the offense shall be committed, and shall also be subject to an indictment; and upon conviction of such offense, shall be punished by fine and imprisonment, at the discretion of the court.

Right reserved to connect other railroads with this road.

SEC. 19. That the right and privilege is hereby reserved to the Territory or State of Michigan, or any company hereafter to be incorporated under the authority of this Territory or State, to connect with the road hereby provided for, any other railroad

1835.

leading from the main route, to any part or parts of the Territory or State aforesaid: *Provided*, That in forming such connection no injury shall be done to the works of the company hereby incorporated: *Provided, further*, That the said company, or companies so connecting may have the free use of said road by paying such a tariff of tolls as may be established by the legislature; and this corporation shall be entitled to the same rights and privileges to any and all roads hereafter connected.

Proviso.

SEC. 20. That the Territory or State of Michigan shall have the right at any time after the expiration of twenty years from the completion of said railroad to purchase and hold the same for the use of the Territory or State, at a price not exceeding the original cost of said road, and fourteen per cent thereon, of which cost an accurate account shall be kept and submitted to the legislature, duly attested by the oath of the officers of said company whenever, and as often as the legislature shall require the same.

Right of territory or state to purchase said road.

SEC. 21. That this act shall be favorably construed to effect the purposes thereby intended; and the same is hereby declared to be a public act; and copies thereof, printed by authority of the Territory, shall be received as evidence thereof.

Construction of this act.

Approved August 25, 1835.

AN ACT to amend an act entitled "An act to authorize the building of a dam across the Flint river," approved March thirty, one thousand eight hundred and thirty-five.

SECTION 1. *Be it enacted by the Legislative Council of the Territory of Michigan*, That so much of the act entitled "An act to authorize the building of a dam across the Flint river," approved March thirty, one thousand eight hundred and thirty-five, as provides for a lock in said dam, is hereby repealed; *Provided*, the person who shall erect the said dam shall build a sufficient apron, not less than sixteen feet in width, for the passage of all rafts.

Provision requiring a lock, repealed.

Approved August 25, 1835.

AN ACT to amend an act to incorporate the Maumee Branch railroad company.

SECTION 1. *Be it enacted by the Legislative Council of the Territory of Michigan*, That the Maumee Branch railroad company are hereby authorized to extend said railroad through the southern tier of counties in Michigan Territory to the mouth of Gallain river on Lake Michigan, and for that purpose and no other, said company are hereby authorized to increase their capital stock to any amount not exceeding fifteen hundred thousand dollars.

Company may extend the road and increase capital stock.

SEC. 2. So much of said road as lies between the mouth of the Maumee river and the point where said road shall intersect the Erie and Kalamazoo railroad, shall constitute the first section of said road; so much of said road as lies between said intersection

What shall constitute the 1st, 2d, and 3d sections of said road.

1835.

and the eastern boundary of St. Joseph county, shall constitute the second section of said road, and the residue of said road shall constitute the third section thereof.

When this act to be void.

SEC. 3. If the second section be not commenced within five years, and completed within fifteen years from the passage of this act, and if the third section shall not be commenceed within fifteen years, and completed within twenty-five years from the passage of this act, then, in either case, this act shall be null and void, so far as it relates to such unfinished part or parts, and no further.

Approved August 25, 1835.

AN ACT to locate the seat of justice for the county of Genesee.

Location of the seat of justice of Genesee county.

SECTION 1. *Be it enacted by the Legislative Council of the Territory of Michgan,* That the seat of justice for the county of Genesee, shall be located on the west side of the Saginaw turnpike, on lands recently deeded by John Todd and wife, to one Wait Beach; known as the Todd farm, at Flint river, at a point commencing at or within twenty rods of the center of said described land on said turnpike; *Provided,* The proprietor or proprietors of said land shall, within six months from the passage of this act, execute to the supervisors and their successors in office, for the use of said county, a good and sufficient deed of two acres of land for a court house and public square, one acre of ground for a burial ground, two churches and two school lots of common size.

Approved August 25, 1835.

AN ACT to amend the act entitled "An act to provide for defraying the public and necessary expenses in the respective counties of this Territory, and for other purposes."

Meetings of the Board of Supervisors.

SECTION 1. *Be it enacted by the Legislative Council of the Territory of Michigan,* That the meeting of the boards of supervisors, in the several counties in this Territory, for the year one thousand eight hundred and thirty-five, shall be held on the second Monday of October, instead of the first Monday of October, as now provided by law; which meetings of said boards shall be held at the places where the same would have been held, if this act had not passed.

Approved August 25, 1835.

AN ACT to authorize the building of a dam across the St. Joseph river, at Niles.

Authority to build a dam.

SECTION 1. *Be it enacted by the Legislative Council of the Territory of Michigan,* That Tallman Wheeler, H. B. Hoffman, C. W. Hoffman, Jacob Beeson, Obed Phacy, and C. K. Green, and their associates, and their heirs and assigns, are hereby authorized and empowered to build a dam across the St. Joseph river, at Niles, in Berrien county.

Size and construction of the dam and lock.

SEC. 2. The said dam shall not exceed five feet in height above common low water mark, and shall contain a convenient lock for the passage of boats, barges, canoes, rafts, or other water craft, not less than one hundred and ten feet in length, and twenty-two feet in width, and so constructed as to receive water craft and rafts in slack water of sufficient depth below the Niles Ripple, and pass them to slack water of sufficient depth above said ripple, for all the purposes of navigation upon said river.

Lock to be kept in repair.

SEC. 3. It shall be the duty of the grantees, at all times, to keep said lock in repair, and to pass any water craft or raft, which can be admitted therein, through the same, free from toll, after the building of said dam shall have been so far prosecuted as to obstruct the navigation of said river; and the said grantees shall be liable to the owner or master of any water craft or raft, in double the amount of damages such owner or master may sustain from such unnecessary detention of said water craft or raft, at said lock, to be recovered, with cost of suit, before any court having competent jurisdiction.

When grantees liable for damages.

Liability of persons injuring said dam.

SEC. 4. Any person who shall, at any time, destroy, or in any wise injure said lock or dam, shall be deemed to have committed a trespass upon the said grantees, and be liable accordingly; and any person who shall willfully and maliciously destroy or injure said lock or dam, shall be deemed guilty of a misdemeanor, and on conviction be punished by fine and imprisonment in the discretion of the court; *Provided*, The imprisonment shall not exceed the term of three months.

How this act construed.

SEC. 5. Nothing herein contained shall be so construed as to authorize the said grantees to enter upon or flow the lands of any other person, without the consent of such person; and the legislature may, at any time, so alter and amend this act as to provide for the further improvement of the navigation of the said St. Joseph River.

Of amendments.

Approved August 25, 1835.

AN ACT to amend an act entitled "An act to incorporate the Shelby and Detroit railroad company, approved March seven, one thousand eight hundred and thirty-four."

Provision of the act extended.

SECTION 1. *Be it enacted by the Legislative Council of the Territory of Michigan*, That the provisions of the above recited act be, and they are hereby continued and extended for the term of two years from and after the seventh day of March, one thousand eight hundred and thirty-six, any law to the contrary notwithstanding.

Approved August 25, 1835.

1835. AN ACT to incorporate the Maumee Branch railroad company.

Commissioners appointed.

SECTION 1. *Be it enacted by the Legislative Council of the Territory of Michigan,* That David White, Salmon Kinney, Jacob A. Barker, John T. Hudson, Stephen G. Austin, John W. Clark, and Charles Townsend be, and they are hereby appointed commissioners, under the direction of a majority of whom, subscriptions may be received to the capital stock of the Maumee Branch railroad company hereby incorporated; and they may cause books to be opened, at such times and places as they shall direct, for the purpose of receiving subscriptions to the capital stock of said company, first giving reasonable notice of the times and places of taking said subscriptions.

Books to be opened and subscriptions received.

Capital stock $100,000 in shares of $50.

SEC. 2. That the capital stock of the said Maumee Branch railroad company, shall be one hundred thousand dollars, in shares of fifty dollars each; and that as soon as one thousand shares of said stock shall be subscribed, the subscribers of said stock, with such other persons as shall associate with them for that purpose, their successors and assigns, shall be, and they are hereby created a body corporate and politic, by the name of the "Maumee Branch Railroad Company," with perpetual succession, and by that name shall be capable in law of purchasing, holding, selling, leasing, and conveying estate, either real, personal, or mixed, so far as the same may be necessary for the purposes hereinafter mentioned, and no further; and in their corporate name may sue and be sued, may have a common seal, which they may alter and renew at pleasure, and shall have, enjoy, and may exercise all the powers, rights, and privileges which appertain to corporate bodies, for the purposes mentioned in this act.

Created a body corporate and politic may hold and sell property.

May sue and be sued and have common seal.

Power to construct and use railroad.

SEC. 3. Said corporation hereby created, shall have power to construct a single or double railroad from, at, or near the mouth of the Maumee river, in the county of Monroe, and from thence on an eligible route until the same shall intersect the Erie and Kalamazoo railroad; and to connect with and use the Erie and Kalamazoo railroad, or any part of it when completed, according to the provisions of the nineteenth section of the act incorporating said Erie and Kalamazoo railroad; and with power to transport, take, and carry property and persons upon the Erie and Kalamazoo railroad, or upon any part of it, when completed, and upon the railroad herein authorized to be constructed, by the power and force of steam, of animals, or any mechanical or other power, or any combination of them.

When this act to be void.

SEC. 4. If said corporation shall not, within two years after the completion of the first section of the Erie and Kalamazoo railroad, commence the construction of the said railroad, and shall not, within four years after the completion of the first section of the Erie and Kalamazoo railroad, construct, finish, and put in operation said railroad, then the rights, powers, and privileges of said company shall cease and be void.

Election of directors.

SEC. 5. That whenever one hundred shares of the aforesaid stock shall have been subscribed, if within two years after the

1835.

passage of this act, the commissioners shall call a general meeting of the subscribers, at such time and place as they may appoint, by giving sixty days' public notice of such meeting; and at such meeting the commissioners shall lay the subscription books before the subscribers then and there present, and thereupon the subscribers or stockholders, or a majority of them, shall elect seven directors by ballot, a majority of whom shall be competent to manage the affairs of said company; they shall have the power of electing a president of said company, either from amongst the directors, or the stockholders, and in said election, and on every occasion wherein a vote is to be taken, every share shall entitle the holder thereof to one vote; and every stockholder may vote himself or by proxy.

Election of president.

How stockholders may vote.

SEC. 6. That to continue the succession of president and directors of said company, seven directors shall be chosen annually, on the first Monday of October, at such place as may be appointed by the directors, and if any vacancy shall occur by death or otherwise, of any president or director, before the year for which he was elected shall have expired, a person to fill such vacant place, for the residue of the year, may be appointed by the directors of said company, or a majority of them. The directors of the said company shall hold and exercise their offices until a new election of president and directors. All elections which are by this act, or by the by-laws of the company, to be made on any particular day, if not made on such day, may be made at any time within thirty days thereafter.

When president and directors to be chosen.

If election be not held on day appointed.

SEC. 7. That a general meeting of the stockholders of said company shall be held annually, at the time and place appointed, for the appointment of president and directors; and a meeting may be called at any time during the interval between said annual meetings, by the president and directors, or by the stockholders owning not less than one-fourth of the whole stock, by giving thirty days' public notice of the time and place of meeting; and when any such meetings are called by the stockholders, the notice shall specify the particular object of the call; and if, at any meetings thus called, a majority in value of the stockholders are not present, in person or by proxy, such meeting shall be adjourned from day to day, not exceeding three days, without transacting any business; and if within said three days, stockholders having a majority of the stock, do not attend such meeting, then the same shall be dissolved.

Meetings to be held annually.

Of extra meetings.

When meeting dissolved.

SEC. 8. That at the regular annual meetings of the stockholders of said company, it shall be the duty of the president and directors in office for the preceding year, to exhibit a clear and distinct statement of the affairs of the company. And at any called meeting of the stockholders, a majority of those present, in person or by proxy, may require similar statements from the president and directors, whose duty it shall be to furnish them, when thus required; and at all general meetings of the stockholders, a majority in value of all the stockholders in said company, may remove from office any president, or any of the directors of said company, and may appoint others in their stead.

When president and directors to account.

When president or directors may be removed.

1835.

Oath of president and directors.

SEC. 9. That every president and director of said company, before he acts as such, shall swear or affirm that he will well and truly discharge the duties of his office, to the best of his skill and judgment.

May appoint and remove officers, agents, etc.

SEC. 10. That the said president and directors, or a majority of them, shall have power to appoint, contract with, and determine the compensation of all such officers, engineers, agents, or servants whatsoever, as they may deem necessary for the transaction of the business of the company, and remove them at pleasure; and the said president and directors, or a majority of them, shall have power to determine the manner of adjusting and settling all accounts against the company; also the manner and evidence of transfers of stock in said company; and they shall have power to pass all by-laws which they may deem necessary for carrying into execution all the powers vested in the company hereby incorporated: *Provided*, Such by-laws shall not be contrary to the laws of this Territory, or of the constitution or laws of the United States.

To settle accounts, make by-laws, etc.

To construct and keep said road in repair.

SEC. 11. That the president and directors of said company shall be, and they are hereby invested with all the privileges, rights, and powers necessary for the location, construction, and keeping in repair said railroad, not exceeding one hundred feet in width; and the said president and directors, or their agents, or those with whom they may contract for making said road, or any part of it, may enter upon, use, and excavate any land which may be wanted for the site of said railroad, or any other purpose which is necessary in the construction or repair of said road, or its works, so soon as the amount is ascertained and tendered, as hereinafter provided.

May contract for, use, and excavate any land, etc.

May agree for materials, etc.

SEC. 12. That the president and directors of said company may agree with the owner or owners of any land, earth, timber, gravel, stone, or other materials, or any article whatsoever, which may be wanted in the construction or repair of said road, or any of its works, for the purchase or occupation of the same; and if such materials (not previously taken or appropriated by the owner to any particular use) as may be necessary for the construction or repair of said railroad, be found on any unimproved land, adjoining to, or near the same, and if the parties cannot agree, or if the owner or owners of any of them be a *femme covert*, under age, *non compos mentis*, or out of the county of which the property wanted may lie, application may be made to any justice of the peace of said county, who shall thereupon issue his warrant, under his hand and seal, directed to the sheriff of said county, or if the sheriff be interested, to some disinterested person, requiring him to summon a jury of twelve freeholders in the county, not in any way interested in the matter, or related to the parties, to meet on or near the property or materials to be valued, on a day named in said warrant, not less than five, nor more than ten days after the issuing of the same, and if at the said time and place, any of the persons summoned do not attend, the said sheriff, or summoner, shall immediately summon as many as may be necessary, with the persons in attendance as jurors, to furnish a panel of twelve jurors, and from them each party, or his, or her, or their agent,

How to proceed when parties cannot agree.

Jury to be summoned, etc.

1835.

or attorney, or if either be not present in person or by agent, the sheriff or summoner for him, her, or them, may strike off three jurors, and the remaining shall act as a jury of inquest of damages; and before they act as such, the sheriff or summoner shall administer to each of them, an oath or affirmation that they will justly and impartially value the damages which the owner or owners will sustain, by the use or occupation of the land, materials, or property, required by said company; and the said jury shall reduce their inquisition to writing, and shall sign and seal the same, and it shall then be sent to the clerk of the circuit court of said county, and by said clerk filed in his office, and shall be confirmed by said court at its next session, if no sufficient cause to the contrary be shown; and when confirmed, the same shall be recorded by said clerk, at the expense of said company; but if set aside, said court may direct another inquisition, to be taken in the manner above prescribed. Said inquisition shall describe the property taken, or the bounds of the land condemned. Such valuation, when paid or tendered to the owner or owners of said property, his, her, or their legal representatives, shall entitle said company to the estate and interest in the same, thus valued, as fully as if it had been conveyed by the owner or owners of the same, for such term of time as said company shall occupy the same as a railroad; and if the valuation be not received when tendered, it may at any time thereafter be received from the company without cost; and the sheriff or summoners and jurors shall be allowed the ordinary fees for like services, to be taxed by the court.

Inquisition to be in writing and sent to circuit court.

Valuation tendered—property to vest in company, etc.

SEC. 13. That whenever in the construction of said railroad, it shall be necessary to cross or intersect any established road, it shall be the duty of said president and directors so to construct the said railroad across such established road as not to impede the passage or transportation of persons or property along the same, or when it shall be necessary to construct it through the land of any individual, it shall be their duty to provide for such individual, proper wagon ways across said road from one part of his land to another.

When company to make wagon ways, etc.

SEC. 14. That if said company shall neglect to provide proper wagon ways across said road, as required by the preceding section of this act, it shall be lawful for any individual to sue said company, and shall be entitled to such damages as a jury may think him or her entitled to, for such neglect or refusal on the part of the company.

Neglect to make wagon ways liable for damages.

SEC. 15. That if it shall be necessary for the said railroad company, in the selection of the route, or the construction of the said railroad to be by them laid out and constructed, or any part of it, to connect the same with any turnpike, road, or bridge, made or erected by any incorporated company, or authorized by any law of this Territory, it shall be lawful for said president and directors to contract with any other corporation for the right to use such road or bridge, or for transfer of any of the corporate or other rights and privileges of such corporation, to the said company hereby

President and directors may contract with any other company for the use of any road, bridge, etc.

1835.

incorporated; and every other such corporation, acting under the laws or this Territory, is hereby authorized to make such contract or transfer, by and through the agency of the person authorized by the respective acts of incorporation to exercise their corporate powers, or by any persons which are, by any law of this Territory, entrusted with the management and direction of such turnpike, road, or bridge, or any of the rights or privileges aforesaid. Every contract or transfer made in pursuance of the power and authority hereby granted, when executed by the several parties, under their respective corporate seals, shall vest in the company hereby incorporated, all such rights and privileges, and the right to use and enjoy the same, as fully as they are now used and enjoyed by said corporations, in whom they are now vested.

Such contracts to be valid.

May purchase machines, etc.

SEC. 16. That the said president and directors shall have power to purchase, with the funds of the company, and place on the Erie and Kalamazoo railroad, or on any railroad constructed by them under this act, all machines, wagons, carriages, or vehicles of any description, which they may deem necessary or proper for the purpose of transportation on said road or roads; and that they shall have power to charge for tolls and transportation, such sums as shall be established by the by-laws of the company hereby incorporated; and it shall not be lawful for any other company, or person, or persons to transport any passengers, merchandise, or property, of any description whatever, along said road, or any part of it, without the license or permission of said president and directors of said company; and the said road, with all their improvements, works, and profits, and all the machinery used on said road for transportation, are hereby vested in said company incorporated by this act, and their successors forever; and the shares of the capital stock of said company shall be considered personal property, and shall be transferrable agreeable to the by-laws of the company.

Power to transport property and persons, and receive toll.

Property vested in the company.

Shares considered personal property and liable for debts.

Of dividends.

SEC. 17. That the said president and directors shall annually, or semi-annually, declare and make such dividend as they may deem proper, of the net profits from the resources of the said company, deducting the necessary current expenses; and they shall make the dividend among the stockholders of said company, in the proper proportions to their respective shares.

Persons injuring said road liable for damages, etc.

SEC. 18. That if any person or persons shall willfully, knowingly, and maliciously, by any means whatever, injure, impair, or destroy any part of the railroad constructed by said company under this act, or any of the necessary works, buildings, or machinery of said company, such person or persons so offending, shall, each of them, for every such offense, forfeit and pay to the company, a sum not exceeding three times the amount of damages caused by such offense, which may be recovered in the name of said company, by an action of debt in any court having competent jurisdiction in the county wherein the effense shall be committed, and shall also be subject to an indictment; and upon conviction of such offense, shall be punished by fine and imprisonment, at the discretion of the court: *Provided*, That the term of imprisonment shall not, in any case, exceed three months.

1835.

SEC. 19. That the right and privilege is hereby reserved to the Territory, or any company hereafter to be incorporated under the authority of this Territory, to connect with the road hereby provided for, any other railroad leading from the main route to any part or parts of the Territory: *Provided,* That in forming such connection, no injury shall be done to the works of the company hereby incorporated: *Provided, further,* That the said company or companies so connecting, may have the free use of said road by paying such a tariff of tolls as may be established by the legislature; and this corporation shall be entitled to the same rights and privileges to any and all roads hereafter connected.

Right reserved to connect other railroads with this road.

Proviso.

SEC. 20. That the Terrritory shall have the right, at any time, after the expiration of twenty years from the completion of the said railroad, to purchase and hold the same for the use of the Territory, at a price not exceeding the original cost of said road, and fourteen per cent thereon; of which cost an accurate account shall be kept and submitted to the legislative council, duly attested by the oath of the officers of said company, whenever, and as often as said council shall require the same.

Right of territory to purchase said railroad.

SEC. 21. The property of every individual member of the said corporation, vested in said corporate funds, shall be liable in the same manner as other personal property is liable by the laws of this Territory, to the payment and satisfaction of his just debts, to any of his *bona fide* creditors; and when any execution shall issue against the personal property of any such individual member, and the creditor is desirous that the same should be levied upon the property of such debtor, in said corporate funds, the officer to whom such execution may be directed, may levy the same, by leaving with the president an attested copy of such execution, and a written notice that the said execution is levied upon the property of the said debtor in said corporate funds; and such property thus levied upon, shall be sold in the same manner as is, or shall by law be provided for the sale of personal property taken in execution; and such corporate funds, thus levied upon and sold, shall be transferred to the purchaser by entering in the proper book of such corporation, a copy of said execution, and a statement of the sale of such property by virtue thereof, which entry the officer serving such execution, shall be permitted to make: *Provided,* That no property vested in said corporate funds, shall be thus taken and sold until all debts due to the said corporation by such debtor shall be fully paid and discharged; and upon any execution being levied on any shares in said corporation, it shall be the duty of the president or secretary of said corporation to expose the proper book of the corporation to the officer, and to furnish him with a certificate, under his hand, in his official capacity, stating the number of shares the debtor holds in the said corporation, and the amount of dividends thereon due.

Members' property liable for debts.

Process for selling same.

Proviso.

SEC. 22. That this act shall be favorably construed to effect the purposes thereby intended, and the same is hereby declared to be a public act; and copies thereof, printed by authority of the Territory, shall be received as evidence thereof.

Construction of this act.

Approved August 22, 1835.

1835. AN ACT to provide for the compensation of the officers of the special session of the sixth legislative council, and for other purposes.

To J. McDonell for expenses and pay officers. SECTION 1. *Be it enacted by the Legislative Council of the Territory of Michigan,* That there shall be allowed to John McDonell, the president of the legislative council, the sum of twelve hundred and twenty-one dollars and fifty cents, for expenses incurred for the pay of officers of said council, and which shall include all other services with the exception of printing and translation performed during the present special session of the legislative council.

J. Norvell. To John Norvell, for postage, thirty dollars and sixty cents.

J. B. Vallee. To J. B. Vallee, for translating governor's message, twenty-five dollars.

S. Wells. To Stephen Wells, for stationery, fifty-two dollars and twenty-five cents.

L. Hall. To Lewis Hall, for stationery, sixty dollars.

E. P. Hastings. To E. P. Hastings, for disbursements by directions of the president of the legislative council, for repairing and securing the basement story of the capitol, and enclosing the same, and fitting up the room in said building, for the district court of the United States, fifteen hundred dollars.

J. McDonell for newspapers. To the president of the legislative council, for the publishers of the National Intelligencer, the Globe, and United States Telegraph, twenty-four dollars.

A. H. Stowell. To A. H. Stowell, for stationery, one hundred and ninety-two dollars and sixty-three cents.

Moore and Chandler. To Moore and Chandler, for repairs to the capitol, eighty-six dollars.

A. Morton and others for publishing the laws. To A. Morton and Son, Addison Phillio, Albert G. Ellis, Edward D. Ellis, George Corselius, Sheldon McKnight, and George L. Whitney, for having published the laws of the extra session in their respective papers, twenty-five dollars each.

H. Hallock. To Horace Hallock, for stationery, five dollars.

S. M'Knight. To Sheldon McKnight, the sum of three hundred dollars, for printing bills, journals, and other documents, for the present special session of the legislative council, and for printing the laws and journals of the same in pamphlet form, which shall include stitching and binding, to be paid by the fiscal agent on the certificate of the president of the council certifying that the same has been duly performed.

C. W. Whipple. To Charles W. Whipple, secretary of the legislative council, for making an index and marginal notes to the laws and journal, passed at the present special session of the legislative council, and furnishing copy of the journal for the press, and for bringing up and completing the journal of the last and present special session of the legislative council, recording the legislative and executive journals, one hundred and twenty-five dollars, which shall be paid by the fiscal agent, on the certificate of the president of the legislative council, certifying that the same has been performed, which is not included in the item specified in the first clause of this act.

To publishers of all papers now published in this Territory, for

1835.

publishing the laws of the present special session of the legislative council, in the respective papers, ten dollars each: *Provided*, That the publication of the same commences immediately after receiving copies of the same from the secretary of the Territory, which compensation and allowance shall include the current accounts of the auditor and treasurer of the Territory, furnished by them on the first day of the next session of the legislature, together with all circulars issued by the auditor relative to the territorial revenue, which compensation and allowance shall also include the proclamations from the executive and all general militia orders, or other documents published by authority; that no extra allowance shall be made to any publisher of a newspaper, hereafter, for the publication of separate copies of any such documents, unless when the executive of the Territory or State shall deem it indispensably necessary, as shall appear by his written instruction to such publisher; which said sums shall be paid by the fiscal agent, on the affidavit of such publisher, made before competent authority, that he has actually performed the services.

To the publishers of papers for publishing the laws.

Proviso.

Approved August 25, 1835.

INDEX.

INDEX.

A.

H.

I.

J.

K.

L.

S.

www.ingramcontent.com/pod-product-compliance
Lightning Source LLC
LaVergne TN
LVHW011231110826
845150LV00006B/1602

* 9 7 8 1 4 2 5 5 1 4 8 7 7 *